NEITHER CALENDAR NOR CLOCK

Neither Calendar nor Clock

PERSPECTIVES ON THE
BELHAR CONFESSION

Piet J. Naudé

WILLIAM B. EERDMANS PUBLISHING COMPANY
GRAND RAPIDS, MICHIGAN / CAMBRIDGE, U.K.

Published 2010 by

Wm. B. Eerdmans Publishing Co.

2140 Oak Industrial Drive N.E., Grand Rapids, Michigan 49505 /

P.O. Box 163, Cambridge CB3 9PU U.K.

Printed in the United States of America

15 14 13 12 11 10   7 6 5 4 3 2 1

Library of Congress Cataloging-in-Publication Data

Naudé, Piet, 1956-

Neither calendar nor clock: perspectives on the Belhar Confession / Piet J. Naudé.

p.   cm.

Includes bibliographical references and index.

ISBN 978-0-8028-6259-4 (pbk.: alk. paper)

1. Belhar confession.

2. Reformed Church — Creeds — History and criticism.

I. Title.

BX9429.B44N38   2010

238'.4268 — dc22

2010013278

www.eerdmans.com

Confession is bound to neither calendar nor clock.
When its hour comes, it may and must occur.

—Karl Barth, *Church dogmatics,* III/4

Contents

Foreword   ix

Preface   xvi

The texts, with commentary   1

Part 1: Tradition

1. The "no!" of the Belhar Confession   23

2. The relation between Belhar and some antecedent
   church witnesses in the period 1948-1982   49

Part 2: Confession

3. The confessional character of the Belhar Confession   77

4. Confessing the one faith? Theological resonance
   between the Creed of Nicea and the Confession of Belhar   104

Part 3: Reception

5. "A gift from heaven": The reception of the
   Belhar Confession in the period 1982-2007   131

6. The echoes of Belhar in the ecumenical church   149

Part 4: Contemporary significance

7. Unity in freedom   169

8. Reconciliation   185

9. Justice   201

   APPENDIX A: *The Belhar Confession, 1982*   219

   APPENDIX B: *The Nicene Creed, 381*   224

   APPENDIX C: *The Cottesloe Declaration, 1961*   226

   APPENDIX D: *A Message to the People of South Africa, 1968*   233

   Bibliography   237

   Index   250

Foreword: The Ongoing Task

The theological interpretation of Belhar — the Reformed confessional document born in the church and theological struggles in apartheid South Africa during the 1980s — is an ongoing task, and much still needs to be done, claims Piet Naudé. This timely book as a whole could be read as a contribution to this ongoing task. In such a case, however, one would have to see the complexity of this task, the many aspects involved, and the rich and instructive way in which Naudé understands the ongoing task and sets about this theological interpretation.

He regards at least *four aspects* of such an ongoing task as important challenges. Together, these four determine the structure of this volume and provide its inner logic and argument.

He is — *firstly* — convinced that the Confession of Belhar can be understood only as an integral part of the confessional tradition of the Christian faith. He therefore does not hesitate to begin his theological interpretation with the creeds of the early church, starting with the faith confessed in the Nicene Creed of the fourth century.

In the instructive second part of the volume, "Confession," he therefore deals with questions of extreme importance for the self-understanding of the Reformed tradition, controversial questions debated today in many circles of the Reformed community worldwide. They concern the confessional nature of the church, the historical nature of Reformed confessions, the human and fallible character of Reformed confessions, and their relative authority in the life of Reformed churches.

Characteristic of Naudé's engaging and often challenging, even confrontational rhetoric (he is with good reason one of the most popular preachers and public speakers in South African church circles today), he develops his own ideas in dialogue with Karl Barth's views on confession. He asks whether Barth would have signed Belhar and then delves into Barth's discussions of confession in his early speeches and essays and later in the *Church dogmatics* itself. This instructive and relevant section alone makes reading the book a worthwhile experience, even for those who may have no interest in Belhar itself.

Integral to both Barth's and Naudé's understanding of Reformed confessions is — *secondly* — their historical character. They are born within particular historical circumstances. In his instructive study *Credo* (2003), Jaroslav Pelikan argues that in most cases these historical circumstances also have a critical political background. In order to interpret such confessions theologically, we must therefore understand them against their historical, mostly political, origins. Both the influence of what Pelikan calls the politics of religion on the formation of creeds and confessions, and its counterpart, the influence of creeds and confessions on the formation of politics, including economic and social realities, belong integrally together.

Again, Naudé makes this crucially important point very clear when many others in the Reformed community worldwide — including South Africa — still regularly treat their own confessions as ahistorical documents with timeless propositions and often regard historical and sociopolitical factors as problematic and irreconcilable with timeless confessional claims and formulations.

While most Reformed believers fully understand and acknowledge that we need responsible hermeneutics when reading Scripture, for some remarkable reason many do not fully agree and appreciate that we similarly need responsible hermeneutics when reading the documents from our confessional tradition.

This book can help raise awareness of these claims in fresh ways. In this way, Naudé contributes to nothing less than the responsible hermeneutics of tradition, which the influential Lutheran and ecumenical theologian Edmund Schlink, another of Naudé's discussion partners, famously called for.

Such an awareness of the historical and political nature of confessions, along with such an attempt toward a responsible hermeneutics of tradition, provokes serious controversies and difficult debates. What are the implications of confessions as sociohistorical documents, written under specific purposes and with specific intentions, using the language and conceptual frameworks available, and reflecting the assumptions and insights of the time, including the supposed falsehood against which confessions speak?

On the one hand, this means that the ongoing theological interpretation should be informed by knowledge about the historical circumstances in which the confession originated, including the political, social, and ecclesial backdrop, and about the theological debates of the time, the issues at stake, the threats to the gospel perceived, and the temptations and one-sided truths challenged and unmasked. For this purpose, Naudé provides some background information in the first section under the heading "Tradition."

Naudé describes Belhar quite correctly as one moment in a much longer history of theological reflection and struggle in South African church and theological circles in the latter part of the twentieth century. He analyzes Belhar's "no!" and explains to readers today precisely what was rejected at the time and why. He pays careful attention to the Accompanying Letter of the Synod, in which the Dutch Reformed Mission Church (DRMC) explained what it was doing, its motivation and expectation, in that historical moment.

All of this is helpful for contemporary readers — for those outside South Africa who do not know the historical circumstances and may appreciate such information; for new generations inside South Africa who today know apartheid "only by hearsay," in the well-known words of the South African scholar and public figure Russel Botman (which he borrowed from Bonhoeffer); but also for many South Africans who, even at the time, did not know what was happening, who did not see and could not understand, and perhaps still struggle to understand.

Naudé clearly has this last group of readers in mind — the members, congregations, and official bodies of his own Dutch Reformed Church. The book is a moving plea to this church to look and listen again, perhaps for the first time. This section therefore also makes the book so timely, not only because people worldwide who are today discussing Belhar could benefit from such an informative introduction, but also because many in South African Reformed churches have not, according to Naudé, really understood what has happened and what is still happening.

On the other hand, the historical background alone never justifies any confessional claims. "No other motives or convictions, however valid they may be, . . . give us the right to confess," the Accompanying Letter acknowledged. The historical and political context occasions the act of confession, but only the gospel itself provides the truth of the "no" and the "yes." A Reformed confession, however political both its origins and its effects may be, can never be at heart a political instrument with political intent and purpose. For such other purposes, including public witness, churches have many other ways of acting and speaking at their disposal.

This implies that the origins do not determine the truth of the content of any confession. The sisters and brothers of the worldwide church participate in the discussion of the meaning of confessional documents, including the question of whether the gospel was truly understood and spoken in them. There is no final authorial intention. In fact, as Naudé approvingly quotes Barth, the authors of any confessional document are not important; the question of who actually wrote any confession is irrelevant and does not add or detract anything from its truth or falsehood.

This is precisely the reason why Naudé can claim that the theological interpretation of Belhar is an ongoing task. It is not the possession of the Uniting Reformed Church in Southern Africa (URCSA, the successor body to the DRMC). Like the Nicene Creed, the Heidelberg Catechism, and the Barmen Declaration, Belhar must find its own way in a process of ongoing theological interpretation; there are simply no voices with final authority that can adjudicate the controversies that inevitably arise in this ongoing story. Together, believers and churches seek to discern. They stand in a shared confessional tradition, but also they face new challenges and questions in the light of that shared tradition.

With that — *thirdly* — we come to Naudé's next theme: the difficult questions concerning the reception of confessional documents. Many scholars have recently argued that this is the single most challenging issue for the whole ecumenical church. For the Reformed community, it is particularly complex and controversial. The author reflects on these difficulties in his third section, "Reception."

When and how do we truly and adequately "receive" in the church the tradition in which we stand and to which we belong, including its confessions; the documents, reports, studies, and decisions of the church; the larger community to which we belong; one another, other believers, other congregations, and other denominations? What does "accept," "receive," or "reception" mean, for example, when Paul pleads that we should receive one another the way Christ received us (Rom. 15:7)?

These questions are related to questions of authority, including the authority of tradition; the authority of the broader ecclesial community; the authority of argument, study, and persuasion; the authority of leaders speaking on behalf of tradition and community; and ultimately the authority of Scripture and its interpretation. For the Reformed community every one of these questions has been notoriously difficult. Today, they are all again controversial and burning, almost everywhere. What does communion mean for Reformed churches — full, visible communion? What does reception mean? How do we truly receive?

Once again, while Naudé is telling the particular story of Belhar, both the story of its initial reception over the first twenty-five years (in the history of confessional documents, still only a brief moment in time) and the story of its growing reception today in contexts outside South Africa, he is raising much broader questions for the contemporary church. What does it mean to be an apostolic church? to stand in continuity with the Christian tradition? to be faithful? To borrow the well-known words of Alasdair MacIntyre in *After Virtue,* how do we participate in responsible ways in "an historically extended, socially embedded argument, . . . an argument precisely in part about the goods which constitute that tradition"?

Naudé's discussion of the ecumenical challenge of reception is informed, informative, and instructive. He suggests that the reception of confessional documents should be understood as a much broader process than merely the formal reception of such documents as official confessions. In fact, Reformed theology should take the potentially radical implications of such an insight very seriously.

It is therefore in principle possible that Reformed churches may officially accept confessional documents and even pride themselves in the possession of those documents yet deny the thrust and claims of those documents in their lives and even in their church structure and order. Conversely, it is also possible that churches may not officially accept confessional documents yet in practice, through their lives and even their structure and order, show that they do believe the promises and follow the claims of those confessions.

Barmen serves as a powerful demonstration of both these possibilities. Eberhard Busch has movingly argued that Reformed churches should not safely store their confessions in cabinets like trophies but, rather, follow them like banners into battle. There may be churches that have officially accepted Barmen without living out the implications of Barmen's claims. Other churches may not have officially accepted Barmen but yet in many ways do live from its promises and claims.

The same is also true of Belhar. It is in principle possible that the URCSA itself may treasure Belhar as a confessional document without

xiii

faithfully seeking to live and to embody the implications of Belhar's promises and claims. Again, it is for such serious reasons that the theological interpretation of Belhar remains an ongoing theological task.

By developing this rich notion of reception, Naudé persuasively shows that the continuing story of the official reception of Belhar in many churches worldwide — a story that by its very nature is already outdated by the time of this book's publication — is just one part of the story. Belhar, like the earlier Reformed confessions, is also received in many other ways, where its history is remembered, where the struggles in which it was born are discussed — in short, where the history of its effects, its so-called *Wirkungsgeschichte,* is present and active and challenging.

With this, readers arrive at the last aspect of Naudé's discussion of the ongoing task of theological interpretation. In his final section he considers — *fourthly* — some contemporary challenges that he personally discerns, standing in this *Wirkungsgeschichte* of Belhar. Under the heading "Contemporary Significance," he reflects on the challenges raised by the call to embody unity in freedom, to practice reconciliation, and to pursue justice.

Although these three claims represent the central issues of Belhar, the way in which he analyzes contemporary challenges is almost provocatively focused on controversial issues. He does not pretend to speak a final word — quite the contrary, since that would contradict his own central conviction about the nature of the Reformed confessional tradition and the ongoing task of theological interpretation.

He writes about issues close to his own heart — what living unity could mean for being human and for human dignity in Africa today; what real reconciliation could mean for gender issues and within a pandemic of HIV/AIDS; what restorative and economic justice could mean, given the situation of Africa within global economic realities. He writes both as a social scientist (a trained philosopher and at present the director of the Business School of the Nelson Mandela Metropolitan University, Port Elizabeth) and as one of the most respected systematic theologians in South Africa. He is outspoken, even provocative, in the deliberate way he weaves these fields together.

Naudé does not provide solutions but, rather, demonstrates how historical decisions and commitments, voices from other moments in history, can remain inspiring today, calling, claiming, challenging us to discern the spirit of our times, to read our moment in history, to recognize the temptations for our church, the threats to our proclamation of the gospel. Not everyone will agree with his analyses and positions; the orientating potential of the confessional tradition does not lie in speaking final words but in opening our eyes, hearts, and minds to speak and search and discern together, and to act.

The title captures this process very well. The expression is from Barth's description of the moment of confession, the dramatic moment of truth, which the church cannot plan or control. The moment overcomes the church, which is forced to speak — "struck on the mouth," Barth says, with no other choice "except credo." Once that has happened, sisters and brothers are called to an ongoing task of theological interpretation, trying to discern what took place and what may perhaps be at stake for them today.

Piet Naudé writes about the ongoing task of interpreting Belhar, but in fact he helps us to see and think about much more: the nature of our tradition, the roots of our faith, the way we belong to one another, and the challenges of our time. This is truly a timely book!

DIRKIE SMIT
Stellenbosch
April 2010

Preface

Until very recently, it never crossed my mind to write a book on the Belhar Confession. Popular essays, sermons, conferences, and academic papers were the ways in which many of us explained, promoted, and defended the confession since the Dutch Reformed Mission Church (DRMC) adopted its draft form in 1982. Up to the present, the superb translated collection *A moment of truth*, edited by Daan Cloete and Dirk Smit and published by Eerdmans in 1984, remains the best guide to many core theological issues raised by the confession. Issues such as *status confessionis*, the need for a confession in the light of the prophetic tradition, the long prehistory of the confession, its biblical roots, and the crisis it caused the family of Dutch Reformed Churches in South Africa[1] are all addressed by various authors closely aligned to the confessing church movement in South Africa.

But much has happened since those early days after the doctrines supporting apartheid were declared a heresy, and since Belhar was formally adopted as a fourth confession of the DRMC in October 1986. In 2012 we celebrate the thirtieth year of the original Belhar text, and we remind our-

---

1. For many years this family consisted of the Dutch Reformed Church ("mother church," of Dutch descent, established in 1652 in the Cape), the Dutch Reformed Mission Church (DRMC, the so-called colored church, 1881), the Dutch Reformed Church in Africa (DRCA, "black church," 1963), and the Reformed Church in Africa (RCA, "Indian church," 1968). The white Reformed community is divided into three further churches: the Gereformeerde Kerk (Reformed Church, 1859), the Hervormde Kerk (Dutch Reformed Church, 1853) (both formed in reaction to events in the Netherlands), and the Afrikaanse Protestantse Kerk (APK, Afrikaans Protestant Church), which split off from the DRC when this church started to move away from its theological support for apartheid after 1986.

selves that it is now just over 150 years after the infamous decision by the Cape Synod in 1857 to separate believers at the table of the Lord on practical and racial grounds. This decision played a significant role in the establishment of separate churches for different racial groups, commencing in 1881 with the Dutch Reformed Mission Church for so-called colored members. Who at that time would have foreseen that, 101 years later, this small and humanly insignificant church would speak a prophetic word against the grounds of its very own formation? A theological interpretation of Belhar is still in its infancy, if compared with the elaborate work done on, for example, the Barmen Declaration (1934) in Germany.

Two specific experiences convinced me that a serious engagement with international readers would happen only if there was a further dedicated collection of essays available. The first was my very fruitful academic time in 2002 as a visiting Alexander von Humboldt scholar at the University of Heidelberg, where I was privileged to present a seminar with my colleague Professor Michael Welker on the relationship between Barmen and Belhar. The enthusiastic reaction from students to the text and its interesting appropriation from the contexts of seven or eight different countries convinced me that some wider reflections were necessary.

The second experience was my sabbatical at the Center of Theological Inquiry, in Princeton, New Jersey, during the first half of 2007. I presented a draft paper on Belhar in relation to Karl Barth's definition of a Reformed confession. The encouraging discussion by fellow resident scholars from different disciplines and backgrounds convinced me to gather some of my work together in one volume.

There are also important impulses, closer to home, behind this essay collection. The reunification process among the Dutch Reformed family of churches in South Africa is still incomplete. The unity of the family to which Belhar so powerfully witnessed will hopefully be realized in the near future. Over the past few years this process of reunification has intensified the discussion around the Belhar Confession, its content, its difficult reception, and particularly its status in a new uniting church. I sincerely hope that this volume might assist at a theological level in moving toward a positive and full reception of Belhar in a reunited South African Reformed Church.

Another impulse arises from the fact that South Africa is now a markedly different place than it was in the 1980s. The doctrine and political system against which Belhar confessed were dismantled twelve years after the draft confession, when South Africa, against many odds, became a full democracy on April 27, 1994. This brought about enormous changes to South African society. We have a widely respected constitution and are quickly learning to foster democratic institutions and practices. However, the legacy of our past, the struggle to forge new personal and collective identities in the present, the devastation of poverty and HIV/AIDS, as well as the ambiguous effects of economic and cultural globalization continue to present us with enormous challenges. It is my conviction that the core issues addressed by the Belhar Confession, namely unity, reconciliation, and justice, are as important now as they were in the early 1980s. We need to hear Belhar's continuing witness as it speaks and guides us today.

Meanwhile, the world has also moved on. The fall of the Berlin Wall in 1989 inaugurated a new world order. China is slowly emerging as the new political and economic superpower. After 9/11 the United States retreated into isolation and engaged in wars that, realistically speaking, it cannot possibly win. In November 2008, during the closing phase of preparing this book, Barack Obama was elected as the first black president of the United States, creating new hope for America and the world. Two issues highlight the fact that we now live in a truly global village. First, climate change is no longer a matter for individual states to address alone. We all face this inconvenient truth. Second, the so-called subprime crisis and the failure of the Doha Round of development talks of the World Trade Organization demonstrate that economies are more intertwined than ever before. We can no longer live as if we were alone on the planet.

The witness of Belhar was never intended to be only a local witness. It did not merely confess about contextual issues of apartheid in late twentieth-century South Africa. Like all confessions, the words are from the local church but are spoken on behalf of and addressed to the universal church. The enduring global significance of this confession needs to be shown by reflections from contexts different from the one in which I write. To this reflection, you as readers are sincerely invited.

Let us turn to the structure of this book, which may be construed as a reading of Belhar from four different perspectives. Each perspective — that of history, earlier creeds, reception, and current significance — opens another view of Belhar. The essays, on which a major portion of this book is based, were published in various journals between 1997 and 2008. I acknowledge the kind permission of the various editors to use the material in this format and indicate such use at the beginning of each chapter. In most cases, the essays have been updated and adapted to fit into an overarching scheme. The reader will sense, however, that this collection is not an organic, fully coherent whole. It is more like a collage of photographs taken from different angles rather than a unified, wide-angle picture. The structure therefore needs some explanation.

Following this preface, we provide the texts — the English versions of the original Afrikaans Accompanying Letter and of the Belhar Confession — along with easily accessible commentaries. Some South African churches have been using these clarifying comments for distribution among laypeople. The explanatory commentaries are themselves an example of minimal theological interpretation in service of a wider understanding and reception of Belhar. It is also important to have the Belhar text and letter available, for reference purposes, while reading the essays from chapter 1 onward. The main chapters of the book are academic in nature and require some theological background and technical expertise, although it is hoped that their basic thrust is sufficiently plain for average readers to discern.

The chapters are divided into four parts: Tradition, Confession, Reception, and Contemporary Significance. Part 1 (chapters 1 and 2) explores the tradition underlying the Belhar Confession. Part 2 (chapters 3 and 4) deals with Belhar's confessional and creedal character. Part 3 (chapters 5 and 6) focuses on the reception of the Belhar Confession. And part 4 (chapters 7-9) explores the enduring significance of the confession for Southern Africa and for issues of global concern today.

Part 1: Tradition

Belhar is a protest confession. It speaks from a confessing tradition against a false representation of the gospel. The first two chapters explore this background: Chapter 1 is a concise explanation of the theological roots and contours of what Belhar spoke against. This chapter ends with a specific discussion of the rejection clauses in the light of theological developments in South Africa since the middle of the nineteenth century. Chapter 2 explores Belhar's relationship with a series of countervoices against apartheid theology, as expressed by important preceding ecumenical witnesses between 1948 and 1982. Two examples are the Cottesloe Consultation statement (now commonly called the Cottesloe Declaration, 1961), and *A Message to the People of South Africa* (1968).

Part 2: Confession

Chapter 3 explores how Belhar fulfills the core criteria for church confessions as explicated by Reformed theologian Karl Barth. This chapter attempts to convince the reader that Belhar is indeed a legitimate confession and not only a declaration or a witness. On this basis, chapter 4 explores Belhar's relation with the oldest ecumenical creed, the Nicene-Constantinopolitan Creed, as adopted in 381. This is meant to demonstrate that Belhar indeed witnesses to the same apostolic faith handed down in the church through the ages.

Part 3: Reception

The next two chapters focus on the reception of the Belhar Confession. After a short explanation of the ecumenical challenges posed by a confession, the reception process outside South Africa and in the DRC specifically is explored in chapter 5. Reference is made to the exciting possibilities of full reception in the Reformed Church in America (approved by its General Synod in June 2009) and the reflections on Belhar planned by the Presbyterian Church (U.S.A.) for 2010. Then in chapter 6 we consider the strong links between Belhar and a variety of recent ecumenical initiatives, mainly stemming from the World Council of Churches (WCC).

Part 4: Contemporary significance

The last three chapters attempt to spell out the enduring message of Belhar for today. The confession's three middle articles — on unity, reconciliation, and justice (considered respectively in chapters 7, 8, and 9) — serve as reference points for discussing important issues of local and global concern. Rather than presenting an exhaustive list of possible topics, these chapters serve as an example of creative rereadings of Belhar with the purpose of speaking into the twenty-first century. Questions concerning unity in freedom, gender reconciliation, and issues related to restorative and distributive justice are briefly touched upon.

An important motive behind this book is to place this beautiful African confession in the global arena and invite theological reflections from others. This is not done for the sake of Belhar as such, but rather for the truth of the gospel, to which Belhar witnessed and is still witnessing today.

Acknowledgments

This book was possible only because others have invested considerable time and spiritual energy in my life. I gratefully acknowledge the immense influence of my late dogmatics professor at Stellenbosch University, Willie Jonker, who shaped my theological thinking at a crucial time in South Africa's history. He equipped me and others in a gentle but sure manner, not only to struggle against false theologies, but also to develop our own voice. He knew how important theology would be after political liberation.

The personal friendship and many discussions with Dirkie Smit over the years have played an indispensable role in my Reformed-ecumenical thinking. His ability to serve us through his prolific work remains a constant fountain of joy, and his willingness to write a foreword adds a special dimension to this book.

Johan Botha, Coenie Burger, and Nico Koopman have been tremendous sources of encouragement through their commitment to Belhar and their untiring work in the difficult processes of church reunification in South Africa.

Michael Welker from the University of Heidelberg in Germany has always opened new vistas during my many visits to that university since 1999. He has the ability to challenge us from the South to really become part of a global theological discourse. He has always trusted me more than I thought my work warranted.

The Dutch Reformed Church is my spiritual mother. Here I learned the gospel of Jesus Christ. I acknowledge the work of God — sometimes hidden — in this church and pray earnestly that we will be joyfully obedient as God leads us in the Reformed family back to one another.

My wife, Elize, has lived the Christian faith at my side and always encouraged me to explore new ideas. She has made huge personal sacrifices for me and our family to enable me to focus on research. I thank God for her life and for the example she set to our children.

I sincerely thank David Morton, who ably assisted me in preparing the first draft of this book and who later compiled the index. His attention to minute detail is most commendable.

The University of Port Elizabeth and now the Nelson Mandela Metropolitan University have been generous in their research support, without which this work would not have been possible.

Finally, I thank Jon Pott from the William B. Eerdmans Publishing Company, who agreed in principle to accept this book proposal when very little had been written. It is a pleasure to acknowledge the professional support I received from Craig Noll, editor at Eerdmans, in preparing the final proofs. More broadly, I thank Eerdmans for its role in facilitating theological discussion in the United States and around the world.

PIET NAUDÉ
Nelson Mandela Metropolitan University
Port Elizabeth, South Africa
November 2008

The texts, with commentary

The text of the Belhar Confession and its Accompanying Letter are the real subjects of this book. These closely interrelated texts will therefore be our constant companions throughout our journey to read and reread the confession for today. In this section I offer a preliminary interpretation with explanatory notes that will serve as guidance for the more in-depth theological analyses that follow in the rest of this book.

Accompanying letter

From its beginning, the Belhar Confession in its concept form (1982) was supported by an accompanying letter. Note also that such letters of explanation have often been sent with confessions:

- The Nicene Creed, as finally accepted in the city of Constantinople in A.D. 381, was sent with a letter to Emperor Theodosius I. As ruler of the empire, Theodosius needed to officially approve the final draft of the creed.
- The Belgic Confession (1561) was sent with an accompanying letter to the Catholic-minded King Philip II to explain the good intentions of the Protestants with regards to their confession.
- The Barmen Declaration (1934) in Germany also has an introduction before the actual confessing text. It explains that it is a declaration of the German Evangelical Church, a federal union of confessional

1

churches. These churches testified against the strong and growing National Socialism of that time.

The Accompanying Letter of the Belhar Confession is an important tool for understanding the confession itself. We must therefore take the letter seriously and must always read it with the confession. The Letter consists of four paragraphs. Here I give a short explanation of each one, followed by the paragraph itself.

The first paragraph emphasizes *the seriousness of the situation,* in which the gospel itself is at stake. It asks for a radical faith-decision in the form of a confession. Those who are confessing at this point are aware that they themselves contributed to the situation, and together they accept responsibility for what is confessed.

1. We are deeply conscious that moments of such seriousness can arise in the life of the church that it may feel the need to confess its faith anew in the light of a specific situation. We are aware that such an act of confession is not lightly undertaken, but only if it is considered that the heart of the gospel is so threatened as to be at stake. In our judgment, the present church and political situation in our country, and particularly within the Dutch Reformed Church family, calls for such a decision. Accordingly, we make this confession, not as a contribution to a theological debate or as a new summary of our beliefs, but as a cry from the heart, as something we are obliged to do for the sake of the gospel in view of the times in which we stand. Along with many, we confess our guilt in that we have not always witnessed clearly enough in our situation and so are jointly responsible for the way in which those things that were experienced as sin and confessed to be so or should have been experienced as and confessed to be sin have grown in time to seem self-evidently right and to be ideologies foreign to the Scriptures. As a result many have been given the impression that the gospel was not really at stake. We make this confession because we are convinced that all sorts of theological arguments have contributed to so disproportionate an emphasis on some aspects of the truth that it has in effect become a lie.

The second paragraph speaks about *the authority, the motive, and the subject of the confession.* This authority — as for any Reformed confession — is derived from the Bible as the Word of God. The motive is purely to proclaim the truth of the gospel and to protect the credibility of the church's message. The subject (the "we") of the confession is the church it-self and not one or another party or theological grouping. The plea is therefore that ulterior motives shall not prevent the positive use or reception of the confession.

2. We are aware that the only authority for such a confession and the only grounds on which it may be made are the Holy Scriptures as the Word of God. Being fully aware of the risks involved in taking this step, we are nevertheless convinced that we have no alternative. Furthermore, we are aware that no other motives or convictions, however valid they may be, would give us the right to confess in this way. An act of confession may be made by the church only for the sake of its purity and credibility and that of its message. As solemnly as we are able, we hereby declare before everyone that our only motive lies in our fear that the truth and power of the gospel itself are threatened in this situation. We do not wish to serve any group interests, advance the cause of any factions, promote any theologies, or achieve any ulterior purposes. Yet, having said this, we know that our deepest intentions may be judged at their true value only by him before whom all is revealed. We do not make this confession from his throne and from on high, but before his throne and before other human beings. We plead, therefore, that this confession should not be misused by anyone with ulterior motives and also that it should not be resisted to serve such motives. Our earnest desire is to lay no false stumbling blocks in the way but to point to the true stumbling block, Jesus Christ the rock.

The third paragraph tells of *the object* (the "to whom" or "to what") *of the confession*. It is not aimed at specific people or groups of people or a church or churches, but against a false doctrine that is occurring now and could occur again in the future. The deceptive nature of false doctrines is that they consist of half-truths that have been accepted as truth by sincere Christian people. Then follows *a plea for reconciliation and also humility* — in particular, by those people who actually pronounce the confession.

3. This confession is not aimed at specific people or groups of people or a church or churches. We proclaim it against a false doctrine, against an ideological distortion that threatens the gospel itself in our church and our country. Our heartfelt longing is that no one will identify themselves with this objectionable doctrine and that all who have been

wholly or partially blinded by it will turn themselves away from it. We are deeply aware of the deceiving nature of such a false doctrine and know that many who have been conditioned by it have to a greater or lesser extent learned to take a half-truth for the whole. For this reason we do not doubt the Christian faith of many such people, their sincerity, honor, integrity, and good intentions, and their in many ways estimable practice and conduct. However, it is precisely because we know the power of deception that we know we are not liberated by the serious-ness, sincerity, or intensity of our certainties, but only by the truth in the Son. Our church and our land have an intense need of such liberation. Therefore it is that we speak pleadingly rather than accusingly. We plead for reconciliation, the true reconciliation that follows on conversion and change of attitudes and structures. And while we do so, we are aware that an act of confession is a two-edged sword, that none of us can throw the first stone, and none is without a beam in his own eye. We know that the attitudes and conduct that work against the gospel are present in all of us and will continue to be so. Therefore this confession must be seen as a call to a continuous process of soul-searching to-gether, a joint wrestling with the issues, and a readiness to repent in the name of our Lord Jesus Christ in a broken world. It is certainly not in-tended as an act of self-justification and intolerance, for that would dis-qualify us in the very act of preaching to others.

The fourth paragraph points to *the implications of the confession.* It asks for repentance and conversion from all. It requires that all should walk together on the unknown road of reconciliation and justice. It also asks for the dismantling of unjust church and social structures that have developed over many years. The letter ends with a prayer and the firm con-viction that the Lord, Jesus Christ, will bring true peace by his Spirit.

4. Our prayer is that this act of confession will not place false stumbling blocks in the way and thereby cause and foster false divisions, but rather that it will be reconciling and uniting. We know that such an act of con-fession and process of reconciliation will necessarily involve much pain and sadness. It demands the pain of repentance, remorse, and confes-sion; the pain of individual and collective renewal and a changed way of life. It places us on a road whose end we can neither foresee nor manip-ulate to our own desire. On this road we shall unavoidably suffer intense growing pains while we struggle to conquer alienation, bitterness,

irreconciliation, and fear. We shall have to come to know and encounter both ourselves and others in new ways. We are only too well aware that this confession calls for the dismantling of structures of thought, of church, and of society that have developed over many years. However, we confess that for the sake of the gospel, we have no other choice. We pray that our brothers and sisters throughout the Dutch Reformed Church family, but also outside it, will want to make this new beginning with us so that we can be free together, and together may walk the road of reconciliation and justice. Accordingly, our prayer is that the pain and sadness we speak of will be pain and sadness that lead to salvation. We believe that this is possible in the power of our Lord and by his Spirit. We believe that the gospel of Jesus Christ offers hope, liberation, salvation, and true peace to our country.

The Confession of Belhar

The confession consists of five subsections, which for citation purposes will be referred to as articles. The first article repeats and confirms the ancient Christian belief in the triune God, who establishes the church. The following three articles deal with the church and its role in the world: the unity of the church (art. 2), reconciliation in the church and society (art. 3), and the bringing about of peace and justice in the world (art. 4). The fifth article calls the church to do what is confessed, even if it means persecution. The confession closes with a brief doxology to God. Each of the five articles has been subdivided into paragraphs: for example, article 3 paragraph 2 will be denoted as article 3.2. A copy of the complete confession without commentary appears in appendix A.

The three middle articles consist of positive confessions, followed by clauses rejecting the doctrine against which confession is made. Here Belhar follows the pattern of previous confessions, which "answer" specific false doctrines. We find distinct examples of such refutations in the Belgic Confession articles 12, 13, 15, 29, and 35; the Heidelberg Catechism (HC), Sundays 29-30; and also the Canons of Dort, with its very clear rejections in each of its chapters.

The Belhar text, as finally adopted in 1986 by the DRMC of that time, is reprinted below. Note that we also include the Scripture references with the various parts in the original confession. The text is interspersed with comments to show the internal logic of the confession. These comments also at-

5

tempt to point out the bond that exists between the Belhar Confession, the Bible, and the Nicene and Apostolic Creeds, as well as the close ties with the Three Formulae of Unity (Belgic Confession, Heidelberg Catechism, and Canons of Dort). Without elaborate interpretation, a few comments are made on why the confession is still very important to us today.

Article 1

The confession begins with the triune God and also closes (in art. 5) with a doxology to God.

> We believe in the triune God, Father, Son and Holy Spirit,

The entire confession is thus founded in and "encircled" by our faith in this triune God. This is how God has revealed himself in the Bible — as Creator, Redeemer, and Holy Spirit. The trinitarian nature of God is clearly confirmed in verses such as Matthew 28:19 and 2 Corinthians 13:14. This was the confession of the church against all kinds of heresies through the centuries.

This statement of one God and three persons is found in the earliest ecumenical creeds of Nicea, Athanasius, and the Apostles. All three of these creeds are built around faith in the triune God. The Reformation affirmed and explained this faith in detail in the Belgic Confession articles 8-11, HC Sunday 8, and the Canons of Dort 1.7.

The plural "we" with which the confession starts indicates that it is not one person who is confessing here but the whole church. Of course, at the beginning in 1986 it was the Dutch Reformed Mission Church who was confessing, but it is hoped that eventually Belhar will be a confession for the whole church catholic, everywhere and also far into the future.

> . . . who gathers, protects and cares for his Church by his Word and his Spirit, as He has done since the beginning of the world and will do to the end.

This is a direct quotation of the HC, question and answer 54: "What do you believe of the holy catholic church? That the Son of God . . . from the beginning to the end of the world gathers, defends, and preserves for himself . . . by his Spirit and Word . . . a church chosen to everlasting life."

The bond between the triune God and all believers — the old and new

Israel — runs like a golden thread through the entire Bible. Yahweh, the God of Abraham, Isaac, and Jacob, is not to be thought of without his people (Gen. 12; Hos. 11). Likewise, the work of Jesus Christ and the Holy Spirit is closely associated with the church in the New Testament (Acts 1:8; 2:1-13; Col. 1:18). This bond between God and the church is also present in the creeds of the early church, with faith in the church being mentioned directly after faith in the Father, Son, and Holy Spirit. In the Nicene Creed the church is a component of our faith in the Holy Spirit. In the HC question and answer 54, God's Word and Spirit bind God to the church as the means through which he brings the church into existence.

The belief in our election without merit, explained in the Canons of Dort 1.7, underlines the fact that in the church we do not belong to ourselves but to God. The church is definitely not the work of humans or merely the result of human initiative. The church is the work of God and therefore belongs to God. The church exists to honor God and not in the first place to satisfy the needs of human beings.

That God not only gathers his church together but also defends and preserves it implies that the church may always be subject to danger. This also points to article 5, which says that obedience to God may lead to struggle and suffering. This was the situation in South Africa if one looks at the background and time from which this confession comes. Today, it is still the same: obedience to the gospel results in struggle and suffering in various forms, ranging from active persecution to secularist indifference.

The safety and future of the church do not rest with its plans or with human efforts to defend it. The church is safe because Jesus Christ, the head, is an eternal king "who can never be without subjects" (Belgic Confession art. 27). Christ is the Alpha and the Omega (Rev. 22:13). For this reason, it is he who preserves the church from the beginning (alpha) of the world to the very end (omega).

Article 2

The second article begins by quoting directly the "signs" of the church as confessed at Nicea and in the Apostles' Creed, and which is confirmed in the Belgic Confession article 27.

> We believe in one holy, universal Christian Church, the communion of saints called from the entire human family.

The addition of "called from the entire human family" is taken from the HC, question and answer 54, which explains this confession and intimates the grace of God among all peoples of the earth.

It is possible to relate the articles of the confession with the marks of the church as confessed through the ages: catholicity is confessed in articles 1 and 5; unity is confessed in article 2; holiness (via reconciliation) in article 3; and the Christian character of the church that does justice is confessed in article 4. Belhar is a confession of and about the church and, following the early church, roots that confession in its vision of the triune God.

> Eph. 2:11-22
> We believe that Christ's work of reconciliation is made manifest in the Church as the community of believers who have been reconciled with God and with one another;

This article emphasizes the unity of the church as a manifestation of Christ's reconciliation. The basis of the community of believers is not how much people like each other or feel attracted to one another. It grows from the work of Christ, who reconciles people with God and with one another. The reference to Ephesians 2:11-22 points out that this unity specifically concerns people who are often enemies (Jews and Gentiles, circumcised and uncircumcised). According to the Bible, they are now reconciled "in one body" through the cross of Jesus Christ. The cost for accomplishing this peace was Christ's body and his death on the cross (Eph. 2:16-17).

> Eph. 4:1-16
> ... that unity is, therefore, both a gift and an obligation for the Church of Jesus Christ; that through the working of God's Spirit it is a binding force, yet simultaneously a reality which must be earnestly pursued and sought; one which the people of God must continually be built up to attain;

This unity of the church has two sides. On the one side it is a gift of the Holy Spirit, built on the unity of and in God (Eph. 4:4-6). But at the same time it is a mission (4:4) and a task to which the church should apply itself (4:3). Unity is not an optional extra on the agenda of the church that emerges only once in a while when people from different churches come together for the sake of common worship. It belongs to the very nature and core of the church's commission. A disunited church is in conflict with what God intended the church to be.

John 17:20, 23

... that this unity must become visible so that the world may believe that separation, enmity and hatred between people and groups is sin which Christ has already conquered, and accordingly that anything which threatens this unity may have no place in the Church and must be resisted;

Belhar draws here on John's version of Jesus' last prayer for his disciples and for those who would believe because of their witness. The unity between Father and Son is the basis for unity among disciples of Christ. The unity of the church becomes the mark of truth by which the very incarnation is measured. Because the world sees this unity in the church, they also believe the mission of the Son. This unity must therefore be visible and not only "spiritual." For what value would a confession of Christ have if Christian people themselves live in separation and enmity and, on top of that, proclaim this separation to be the gospel?

Phil. 2:1-5; 1 Cor. 12:4-31; John 13:1-17; 1 Cor. 1:10-13; Eph. 4:1-6; Eph. 3:14-20; 1 Cor. 10:16-17; 1 Cor. 11:17-34; Gal. 6:2; 2 Cor. 1:3-4

... that this unity of the people of God must be manifested and be active in a variety of ways: in that we love one another; that we experience, practice and pursue community with one another; that we are obligated to give ourselves willingly and joyfully to be of benefit and blessing to one another; that we share one faith, have one calling, are of one soul and one mind; have one God and Father, are filled with one Spirit, are baptised with one baptism, eat of one bread and drink of one cup, confess one Name, are obedient to one Lord, work for one cause, and share one hope; together come to know the height and the breadth and the depth of the love of Christ; together are built up to the stature of Christ, to the new humanity; together know and bear one another's burdens, thereby fulfilling the law of Christ that we need one another and upbuild one another, admonishing and comforting one another; that we suffer with one another for the sake of righteousness; pray together; together serve God in this world; and together fight against all which may threaten or hinder this unity;

One might now ask: What does visible unity actually look like in practice? This section of the confession consists of a long list of New Testament directions on how to embody unity in the life and practices of the church. Nine of the ten Scripture references here come from the New Testament

THE TEXTS, WITH COMMENTARY

corpus of letters, written to congregations to help them struggle against enmity and forge a community united in Christ and the sacraments. There is a clear emphasis on the status of being one already through their faith in Christ and of their having one God and Father. From this deep reality flow the other practical actions: give yourselves up for others like Jesus did; carry each other's burdens; pray together; build each other up; admonish and comfort one another; and, if need be, suffer together. The section ends with a call to also fight together against all that may hinder this unity from being manifest and visible.

> Rom. 12:3-8; 1 Cor. 12:1-11; Eph. 4:7-13; Gal. 3:27-28; Jas. 2:1-13
> . . . that this unity can be established only in freedom and not under constraint;

All parts of the Bible quoted here are from the "ethical" parts of the letters and from the wisdom of the book of James. It explains what the confession really wishes to say: only by reason of the grace given to us (Rom. 12) and by reason of the work of the Spirit (1 Cor. 12; Eph. 4) are people free to become one. Unity cannot be forced upon people by impressing it as a political or cultural ideal. It comes from the "constraint" of the gospel, which frees us from our selfishness to reach out to one another in freedom.

> . . . that the variety of spiritual gifts, opportunities, backgrounds, convictions, as well as the various languages and cultures, are by virtue of the reconciliation in Christ, opportunities for mutual service and enrichment within the one visible people of God;

The quoted Bible verses deal with the differences in the congregations of the early church: Jews as opposed to Greeks (culture), master as opposed to slaves (authority and position), educated as opposed to uneducated (class), men as opposed to women (gender), and many more. These verses also indicate how this variety of states in life can be used positively: the body has many members, each with its own function, and in their distinctiveness they serve the unity. Throughout Scripture the message comes through loud and clear that, in Christ and through the Spirit, we are and remain one body. As a result, then, our background or class is of little consequence. In Christ we are all children of God. The language that turns racial and cultural divisions into "opportunities for mutual service" comes from HC question and answer 55, where "the communion of saints" is explained. All believers and each one separately share in the Lord's treasures and gifts. For this reason everyone is under obligation to use his or her gifts "freely and cheerfully for the benefit and welfare of other members."

> . . . that true faith in Jesus Christ is the only condition for membership of this Church.

Because the church is the fruit of God's reconciliation in Jesus Christ, it is only logical that admission to the body would be open for all who accept Jesus Christ in faith. Any other condition would mean that the work of Jesus Christ was not sufficient. Then the church would be like a religious club where all kinds of humanly set requirements apply in order to become a member.

Now that the unity of the church has been confessed, Belhar expresses what is no longer acceptable, doing so by rejecting four false beliefs.

> Therefore, we reject any doctrine which absolutizes either natural diversity or the sinful separation of people in such a way that this absolutization hinders or breaks the visible and active unity of the Church, or even leads to the establishment of a separate church formation;

The confession has already brought differences among people within the reconciliation of Christ. Christians who perceive a God-ordained natural differentiation as a basis for separation deny the one new humanity in Christ. There is no other way but to reject a doctrine that weakens or denies this reconciliatory work. A belief that sinful separation is acceptable to God has direct consequences for the visible unity of the church: it prevents such unity and indeed, since 1881, has led to the establishment of separate churches in the Dutch Reformed Church family.

> . . . which professes that this spiritual unity is truly being maintained in the bond of peace whilst believers of the same confession are in effect alienated from one another for the sake of diversity and in despair of reconciliation;

Of course the unity of the church is a spiritual (and Spirit-like!) matter. For example, churches of various confessional traditions are spread all over the world but still maintain a bond of spiritual unity that is expressed visibly in ecumenical bodies or internally in bodies of governance and decision-making. Where churches exist near to one another and share the same confessions, they cannot hide behind separate, racially defined churches or "spiritual unity," which is simply a smokescreen for alienation. A doctrine that confesses irreconcilability rather than unity, which considers church unity as merely "spiritual" (invisible) and not a visible reality, must therefore be rejected.

> . . . which denies that a refusal earnestly to pursue this visible unity as a priceless gift is sin;

A doctrine that implies that we should not seek earnestly for visible unity stands in opposition to the gospel of Jesus Christ. It is a sin to consider visible unity as something that asks too much or takes too long to happen. To abandon the journey toward visible unity is like giving away a priceless gift before it is even opened!

> . . . which explicitly or implicitly maintains that descent or any other human or social factor should be a consideration in determining membership of the Church.

A doctrine that adds something to "faith alone" is a false doctrine. It is a denial of Scripture and of a core insight of the Protestant Reformation. There are believers who do agree that "faith alone" ensures admission to the church but who, in practices of exclusion based on class or race, close their church or congregation so that only certain people are in fact allowed there. These people deceive themselves (Jas. 1:22). They do not act as the Word tells them. "My brothers and sisters, hold the faith of our glorious Lord Jesus Christ without acts of favoritism. . . . But if you show partiality, you commit sin" (Jas. 2:1, 9 mg.).[1]

Article 3

Where article 2 establishes the bond between reconciliation and unity for "the inside" of the church, article 3 looks at reconciliation on "the outside," beyond the confines of the church. In other words, the emphasis falls on the significance of the church as a reconciling community for the world in which it lives.

---

1. Throughout, unless noted otherwise, Bible quotations are taken from the New Revised Standard Version.

2 Cor. 5:17-21; Matt. 5:13-16; Matt. 5:9; 2 Pet. 3:13; Rev. 21–22

We believe that God has entrusted to his Church the message of reconciliation in and through Jesus Christ; that the Church is called to be the salt of the earth and the light of the world; that the Church is called blessed because it is a peacemaker; that the Church is witness both by word and by deed to the new heaven and the new earth in which righteousness dwells;

The article commences with a direct incorporation of five parts of Scripture. It begins with the well-known and significant 2 Corinthians 5, where the church is entrusted with the ministry of reconciliation. In other words, what Christ has done, must be put into practice now. How does the church accomplish this? The answer comes from other passages: by being the salt and the light of the world (Matt. 5:13-16), by being peacemakers (Matt. 5:9), by living in the world with godliness and dedication (2 Pet. 3) so that the promises of the future — righteousness in particular (Rev. 21–22) — may be realized here and now.

Eph. 4:17–6:23; Rom. 6; Col. 1:9-14; Col. 2:13-19; Col. 3:1–4:6

. . . that God by his lifegiving Word and Spirit has conquered the powers of sin and death, and therefore also of irreconciliation and hatred, bitterness and enmity;

For the people of New Testament times, sin was associated with a struggle between powers, authorities, forces, and spirits — "for our struggle is not against enemies of blood and flesh . . ." (Eph. 6:12). The ministry of Jesus (e.g., his healing powers and miracles) shows that he struggled against these forces and eventually conquered them on the cross (Col. 2:13-19). He is now Lord "of all creation" (Col. 1:15), and Christians are exhorted to put on the armor, even while they know that the victory has already been attained (Eph. 6).

This part of article 3 reaches back to the same Word and Spirit the triune God uses to gather and protect the church (art. 1). Here it is confessed that the power of sin and death has already been conquered. In Romans 6, referred to here, this conquering is connected with our baptism in Christ. Nicea specifically names the Spirit "the Lord and Giver of Life." This reference is repeated twice in this article in the very context where Belhar clearly states which powers still alienate people even today: irreconciliation, hatred, bitterness, and enmity. They have, however, been conquered

13

through the lifegiving Word and Spirit and no longer have a hold over Christians.

> ... that God by his lifegiving Word and Spirit will enable his people to live in a new obedience which can open new possibilities of life for society and the world;

Where and how will people know that God really conquered the forces of enmity? The confession answers clearly: The "where" is the church, and the "how" is the lifestyle, the example of God's people who live in the power of the Word and the Spirit. Yes, this life of unity and mutual reconciliation must speak so clearly that it will give hope to a society and a world that are seeking new life possibilities.

> ... that the credibility of this message is seriously affected and its beneficial work obstructed when it is proclaimed in a land which professes to be Christian, but in which the enforced separation of people on a racial basis promotes and perpetuates alienation, hatred and enmity;

Here Belhar moves beyond the church to society and, specifically, to the South African society of the time, which claimed to be Christian, despite evidence to the contrary. In a political order that legitimated enforced separation on a racial basis, the "forces of estrangement" that were conquered in Christ were kept alive. They were in fact promoted and perpetuated. This meant that people no longer accepted the power of the gospel and that the positive fruit of reconciliation was being corrupted. The result was a legitimacy crisis for the gospel.

> ... that any teaching which attempts to legitimate such forced separation by appeal to the gospel and is not prepared to venture on the road of obedience and reconciliation, but rather, out of prejudice, fear, selfishness and unbelief, denies in advance the reconciling power of the gospel, must be considered ideology and false doctrine.

Belhar is a theological confession and does not attempt to judge political models per se. However, it does condemn false doctrines that use the gospel to defend enforced separation as if it were the will of God in Christ. According to the confession, such a doctrine is not based on victory in Christ. It results from prejudice (fixed ideas about what other people are like), fear (afraid of contact and living with "them," "the other"), and selfishness (a desire to retain privileged positions). In a fundamental sense, however, this false doctrine is based on an inability to believe that the power of the gospel can actually bring people together. According to this view, even Christians are unable to transform enmity and separation into friendship and fellowship. Such a doctrine eventually becomes an alien gospel, an ideology, and is therefore rejected as heresy, a false doctrine.

> Therefore, we reject any doctrine which, in such a situation, sanctions in the name of the gospel or of the will of God the forced separation of people on the grounds of race and colour and thereby in advance obstructs and weakens the ministry and experience of reconciliation in Christ.

Any doctrine that presents enforced racial separation as gospel or as the will of God must be rejected. The reason for this rejection is not political in nature, although, as the Accompanying Letter states explicitly, such a doctrine has severe negative social implications. This doctrine is rejected because it vitiates the church's ministry of reconciliation in the world. How can you make the gospel of reconciliation practical when some people teach that the gospel asks the exact opposite? Even more: this false doctrine teaches that people in a divided community can experience, in that very division, reconciliation in Christ. This clearly obstructs and weakens the true gospel and must therefore be rejected.

Article 4

In this article, belief in the triune God (art. 1), the unity of the church (art. 2), and reconciliation in church and society (art. 3) are taken further to promote justice and peace. This article first confesses faith in God, in whom justice lives. It then, as a consequence of this, makes clear that the church — by imitation of God — must bring this justice into practical effect in the world.

> Deut. 32:4; Luke 2:14; John 14:27; Eph. 2:14; Isa. 1:16-17; Jas. 1:27; Jas. 5:1-6; Luke 1:46-55; Luke 6:20-26; Luke 7:22; Luke 16:19-31
> We believe that God has revealed himself as the One who wishes to bring about justice and true peace among men;

How does God reveal himself? In the Bible of course, we say. What does this God of the Bible look like? We cannot see God, but we can understand God from his deeds. This is how God is described in the Scriptures: "He is the Rock, his works are perfect, and *all his ways are just.* A faithful God who *does no wrong,* upright and just is he" (Deut. 32:4 NIV). In God there is no injustice. And for this reason he cannot tolerate injustice or close his eyes to it. In Bethlehem, at the birth of Jesus, the angels sang of peace on earth (Luke 2:14). This is what Jesus also teaches in his last instruction: "Peace I leave with you" (John 14:27), and this is what Eph. 2:14 confesses about the new humanity: "For he is our peace." God wants to establish this justice and peace among all people and in the whole cosmos.

> . . . that in a world full of injustice and enmity He is in a special way the God of the destitute, the poor, and the wronged and that He calls his Church to follow Him in this;

How can God establish this justice and peace (*shalom* as cosmic peace) in a world full of injustice and discord? God does so by choosing justice in situations of wrongdoing, by changing enmity into peace and healing. Therefore, where people suffer or are poor as a result of injustices in systems and society, God will be there for them in a special way: He "executes justice for the oppressed, [he] gives food to the hungry. . . . The LORD watches over the strangers; he upholds the orphan and the widow, but the way of the wicked he brings to ruin," as Israel sings in Psalm 146. And also today, the people of God and the church are called for this purpose: "Cease to do evil, learn to do good; seek justice, rescue the oppressed" (Isa. 1:16-17).

Some people link this part of the confession in a vague way with "liberation theology" and a "partisan God" and as a result oppose and even reject the confession. Their viewpoint must be questioned for at least two reasons. First, such an opposition makes no allowance for the continuous evidence in the Bible of how God accepts responsibility for justice and makes special legal provisions for those without rights. It can therefore truly be confessed that God *reveals* himself as such. This is a theme in Scripture that is as clear, for example, as justification by faith alone. That God is responsible for justice is a perspective that corresponds closely with our Reformed heritage, with its emphasis that God rules over all and everyone. And today this is a perspective that is inscribed in ecumenical (interchurch) agreements about our Christian faith. Second, criticism against Belhar's wording does not take into account that the confession itself gives testimony here of God's "distinctiveness" in a world full of injustice and enmity. God does not stand by the poor because they are poor or because — as in a class struggle — he is in a particular way the God of the working class. In God, there is no injustice. God stands with the people who suffer in situations of injustice, because of this injustice. God can do no other. This is how God is.

> . . . that He brings justice to the oppressed and gives bread to the hungry; that He frees the prisoner and restores sight to the blind; that He supports the downtrodden, protects the stranger, helps orphans and widows and blocks the path of the ungodly; that for Him pure and undefiled religion is to visit the orphans and the widows in their suffering; that He wishes to teach his people to do what is good and to seek the right;

This moving, stirring description of how God stands for justice is nothing but a successive quotation of Bible verses. He brings justice to the oppressed (Isa. 1:16-17). He gives bread to the hungry; he frees the prisoner and restores sight to the blind (Ps. 146:7-8). They become the signs whereby people will know that Jesus is the Messiah (Luke 7:21-23). God raises those who are bowed down (Ps. 146:8) and exalts the lowly (Luke 1:52). God has a very special place in God's heart for those without rights such as widows, orphans, and strangers. This is apparent in many of the laws in the Old Testament and becomes the test for faith that proceeds to deeds, a testimony of true religion before God (Jas. 1:27). God showers the poor with good things (Luke 1:53), blesses them and promises them the kingdom of God (Luke 6:20; 16:19-31). He condemns the rich who focus on self-enrichment and who collect their riches by unfair practices, such as the exploitation of their workers (Jas. 5:1-6). The people of God are called to conversion and repentance so that God can teach them to stand up for right and freedom, thereby acting as God would act (Isa. 1:16-20).

> Ps. 146; Luke 4:16-19; Rom. 6:13-18; Amos 5
> . . . that the Church must therefore stand by people in any form of suffering and need, which implies, among other things, that the Church must witness against and strive against any form of injustice, so that justice may roll down like waters, and righteousness like an ever-flowing stream; that the Church as the possession of God must stand where He

stands, namely against injustice and with the wronged; that in following Christ the Church must witness against all the powerful and privileged who selfishly seek their own interests and thus control and harm others.

What are the practical implications when the church — like God — stands up for righteousness? The confession gives three clear guidelines from Scripture. First, the church must *make a choice* to stand where Christ stands. As he is the source of justice, he stands with the victimized in situations of injustice. So God is praised in his greatness (look again at Ps. 146), which is how Jesus proclaims his ministry in Luke 4 (with a reference to Isa. 61). As followers of Jesus, as people in the service of God (Rom. 6:13), the church is called upon to uphold the year of grace, the year of reparation. The church stands where God stands. Second, the church must be able to *testify against injustice and for that which is right.* As illustrated in the Bible by Amos, Hosea, Jeremiah, Jesus, James, and others, this includes a very clear testimony against people with power who determine the destinies of other people for their own interests and who wrong others for their own advantage. Third, the church must *give assistance and practical support* to people who suffer — it does not matter what kind of suffering, and it does not matter who is in need. Look at the Good Samaritan and heed the call of Jesus that we must be perfect by loving our enemies, irrespective of persons (Matt. 5:43-48).

> Therefore, we reject any ideology which would legitimate forms of injustice and any doctrine which is unwilling to resist such an ideology in the name of the gospel.

An ideology is a system that favors only some people, but it is these people who usually wield the power and fight to retain this position at other people's expense. Where a political or economic system openly allows injustice and where people will do anything to maintain this system, which is favorable to them alone, such a system usually becomes an ideology. Furthermore, when they say that it is God's will that it should be so, it becomes even more dangerous. People are then prepared to lay down their lives to keep this power. We see many examples of this in the world today inside Christianity and in other faiths. The gospel, the good news of a righteous God, is in opposition to such an ideology. A doctrine that calmly allows and maintains such an ideology, and in fact persecutes those who resist this ideology, must be rejected in light of the true gospel.

Article 5

The confession concludes that the church must now confirm all the preceding things through word ("confess") and deed ("do"). This is what following and obeying Jesus Christ means.

> Eph. 4:15-16; Acts 5:29-33; 1 Pet. 2:18-25; 1 Pet. 3:15-18
> We believe that, in obedience to Jesus Christ, its only Head, the Church is called to confess and to do all these things, even though the authorities and human laws might forbid them and punishment and suffering be the consequence.

Those who stand up for what Belhar confesses — unity, reconciliation, and justice — can expect resistance. The authorities (people in control) and human laws may let those who stand for the truth of the gospel be punished and have them suffer. In many situations today, the true gospel is suppressed, and both discord and injustice reign.

Only one head rules the church, however, namely Jesus Christ, and from him the whole body grows (Eph. 4:15-16). As with the apostles from long ago, the church may be asked to say: "We must obey God rather than any human authority" (Acts 5:29). Christians should be able to explain their conduct to any outsider (1 Pet. 3:15). As Peter testifies, "But if you endure when you do right and suffer for it, you have God's approval" (1 Pet. 2:20).

> Jesus is Lord.

This ancient confession from the very first congregations was a clear protest against the worshipping of the Roman emperor. This short statement is an expression of the lordship of Jesus alone. Many Christians were condemned to death because of maintaining this allegiance. Against all powers and authorities and systems — including today against all the forces of globalization — the church still has to testify that one Lord, Jesus Christ, rules us, and he is the head of all creation.

> To the one and only God, Father, Son and Holy Spirit, be the honour and the glory for ever and ever.

The confession ends as it began, with a testimony to the triune God. To this God, as the final words of the Lord's Prayer say, be the power and glory forever. By proclaiming the glory of God "for ever and ever," the confession follows the Nicene Creed in reaching beyond our history to "the life of the world to come."

We have now been introduced to the letter and the confession, and we have become more familiar with them. The rest of this book, then, will provide a deeper theological reflection of these documents. To this journey, the reader is warmly invited.

Part 1

TRADITION

Chapter 1

The "no!" of the Belhar Confession

Therefore we reject any doctrine which absolutizes either natural diversity or the sinful separation of people in such a way that this absolutization hinders or breaks the visible and active unity of the Church, or even leads to the establishment of a separate church formation.

— Belhar Confession, article 2

Karl Barth wrote that one needs to understand the "no" of a confession before one can claim to support the "yes."[1] The Belhar Confession, as we saw above, is first and foremost a positive affirmation of our belief in the triune God, followed by the task of the church in establishing unity, reconciliation, and justice. The confession closes with a positive call to obedience under the lordship of Jesus Christ, irrespective of the cost of standing against human ordinances.

In line with the classic tradition of credos and confessions, the three middle articles express the doctrinal "no" of the confession in clear rejection clauses. The Accompanying Letter makes clear that the confession

---

1. Karl Barth, *Church dogmatics,* I/2: *The revelation of God* (Edinburgh: T. & T. Clark, 1956), pp. 630-31.

This chapter is a substantial redrafting of Piet J. Naudé, "From pluralism to ideology: The roots of apartheid theology in Abraham Kuyper, Gustav Warneck, and theological Pietism," *Scriptura* 88 (2005): 161-73.

does not speak out against a specific church or political system as such. The confession is a "no" against a false gospel that is held as truth.

Against what did Belhar actually profess in the historical situation of South Africa in the 1980s? How is it possible that Christians can turn the gospel into a heresy? The fact that we take the specifics of the South African context into account in no way detracts from the universal significance and warning expressed by Belhar. We know that many false gospels have emerged in the course of history, and the temptation to make the Word of God a servant of narrow human or national interests is always lurking beneath the intentions of well-meaning Christians. Elsewhere, the Christian faith has been turned into an ideology, and it can happen again. But it is important that the specifics of our history are understood in order to give flesh to the rejection clauses in Belhar.

In very broad terms, one could say that Belhar fought against a specific brand of Afrikaner Calvinism,[2] or a specific trajectory of Afrikaner civil religion that emerged in the period between 1860 and 1960.[3] Classic works have been written on the rise of a theology that supported racism and apartheid, and the literature on this topic, from both inside and outside South Africa, is vast.[4] A few of these immediately come to mind: T. Dunbar Moody, *The rise of Afrikanerdom* (Berkeley: University of California Press, 1975); W. A. de Klerk, *The Puritans in Africa* (London: Rex Collings, 1975); Irving Hexham, *The irony of apartheid: The struggle for national independence of Afrikaner Calvinism against British imperialism* (New York: Edwin Mellen, 1981); the groundbreaking first edition of John W. de Gruchy, *The church struggle in South Africa* (Cape Town: David Philip, 1979); and de Gruchy's later theological reflections in *Liberating reformed theology: A South African contribution to an ecumenical debate* (Grand Rapids: Eerdmans, 1991). For those able to read Afrikaans, *Die N. G. Kerk en apartheid*, edited by Johann Kinghorn (Cape Town: Macmillan, 1986), remains one of the best insider analyses available. Readers are encouraged to read these

---

2. See Irving Hexham, *The irony of apartheid: The struggle for national independence of Afrikaner Calvinism against British imperialism* (New York: Edwin Mellen, 1981); and John W. de Gruchy, *The church struggle in South Africa* (Cape Town: David Philip, 1979).

3. See David Bosch, "Nothing but a heresy," in *Apartheid is a heresy*, ed. John W. de Gruchy and Charles Villa-Vicencio, pp. 25-38 (Cape Town: David Philip, 1983).

4. See Dirk J. Smit, "Südafrika," *Theologische Realensiklopädie* 32 (2000): 322-32, for a far greater representative selection of material; see also the older, but still very useful, bibliography compiled by Johann Kinghorn, ed., *Die N. G. Kerk en apartheid* (Johannesburg: Macmillan, 1986).

and other fascinating and far more detailed historical and theological accounts.

The aim of this chapter is to give a condensed account of South Africa's theological history to enable a better understanding of the "no" clauses in Belhar. Building on a mixture of secondary and primary sources, a very broad but hopefully credible picture is drawn of how a "theology of apartheid" was constructed in the first half of the twentieth century in South Africa from a combination of three nineteenth-century European theological currents. These theologies were the neo-Calvinism of the highly influential Dutch scholar Abraham Kuyper, the missiological thinking of the German Lutheran Gustav Warneck, and evangelical Pietism, emerging primarily from Scotland. These ideas are placed in the context of the history of the Afrikaner people around the turn of the nineteenth and early twentieth centuries in order to illustrate the close interaction between theological convictions and certain significant socioeconomic factors.

Abraham Kuyper

Abraham Kuyper (1837-1920), a self-professed (neo-)Calvinist since 1870, exerted enormous influence on the church and society of the Netherlands during his lifetime.[5] Kuyper was a pastor, a brilliant scholar and theologian, and an active public figure who still today inspires the new movement toward "public theology," as for example at the Abraham Kuyper Center for Public Theology at Princeton Theological Seminary. Kuyper worked with the weekly church paper *De Heraut* from 1869, and he was the power behind the 1886 schism in the Nederlandse Hervormde Kerk, known as the Doleantie (lit. "grieving"). In the political sphere, Kuyper founded a public newspaper, *De Standaard,* in 1872. He also established the Free University in Amsterdam (1880), started the Anti-Revolutionaire Partij (1879, a Protestant Christian democratic political party), and ultimately became prime minister of the Netherlands (1901-5). He commenced his reflections on Calvinism with a series of Bible studies in which he worked out the basis for what became his formal dogmatic works pub-

5. For an overview and evaluation of Kuyper's life and work, see Luis E. Lugo, ed., *Religion, pluralism, and public life: Abraham Kuyper's legacy for the twenty-first century* (Grand Rapids: Eerdmans, 2000); and Cornelis van der Kooi and Jan de Bruijn, eds., *Kuyper reconsidered: Aspects of his life and work* (Amsterdam: V. U. Uitgeverij, 1999).

lished between 1888 and 1917.[6] In highly simplified terms, three elements of Kuyper's vast thinking are relevant here: his cosmology, his ecclesiology, and his view of human and social development.

One of the key thrusts of Calvinism, and the driving force behind Kuyper's thinking, is its conviction that the whole world exists under the reign of God. Christian faith therefore not only has personal significance but exerts social, transformative power. In the words of John Hesselink, "Calvinism can never be accused of having a God who is too small, or a vision that is too narrow. . . . In contrast to Lutheranism's quest for a gracious God, Pietism's concern for the welfare of the individual soul, and Wesleyanism's goal of personal holiness, the ultimate concern in the Reformed tradition transcends the individual and his salvation. . . . The concern is for the realization of the will of God also in the wider realms of state and culture, in nature and in the cosmos."[7] One of many examples of Kuyper's cosmological thinking is found in the second chapter of his well-known Stone Lectures, published as *Calvinism: Six lectures delivered in the Theological Seminary at Princeton* (1899).[8]

In line with this tradition, Kuyper's aim was to provide a theological basis for bringing the whole of reality under the rule of God. He accomplished this by constructing a cosmology in which there is a close analogy between Creator and creation, based on the notion of common grace *(gemeene gratie)*. From eternity, all principles of life are hidden in God, carrying a particular essence and potential. Through creation, the Holy Spirit brings this essence into physical reality. This reality, or created order, is marked by a rich pluriformity and develops through time according to different particular life-principles. God-willed orders of creation like family, state, and church exist in sovereign spheres but are held together by God's common grace, which prevents the world from degenerating into chaos. Common grace (sometimes called general grace) allows for the evolutionary development of life-streams inherent to creation. In this way,

6. The most encompassing exposition of Kuyper's thought is the broad overview of theology as a science in three volumes, *Encyclopaedie der Heilige Godgeleerdheid* (Amsterdam: J. A. Wormser, 1894), and his discussion of common grace in three volumes, published as *De gemeene gratie* (Amsterdam: Höveker & Wormser, 1902-4). For fuller literature information, see W. H. Velema, "Kuyper as theoloog. Een persoonlike evaluatie na dertig jaar," *In die Skriflig* 23, no. 91 (September 1989): 56-73.

7. I. John Hesselink, *On being Reformed* (Ann Arbor, Mich.: Servant Books, 1983).

8. Abraham Kuyper, *Calvinism: Six lectures delivered in the Theological Seminary at Princeton; The L. P. Stone lectures from 1889 to 1899* (New York: Revell, 1899).

creation, including the different peoples of the world, fulfills its potential in nature and culture, under God's reign and to God's glory.[9]

Let us turn now to Kuyper's ecclesiology. For him, the church exists as both institution and organism. As institution, he considered the church to be the result of God's particular grace. Where members of the church act as believers in broader society, the church acts as an organism as a result of particular (also called special) grace. But where positive developments in the world occur, even in the absence of overt Christian faith, one finds the church as organism functioning via God's common grace. It is important to note that for Kuyper, the institutional (i.e., external) form of the church does not belong to its essence. This implies that the traditional marks of unity, holiness, catholicity, and apostolicity are marks of the unseen church that will be realized only eschatologically.

According to Kuyper, the formation of various institutional churches (as occurred after 1886 in the Netherlands) is no threat to the spiritual unity of the church. In fact, the search for external, institutional unity is a form of "churchism" *(kerkisme)* that is to be resisted. The freedom of people to form their own churches should not be diminished. Kuyper argued that differentiation among peoples would naturally lead to the development of different institutional churches. "The people among whom the church is formed are not the same. They differ according to origin, race, country, region, history, potential, and psychological orientation, and they also do not stay the same but go through various stages of development."[10] Because of this, the differences that separate person from person form a wedge in the unity of the external church. Kuyper argued that this pluralistic church-formation is "according to my firm conviction a phase of development to which the church should have come."[11]

Regarding human and social development, Kuyper was a man of his times, sharing the cultural biases of Europe in the latter half of the nineteenth century. He believed that, based on common grace, all people have a natural knowledge of God, and in principle the human race and all nations stand equal before God. This common grace forms the basis and stepping-stone for particular grace, which leads to a higher knowledge of God in

9. See Velema, "Kuyper as theoloog," p. 58; Willie D. Jonker, *Die Gees van Christus* (Pretoria: N. G. Kerkboekhandel, 1981), pp. 93-94; Cornelis van der Kooi, "A theology of culture: A critical appraisal of Kuyper's doctrine of common grace," in van der Kooi and de Bruijn, *Kuyper reconsidered*, p. 98.

10. Kuyper, *Die gemeene gratie*, vol. 3, p. 223, my translation.

11. Kuyper, *Die gemeene gratie*, vol. 3, p. 231, my translation.

Christ. On the one hand, Kuyper maintained that the unity of humanity was based on God's counsel.[12] On the other hand, his conception of common grace allowed him to see the confusion of the Babel events as setting forth each nation or people according to its own type and cultural law (*wetstroom*).[13]

According to Kuyper, a hierarchy then follows. The first level consists of people (e.g., in Africa) where common grace has not yet developed to its full potential. Then there is a second level, where one finds a greater impact of common grace, with pockets of developed areas (e.g., in India and Japan). Following this is a level consisting of social systems where special grace dominates. This is the highest level of development, experiencing maximum Christian effect on the whole of society. The pivotal examples of this for Kuyper were the European and North American civilizations.[14]

This differentiation among people based on their participation in levels of grace is the hermeneutical key to understanding, for example, Kuyper's view of the three children of Noah. They reflect the various developmental levels. The children of Shem received both common and special grace; those of Japheth benefited to a lesser degree from special grace; and the descendants of Ham showed a lack of both forms of grace. The descendants of Ham are therefore to be temporarily subservient to the other groups until they have reached the same level of development and civilization.[15]

It does not require a lot of imagination to see why Kuyper's theology became so influential in Afrikaans South African churches of Dutch origin.[16] His own glowing respect for the Boers, who resisted British coloni-

---

12. Velema, "Kuyper as theoloog," p. 66.

13. Piet J. Strauss, "Abraham Kuyper, apartheid, and the Reformed churches in South Africa in their support of apartheid," *Theological Forum* 23, no. 1 (March 1995): 12.

14. See Strauss, "Abraham Kuyper, apartheid," p. 11, and the discussion of the Stone Lectures by D. T. Kuiper, "Groen and Kuyper on the racial issue," in van der Kooi and de Bruijn, *Kuyper reconsidered*, pp. 74-75.

15. See Strauss, "Abraham Kuyper, apartheid," p. 14, and the fine analysis by Kuiper, "Groen and Kuyper," pp. 74-78, based on original Kuyper sources.

16. As early as 1882 S. J. du Toit attempted to translate Kuyper's ideas into the political and ecclesial situation of the time. After 1907, postgraduate students in South Africa chose to attend the Free University in Amsterdam rather than the State University in Utrecht. Some of them returned to South Africa as avid Kuyperians. In the Gereformeerde Kerk, Kuyper's ideas were carried forth by J. D. du Toit and H. G. Stoker, professors of theology and philosophy respectively. The most significant proponents of the neo-Calvinistic revival in the 1930s and beyond were the Dutch Reformed Church academics F. J. M. Potgieter and A. B. du Preez, along with church leaders J. D. Vorster and A. P. Treurnicht (see Kinghorn, *Die N. G. Kerk*, chap. 6).

zation and who — inspired by God — trekked into the darkness of Africa to set up republics as a result of their Calvinistic heroism,[17] added a very personal dimension to this relationship.

One should be careful, however, not to draw a simple, direct line between Kuyper and Afrikaner Calvinism. As will become evident from the discussion below, Kuyper's influence should be read in the wider context of other theological influences, as well as the sociopolitical history of the Afrikaners. It would perhaps be fair to say that Kuyper himself cannot be held responsible for the brand of Kuyperianism that became a specific contextual theology for Afrikaans churches in South Africa in the first half of the twentieth century.

The weaknesses in Kuyper's theology, however, did create the opportunity for interpretations that could legitimately invoke his authority and blessing. W. H. Velema's critique of Kuyper is unambiguous, arguing that the dialectic relationship between common and special grace is an element of Kuyper's idealistic philosophy and cosmology, couched in Calvinistic terms. The only way out of this idealistic system, says Velema, is a radical break with common grace in order to restore some of Kuyper's Reformed intentions.[18] This is supported by Kees van der Kooi, who refutes Kuyper's claim that he merely developed Calvin's notion that some divine indulgence remains beside the total corruption of creation and humankind: "It should be clear, however, that Calvin's point in speaking about general grace is entirely the opposite of Kuyper's. While in Calvin this general grace receives no further attention and the focus remains on mankind's total dependence on God's grace, Kuyper turns his attention to the subject of this common grace."[19] Common grace in fact becomes a broad theory of culture, based on an optimistic view of Western society, civilization, and scientific achievements.[20] If through common grace God establishes orders of creation such as family, state, and church, surely one can further argue that the existence, development, and protection of different peoples — each as a separate people according to its own potential and cultural law — can be seen as the will of God. This was especially relevant for a people like the Afrikaners, who as devout Christians believed that it is through God's providence that they were planted on the southern tip of Africa to be bearers of the light of the gospel.

---

17. Strauss, "Abraham Kuyper, apartheid," p. 13; Kuiper, "Groen and Kuyper," p. 78.
18. Velema, "Kuyper as theoloog," p. 69.
19. Van der Kooi, "A theology of culture," pp. 97-98.
20. Van der Kooi, "A theology of culture," p. 98.

Afrikaners reinterpreted their own history as sacred history, analogous to the Israelite people of God. They were in the "bondage" of British colonialism. To escape this bondage, they trekked through the "desert" of unoccupied territories to finally reach the "promised land" of their own republics. God sent them into exile during the British War of 1899-1902, but they were restored as a people. God reestablished them and made them a blessing to the heathen nations of Africa, to whom they owed the witness of the gospel. In short, "the blending of Afrikaner 'sacred history' and neo-Calvinism with its 'sovereignty of spheres' thus provided a powerful ideological base for Afrikaner nationalism and apartheid," writes John de Gruchy.[21]

Willie Jonker, an influential South African systematic theologian in the period after 1960, notes that Kuyper did not construct the pluriformity of the church on Scripture or on the intention of the Reformation. Rather, it was based on his evolutionist and organic concept of history and concomitant social realities. Kuyper, under the influence of nineteenth-century individualism and idealism, introduced a subjectivist element into his ecclesiology. Church formation becomes an issue of personal choice and the exercise of personal freedom. This can lead to the conclusion that it is a normal and God-willed development to establish separate institutional churches for groupings based on culture, psychology, or any other human factor. As Kuyper himself argues, these separate churches in no way detract from the unity of the church as a fundamental spiritual reality in Christ.[22] We shall see below how the idea of separate churches for different racial groups was firmly established through the mission theology of the nineteenth century — even before Kuyper's work became known in South Africa.

Based on the analysis of Roman Catholic scholar Alexandre Ganoczy, John de Gruchy points to the ambiguity of Calvin's life and work.[23] On the one hand stands the "young Calvin," with his positive, evangelical, and liberating theology. On the other hand, we find the "older Calvin," who shows trends of domination and constriction. This same ambiguity is evident in the reception of Kuyper in South Africa.[24] Scholars like Allan

21. John W. de Gruchy, *Liberating Reformed theology: A South African contribution to an ecumenical debate* (Grand Rapids: Eerdmans, 1991), p. 27.

22. Jonker, *Die Gees van Christus*, pp. 91-94; Willie D. Jonker, "Die pluriformiteitsleer van Abraham Kuyper. Teologiese onderbou vir die konsep van aparte kerke vir aparte volksgroepe?" *In die Skriflig* 23, no. 3 (1989): 16-18.

23. De Gruchy, *Liberating Reformed theology*, p. 32.

24. Kuyper has left a wide-ranging, complex, and even contradictory legacy, which is,

Boesak,[25] John de Gruchy,[26] and Russel Botman[27] clearly attempt to retrieve the liberating elements of Kuyper's theology in their struggle to turn Afrikaner civil religion against its own source.

But the first and dominating reception of Kuyper in South Africa was via "imperial Calvinism," which was in essence "fearful of spontaneity, openness, equalities and diversities."[28] The neo-Calvinism espoused by Kuyper found its clearest public expression in his political activities. Jan de Bruijn argues that Kuyper was a child of European Romanticism and that his Calvinist politics were in part imbued by his romanticizing of the "glorious" past of the Netherlands and a specific brand of Dutch nationalism.[29] This nationalism was based on a theology that accorded undue weight to "a value of separateness."[30] And because it was embedded in a hierarchical view of civilizations, it paved the way for Afrikaner nationalists to claim legitimate *voogdyskap* (rule over) black people in South Africa as an expression of God's will, as well as a practice of equal but separate justice. As in Kuyper's case, "circumstances claimed victory over doctrine."[31] When these ideas struck a chord with the socioeconomic position of the

---

like any comprehensive oeuvre, open to more than one interpretation. Russel H. Botman argues that Kuyper was indeed both liberative and oppressive. See Botman's "Is blood thicker than justice? The legacy of Abraham Kuyper for Southern Africa," in *Religion, pluralism, and public life: Abraham Kuyper's legacy for the twenty-first century,* ed. Luis E. Lugo, p. 354 (Grand Rapids: Eerdmans, 2000). The bases in Kuyper's work for a liberative understanding of Calvinism must be seen against the historical context and specific occasion for which they were constructed. See specifically the discussion of Kuyper's rhetorical strategies for American and French audiences by Kuiper, "Groen and Kuyper." The reclaiming of Kuyper for liberation in South Africa should also be seen in its rhetorical context of fighting Kuyperianism at its worst by appealing to Kuyper himself. Whatever the evidence, even direct quotations, that may be found to support contrasting views, it is ultimately the underlying and permeating structure of Kuyper's thought that should guide our interpretation. I declare my South African Reformed presuppositions openly and probably err in the direction of a more critical, rather than an appreciative, reading of him.

25. Allan Boesak, *Black and Reformed: Apartheid, liberation, and the Calvinist tradition* (Maryknoll, N.Y.: Orbis Books, 1984), p. 87.

26. John W. de Gruchy, *Bonhoeffer and South Africa: Theology in dialogue* (Grand Rapids: Eerdmans, 1984), p. 107.

27. Botman, "Is blood thicker?" p. 354.

28. N. Wolterstorff, as quoted by de Gruchy, *Liberating Reformed theology,* p. 18.

29. Jan de Bruijn, "Abraham Kuyper as a romantic," in van der Kooi and de Bruijn, *Kuyper reconsidered,* pp. 45-58.

30. Botman, "Is blood thicker?" p. 355.

31. Kuiper, "Groen and Kuyper," p. 81.

Afrikaner people after 1929,[32] the scene was set for the development of Kuyper's legacy into a theologically guided ideology. But to fully understand why this happened, we must note the merger with a second stream of thought, this one arising from Germany.

Gustav Warneck

The churches of European origin in South Africa were faced with the issue of differentiation among people from the very beginning, although this was more in a cultural-economic sense than in a racially specific sense.[33] The doctoral dissertation by W. J. van der Merwe, later himself a missiologist of note, contains a careful analysis of social and racial attitudes in the Dutch Reformed Church (DRC) from the settlement in the Cape (1652) up to the early twentieth century.[34] This problem of how to deal with different racial groups intensified as church members began to spread beyond the confines of the early Cape settlement and as missionary work led to new converts all over Southern Africa.[35]

After the formation of the Zuid Afrikaanse Zendingsgenootskap as a separate missionary arm of the DRC (1799), a binary system of ministry developed. This consisted of the normal ministry to white congregants, augmented with a missionary ministry to mostly colored and black people, who were accommodated in separate meetings *(oefenhuise),* although always accepted as members of the same congregation.

As the missionaries developed a more autonomous ministry, whole congregations of converts were formed. It is of great interest to note that

32. I refer here to the rapid urbanization of Afrikaners when both economic depression and severe droughts forced them to turn from an agricultural economy to an industrial one. They were not skilled for this, and they found themselves in an environment dominated by English capital. The well-known Carnegie Commission was set up to investigate the problem and make recommendations. It found that by the early 1930s about 300,000 Afrikaner people were living in poverty. A similar study undertaken for black people in the late 1980s showed an even greater proportion of black South Africans living in abject poverty. See Francis Wilson and Mamphela Ramphele, *Uprooting poverty: The South African challenge; Report for the Second Carnegie Inquiry into Poverty and Development in Southern Africa* (Cape Town: David Philip, 1989).

33. Bosch, "Nothing but a heresy," p. 31; and Kinghorn, *Die N. G. Kerk,* p. 72.

34. See Willem Jakobus van der Merwe, *The development of missionary attitudes in the Dutch Reformed Church in South Africa* (Cape Town: Nasionale Pers, 1936).

35. See Smit, "Südafrika," pp. 323-24.

the real question facing the first (1824) and subsequent synods of the Cape Dutch Reformed Church (1826, 1829, and beyond) was not the issue of separate congregations but the administration of Holy Communion. This was a complicated issue. It involved both the officiation rights of missionaries vis-à-vis ordained ministers and whether communion should be enjoyed together in one place of worship. The synod of 1829 clearly affirmed that communion was to be served to all people, irrespective of their origin, in the same place of worship and at the same time. This was derived from an "unchangeable principle based on the infallible Word of God."[36]

By the late 1850s a practice developed whereby colored congregants gathered in separate buildings to hear the Word and receive the sacraments. As the church's mission developed, it was necessary for practical reasons to accommodate the church services of converts from different language groups in different locations. David Bosch remarks that Protestantism acquired a much greater diversity of churches exactly because it focused on the preaching of the Word in the language of the hearer and functioned without an overarching uniform authority, as in the case of Roman Catholicism.[37] This led to the formation of "national churches" in Europe with separate circuits and synods for different language groups. In the missionary situation the question of diversity was intensified and posed serious challenges to the Reformed notion of the church. At that time, however, the idea of separate congregations or separate institutional churches was not on the horizon.

The synod of 1857, which has received notoriety in the expansive literature covering the topic, opened the door for greater separation. The synod's decision does not mention or propose the setting up of separate churches.[38] It merely regulated formally what was already in practice in

36. See Kinghorn, *Die N. G. Kerk,* p. 74, my translation.

37. Bosch, "Nothing but a heresy," pp. 24-25.

38. "Synod considers it to be desirable and in accordance with Scripture that our converts from paganism be received and incorporated into existing congregations, wherever possible; however, where this practice, because of the weakness of some, constitutes an obstacle to the advancement of Christ's cause among pagan congregations formed or still to be formed, converts from paganism should be given the opportunity to enjoy their Christian privileges in a separate place of worship" (translation from Dutch by Bosch, "Nothing but a heresy," p. 32). Other interpretations see "the weakness of some" as referring not to white resistance but to the inability ("weakness") of new converts to understand the Dutch language used during worship.

many areas. In fact, the synod still held as "preferable and scriptural" that converts from paganism become members of existing congregations. The situation of separate church services was for some merely a transitional measure, "because of the weakness of some," until the practical situation would enable a return to the "normal" rule of the church.

But in the end, the practical situation (separate ministries) and not the theological starting point (unity in Christ) led the DRC synod of 1880 to decide on the formation of a separate church for coloreds. The Dutch Reformed Mission Church (DRMC) was founded on October 5, 1881, the first of many such separate institutional church formations that would follow as part of the so-called family of Dutch Reformed churches. Within the borders of South Africa, the Dutch Reformed Church in Africa (DRCA) for black members and the Reformed Church in Africa (RCA) for Indians were founded in 1963 and 1968 respectively.

The "Bantu"[39] question slowly emerged as an agenda point in the DRC after 1920. The period 1921-35 is well described in Kinghorn and his original sources.[40] It is crucial to understand that the changing political landscape[41] and the deteriorating socioeconomic situation of DRC members forced the DRC to provide some clarity for itself on the social implications of its understanding of the gospel.

The church did not have a developed social ethic at that time. The channel through which it made its most far-reaching policy decisions was the area of mission. The emerging mission policy, adopted in 1935, proved to be far more than a mere mission document. It was a theological interpretation of the sociopolitical events of its time. And it is in relation to this and preceding policies that the influence of Warneck must be counted together with that of Kuyper.

Gustav Warneck (1834-1910) was the intellectual giant of nineteenth-century missiology. His three-volume *Evangelische Missionslehre* (*EM*, 1879-1903) had an influence far beyond Germany and far beyond his own

---

39. Archaic and sometimes derogatory reference to blacks, from the isiXhosa word *abantu*, meaning "the people."

40. Kinghorn, *Die N. G. Kerk*, p. 79.

41. Note the formation of the South African Native National Congress in 1912 (renamed the African National Congress from 1923) and the establishment of several Afrikaner organizations around 1915, including *Die Burger* (newspaper), the Broederbond (secret political organization), and the National Party. Two "nationalisms" — black and white — were in the making, with the first legal provisions (Natives Land Act, 1913; and Location Act, 1923) protecting white interests against black aspirations.

time.[42] It is clear from the dates of publication that Warneck did not influence the actual missiological practices as described above. For instance, by the time of this, his major publication, the DRMC was already constituted as a separate church.

Warneck's work, however, unmistakably provided a theological rationale for defending the earlier establishment of separate churches for different race groups, based on the notion that the ultimate aim of mission is *Volkschristianisierung*, that is, the Christianization of people *as ethnic groups*. Later, it was only a small step to move from separate *Volkskirchen* (ethnic churches) to the political design of society on the basis of different ethnic groups.

As in the case of Kuyper, a short chapter like this cannot deal adequately with all the complexities of interpreting Warneck. The aim here is to show a certain trend, to follow the trajectory of how commitment to pluralist forms can lead to holding ideological constructs. Apart from certain chapters in the *EM* (part 3, sec. 1, published in 1897), I rely here on the doctoral dissertation of the well-known Dutch missiologist Johannes Christian Hoekendijk, published as *Kerk en volk in de Duitze Zendingswetenschap* (1948), and the insightful article "Nothing but a heresy" (1983) by the world-renowned South African missiologist David Bosch.

The crux of Warneck's argument is as follows. Already in 1874 Warneck chose the well-known text from Matthew 28:19 as programmatic for mission. This missionary call by Jesus was to form the basis of Warneck's biblical missiology. In his explication of this text, Warneck was led by two considerations, namely, the practical situation in the mission field and a popular idealistic notion that society is structured in concentric circles with the following categories: (1) individual, (2) family, and (3) *Volk*. This is motivated by referring to the same structure in the Old Testament, namely (1) Abram/individual, (2) clan/extended family, and (3) people of Israel/*Volk* and the New Testament, namely (1) Jesus, (2) house churches, and (3) *Volkskirchen*. He therefore logically concluded that mission is "making disciples (Gk. *mathēteuein*) of heathens *as peoples*."[43]

In subsequent work up to 1891, Warneck retained a tension between the conversion of single persons and the teaching of the gospel to peoples in their ethnic sense *(Völkerpädagogie)*. This tension is finally resolved in

---

42. See Johannes Christiaan Hoekendijk, *Kerk en volk in de Duitse zendingswetenschap* (Amsterdam: Rodopi, 1948), p. 94, n. 66.

43. Hoekendijk, *Kerk en volk*, p. 85, my translation and emphasis.

the work of Reinhold Grundemann, notably his two-volume *Missions-Studien und Kritiken* (1894-98),[44] where he explicitly argues against mission as the conversion of single persons: "The ways of God lead to the establishment of churches for peoples [*Volkskirchen*]." This point is then confirmed by his interpretation of Matthew 28:19 as "making Christians of peoples as peoples," where the Greek *ethnē* (peoples) is clearly understood in an ethnographic-nationalist sense, and *mathēteuein* as "making disciples of peoples as peoples."[45] Making disciples of a heathen people *as an ethnic group* is a slow process whereby the heathen norms and ideas are gradually replaced by Christian ones,[46] in a dialectic of learning to abdicate old habits and to accept new ones.[47]

By the time Warneck started work on his *EM,* the debate was wide open. Zinzendorf had taken the biblical passage on the Ethiopian convert (Acts 8) as the appropriate model,[48] with the mission to the individual as the means of winning souls for the kingdom; the converting of nations *as nations* is only an eschatological possibility. Warneck's colleague Grundemann, however, raised two crucial questions: Is the object of mission to reach individuals or to reach peoples *(Völker)?* And must the latter be understood in a religious or an ethnographic sense? In other words, are the people to whom Jesus sent his disciples existing ethnic groups, or are they anyone who would respond in faith to their message, irrespective of ethnic origin? In which direction would Warneck lean?

Warneck starts his chapter entitled "Die Missionsaufgabe als Volkschristianisierung" by keeping individual conversion *(Einzelbekehrung)* and ethnic group conversion *(Volkschristianisierung)* in a fine balance, with the former serving as a basis for the latter (pp. 234-35).[49] He then builds an ar-

---

44. Reinhold Grundemann, *Missions-Studien und Kritiken,* 2 vols. (Gütersloh: C. Bertelsmann, 1894-98).

45. Hoekendijk, *Kerk en volk,* p. 88, refers to Grundemann, *Missions-Studien,* 1:3, my translation.

46. Note how close this is to Kuyper's idea of the slow developmental impact of special grace on the already-existing natural grace.

47. Hoekendijk, *Kerk en volk,* p. 89.

48. See Warneck's criticism of Zinzendorf and Pietism in general as harboring an unrealistic missionary ideal of converting individual persons — which is disproved by the historical results of their very own missionary efforts! See D. Gustav Warneck, *Evangelische Missionslehre. Ein missionstheoretischer Versuch,* part 3: *Der Betrieb der Sendung* (Gotha: Berthes, 1897), p. 254.

49. Page references in the text are to Warneck, *Evangelische Missionslehre,* with my translation throughout.

gument in two phases, one exegetical and one historical, to show that, although mission might have started with the conversion of individuals, it clearly developed into *Volkschristianisierung,* and that the latter sentiment is to be found in the New Testament as well. He also shows that although exegetical results are mixed, the historical situation of mission leads him to accept "peoples" as ethnographic entities that are to be Christianized. Let us follow his argument.

Warneck engages in quite an extensive exegesis of New Testament texts, focusing on the meaning of *ta ethnē,* "the peoples." The core question is whether this is a salvation-historical (and therefore religious) concept or an ethnological one. His conclusion is that the two meanings are so intermingled that they can hardly be used apart from each other. He then argues that, just as Israel is an ethnic people, so Jesus would consider the heathens as structured in terms of peoples because this was an order of nature. It would therefore be "unnatural to state that the concept of peoples did not have an ethnographic dimension for Jesus" (p. 237). With this, the door for an ethnographic interpretation (and misinterpretation!) was opened.

Warneck subsequently clarifies the question of individual conversion versus the evangelizing of a group of ethnic people by his historical argument. He suggests that historical proof will provide for whatever the biblical-theological investigation may overlook. "The facts of history are also an exegesis of the Bible, and they speak a word of discernment in cases where theological exegesis remains unclear" (p. 245).

This is an important point, because Warneck concludes that the whole history of mission (which he discusses from apostolic times to his day) always shows that mission work is the Christianization of peoples. He consequently casts serious doubt on the theory of individual conversions, which is contradicted by mission realities (p. 255). This allows him to make a crucial move by collapsing the possible historical result of mission into the very method of mission: "If the Christianization of people communities [*Volksgemeinschaften*] is always and everywhere the actual outcome of mission, one has to draw the conclusion that it is also the task of mission" (p. 254). It is clear from the implications for a mission program that Warneck had ethnic groups in mind. The emphasis is placed on the specific language, the family structure as the foundation of the community of peoples, and the direct cooperation with indigenous people themselves (pp. 256-69). In this way, Warneck provides two points of connection to the South African situation of the early twentieth century.

37

First, he provides a missionary method where the ethnological reality and the religious ideal are naturally linked, with the former providing the basis for the latter. "When Jesus commands that we should make disciples of the nations, he wants us to make them Christians on the basis of their distinctive nature as a people. The better the people's own nature is addressed, the better are the prospects for Christianity to become indigenous to the specific people" (pp. 268-69).

The move from here to separate churches for different peoples in South Africa was just as natural: "The indigenous church [*inboorlingkerk*] must be grounded in the life of the people . . . and be considered as flowing from the life of the *volk*, and not as an imported or foreign institution," writes Du Plessis in 1932 in his popularized Warneck interpretation, with the title "Wie sal gaan?" (Who shall go?).[50] This assumption is the basis for a mission policy that clearly takes the ethnic reality (i.e., the ethnic "nature") as the basis for thinking about the church ("grace"). The German missiologist Christian Keysser goes so far as to state categorically: "The tribe is at the same time the Christian church."[51] In a note that reminds one of Jonker's critique of Kuyper's idea of the church, David Bosch writes that, theologically speaking, the Achilles' heel of nineteenth-century missionary thinking was its weak ecclesiology.[52]

Second, Warneck establishes an ethnographic pluralism based on a romantic notion of the *Volk*.[53] This opened his idea of mission to be interpreted as a form of cultural propaganda,[54] which in the end made possible a theological defense of a political structure based on *Volk* in an ethnic sense.

We must note that German Romanticism reached its zenith by 1850. As a reaction against rationalism, it was noted for its emphasis on feelings, the nonrational dimension of human existence, and the idealizing of "the

50. Kinghorn, *Die N. G. Kerk*, p. 68, my translation.

51. Quoted in Bosch, "Nothing but a heresy," p. 28.

52. Bosch, "Nothing but a heresy," p. 33.

53. In the context of nineteenth-century idealism and Romanticism, the Oxford Missionary Conference of 1938 rightly remarks: "The word *Volk* is quite untranslatable because it designates both a sentiment and a body of convictions to which there is no exact, or even approximate, parallel elsewhere" (see Hoekendijk, *Kerk en volk*, p. 99, n. 9).

54. See Hoekendijk's *Kerk en volk*, p. 104, for an interesting reference to Harnack's notion of cultural hierarchy and the supremacy of civilized cultures over "barbaric" China after the Boxer Revolution of 1900: "This culture does not deserve to be conserved!" (my translation).

own."[55] I am not suggesting that Warneck was a Romantic scholar in the historical or technical sense. He merely reveals the traits of a Romantic idea of the *Volk* in his missiological design. Consider, for example, the way in which he extols the virtues of his own people in mission: "The Germans have a special gift of respecting foreign nationalities. This enables them to understand, in a selfless manner, the specificities of other peoples from the inside out."[56]

The basic outlines of the Warneck construction found its way into DRC missionary thinking. Already in 1932 we find exactly the same "method" outlined in the missionary policy of the Cape DRC. It starts with mission as "the collection of souls for God's kingdom" (i.e., the conversion of individuals). The "necessary result" was the setting up of organized congregations that had to become "self-reliant and self-governing" churches in accordance with the nature of the *volk* because of the gradual development of the *volk* under the sanctifying influence of the gospel. The move beyond the church to society is then a small step: Separate societal structures for different peoples were aimed at the well-being of each "in order that both the colored and the black can increasingly take their rightful place in each area of society."[57]

When the Federal Mission Policy, in which all DRC synods participated, was developed in 1935, it was stated unambiguously that evangelization could never imply denationalization. The reason was that "Christianity does not want to rob the *bantu* of his language and culture, but wants to permeate and cleanse [*deursuiwer*] his whole nation."[58] For this reason there could be no social integration, as this implied the rejection of a God-created and God-willed social differentiation.

Hoekendijk's critical note on Warneck and other nineteenth-century German missiologists is clear. By relinquishing the eschatological proviso, missiological praxis became normative via a romanticized and ethnologically structured idea of the *Volk*. The church was no longer the sign of

---

55. See Gunther Seubold, "Romantik," *Lexikon für Theologie und Kirche* 8 (1999): 1268.

56. Warneck, *Evangelische Missionslehre*, p. 23, my translation; see Hoekendijk, *Kerk en volk*, p. 101. Werner Elert later goes even further to put cultural grounding in the people as a precondition for a good missionary: "Where the missionary has no understanding of his own specific people, one cannot expect him to understand foreign peoples" (see Hoekendijk, *Kerk en volk*, p. 101).

57. My translation of the original as contained in van der Merwe, *Missionary attitudes*, pp. 261-63.

58. Kinghorn, *Die N. G. Kerk*, p. 87, my translation.

the coming of the kingdom in this world but was seen as an extension of the *Volk,* as a blessed fulfillment of its naturally evolving ethnic structure.[59]

The foundation for a theology of apartheid that would have disastrous consequences for both church and state over the next fifty years was now firmly laid. The structured pluriformity of Kuyper, with a concomitant notion of an unequally structured civilization, was built on his dialectic of common and particular grace. The ethnological pluriformity of Warneck was built on his notion of *Volkschristianisierung,* where history and missiological praxis became the determinant for interpreting Scripture as calling for a form of "ethnic mission."

An interesting point is that both Kuyper and Warneck went to great lengths to show that their respective theologies were indeed based on Scripture. I already referred to the fact that Kuyper begins his theological work with six volumes all entitled *Uit het Woord. Stichtelijke Bijbelstudien* (From the Word: Pious Bible studies, 1873-86). Equally, Warneck chooses Scripture as a basis for his missiology from the beginning and engages in serious exegesis throughout his *EM.* His legacy is even described as seeking an answer for each missiological question "in the light of God's revelation," in a pietistic-biblicist sense![60]

How is natural theology possible in the light of Scripture? How can destructive, ethnic pluralism be seen as a biblical injunction? The answer might be constructed as follows. When the presupposition of hermeneutics is constituted by an ideological pluralism, God becomes the Great Divider, Scripture is consistently read from the perspective of creation and not re-creation, and unity in the church is spiritualized and reduced to an unseen reality.

The link between Kuyper and what Loubser has called *The Apartheid Bible* (1987)[61] is much more direct than in the case of Warneck. But behind the "model reading" that follows below lies the enabling shadow of Warneck's design, perhaps far beyond his own intentions. If you approach Scripture with an ideological presupposition to which you are not open and critical, you will generally find what you are looking for.

The differentiations in creation (light/darkness, sea/land, plants/animals, man/woman) are emphatically confirmed in the events of Babel,

---

59. See Hoekendijk, *Kerk en volk,* p. 107.

60. See Hoekendijk's *Kerk en volk,* p. 95, for the reference to J. Warneck: *Zu G. Warnecks 100. Geburtstag* (1934), and his own comments on p. 106.

61. J. A. Loubser, *The apartheid Bible* (Cape Town: Tafelberg, 1987).

where God specifically opposed a false unity among peoples. This is set forth in the clear injunction to Israel to retain its national and religious identity among, and in opposition to, other nations. This is equally confirmed with the differentiated and pluralistic work of the Spirit during Pentecost, where the existence of separate peoples is not abolished but is affirmed, as each nation hears the gospel in its own language. The land where each *Volk* lives is the predestined work of God's promise to Abraham (Gen. 12) and others (Amos 9:7), as God alone determines the time and place where each shall live (Acts 17:26).

The unity of the church in Christ is both a higher spiritual unity and a nonrealizable eschatological vision of a heaven in which all peoples and nations shall come before God and praise him (Rev. 7). Even God as triune God demonstrates the uniqueness and differentiation of each person in the Trinity, where one person can never be fully identified with either of the other two. The rule of one *Volk* over another is not directly stated in Scripture but can be derived from the subjugation of the heathen nations to Israel and from the principle of love, which is especially required from the more developed nations toward the less developed nations.[62]

Readers of this chapter will be able to construct the relationship between the theological framework described above and the way in which Scripture is interpreted here. Why did this very obvious ideological reading find its way so relatively easily into the Afrikaans-speaking Reformed churches, which had always claimed the absolute authority of Scripture? To understand this, it is necessary to give a short overview of Pietism.

Pietism

The second half of the nineteenth century brought to light two important and deeply contrasting Bible-reading strategies. The one was the very influential and fast-growing body of historical-critical scholarship that asked difficult and overtly critical questions about historicity, truth, and the authority of Scripture. At the same time, one finds a maturing Pietism, not only in Germany, but all over Europe, and specifically in Scotland. In

---

62. Please note this is my own constructed paraphrase of the many threads that are woven together to support an apartheid exegesis. The best examples — all discussed by Kinghorn, *Die N. G. Kerk* — are J. D. du Toit's speech at the Volkskongres of 1944, F. J. M. Potgieter's opening speech at the Stellenbosch seminary in 1958, and the more refined DRC document *Ras, Volk en Nasie* (1974), in which apartheid theology found its culmination.

fact, much of the Protestant missionary zeal of the early nineteenth century had its roots in pietistic communities.[63] In these communities, a great, almost biblicistic respect for Scripture held sway, clearly setting itself apart from "liberal" and "critical" scholarship. Strong emphasis fell on a pious personal lifestyle, an active striving toward holiness, and an enthusiasm to win souls for Jesus through evangelization and mission.[64]

At this point readers must be made aware of a very important link between the spirituality of the DRC and evangelically oriented Pietism.[65] Before the DRC began training its own theological students, it had to rely on "imported" ministers. In the early years, ministers mostly came from the Netherlands. By the middle of the nineteenth century, however, this shifted to the theologically conservative Scotland, from where preachers, academics, and church leaders of great holiness came. Andrew Murray Jr., the best-known theologian from this period, studied in Holland and was exposed to Dutch Pietism. He became the founder of an evangelical spirituality and a distinct theological tradition that stood alongside the Reformed origins of the DRC. It was Scottish Pietism that provided the theological foundations for the revivals that swept through the Cape Church after 1860.

Pietism has had many faces in history. The Reformed evangelical Pietism that became contextualized in South Africa sought initially to be politically neutral, with a clear emphasis on personal salvation and the spiritual well-being of the church. Evangelical pietists showed a huge commitment to mission, in the context of which they involved themselves in education, medical care, and other forms of social philanthropy. After the pain and humiliation of the British War, the idea of a *volkskerk* also emerged from within these ranks. In its close solidarity with the dire socioeconomic and spiritual needs of Afrikaners, Pietism provided some theological foundations for a rising white nationalism and became part of a larger political project.[66]

This type of Pietism had two weaknesses. First, because of its focus on individual salvation, it could not provide a social vision for the problems of Afrikaners, the converted indigenous peoples, or the question of race in South Africa. This vacuum was filled by the optimistic and encompassing

---

63. See Bosch, "Nothing but a heresy," p. 25.

64. See Christian Peters, "Pietismus," *Lexikon für Theologie und Kirche* 8 (1999): 291-93.

65. See Willie D. Jonker, "Kragvelde binne die kerk," *Aambeeld* 26, no. 1 (June 1998): 11-14.

66. De Gruchy, *Liberating Reformed theology*, p. 24.

Kuyperian cultural theory-cum-cosmology and the mission policy that emerged after 1930. Second, although Pietism always showed a deep respect for Scripture, it was never able to develop the instruments to deal with the rise of historical-critical readings of the Bible.

One must take into account that Kuyper himself was quite critical of certain elements of modern biblical scholarship of his time. A translation of the title of his eloquent farewell speech as rector of the Free University on October 20, 1881, reads as follows: "The contemporary critique of Scripture and its precarious implications for the congregation of the living God." He expresses his concern that critical literary studies of the Bible shift the locus of theology from God's revelation to human consciousness, thus falsifying theology to become mere religious studies. Such critical studies question the inspiration of Bible writers to the point where the Bible as God's Word is stolen from ordinary Christians and congregations.[67] Kuyper, however, was too much of a Calvinist to be pietistic in the classic sense of the word. According to him, a critical mind-set remains important, and Pietism's reaction against rationalism, understandable as it was, led to an antitheological attitude that actually left the forces outside the church free play in the world.[68]

This problem of dealing with critical scholarship in South Africa is illustrated by the well-known case of Professor Johannes du Plessis, who was dismissed from his teaching position at the Stellenbosch seminary because of his perceived alignment with critical scholarship, specifically regarding the Old Testament.[69] The church's action against du Plessis restricted the opportunity for critical and especially self-critical reading, stemming, inter alia, from Barth's critique of religion and Bultmann's notion of *Vorverständnis* (preunderstanding). A hermeneutical opening was created in the early 1930s into which the pluralism of Kuyper, as an all-encompassing Christian worldview based on Scripture, could enter. These views went unchallenged by a largely pietist audience, who ac-

---

67. Abraham Kuyper, *De hedendaagsche Schriftkritiek in hare bedenklijke strekking voor de gemeente des levenden Gods* (Amsterdam: J. H. Kruyt, 1881), pp. 6-21, my translation of the title.

68. Kuyper, *Encyclopaedie,* pp. 623-24.

69. Much has been written on this case, including dissertations. The point here is not the details of the case itself but the effect that it had on the development of critical scholarship. This has been espoused by Andrew Nash in his excellent contribution "Wine-farming, heresy trials, and the whole personality: The emergence of the Stellenbosch philosophical tradition, 1916-1940," *South African Journal for Philosophy* 16 (1997): 55-69 and 129-39.

cepted the Word "as it stands." This in fact allowed a natural theological construct to destroy a sense of the historical and salvation-historical modes of Scripture.[70]

It took the DRC more than fifty years to escape from this hermeneutical trap. This type of hermeneutics provided the moral legitimacy and authority not only to set up different churches for different races but, under the guise and in the name of Christ, to give Afrikaner political leaders from 1948 onward the go-ahead to intensify and complete construction of the whole of South African society along racial/racialist lines.

The deconstruction and eventual dismantling of this massive ideological pluralism came from many theological sources, and also through the work of Bennie Keet, Willie Jonker, and Beyers Naudé from within the DRC itself.[71] The most important German influences were without doubt the christological focus of Karl Barth's theology, the Barmen Declaration, and the inspiring example of Dietrich Bonhoeffer in the Confessing Church. The Belhar Confession has been one of the most creative internal theological responses, following on many antecedent witnesses.[72] It was the first addition to the confessional base of the DRC family since the Canons of Dort in 1618-19, and the first Reformed confessional cry from the African soil by a church created exactly as a result of an ideologized theology 105 years earlier.

---

70. See Bernard Lategan, well-known hermeneutical scholar from South Africa, who makes a compelling case that a "structural deficit" arose in Reformed hermeneutics when historicity became a central issue in critical scholarship after the Enlightenment. The reason is that the indivisibility of truth applied to the totality of Scripture was the basis on which Scripture's authority was based. There was thus very little room for internal criticism and Sachkritik, as practiced, for example, in the Lutheran tradition by people like Lessing, Reimarus, Strauss, and Baur. See Bernard C. Lategan, "History, historiography, and Reformed hermeneutics at Stellenbosch," in *Reformed theology: Biblical interpretation in the Reformed tradition*, ed. Wallace M. Alston Jr. and Michael Welker, pp. 157-71 (Grand Rapids: Eerdmans, 2007). Also see Kinghorn, *Die N. G. Kerk*, pp. 55-58.

71. Beyers Naudé (no relation) was forced to leave the DRC in 1964, among other reasons because of his involvement in the Christian Institute, an ecumenical body Naudé founded in 1963 to unite South Africans against apartheid.

72. A selection of these precursor witnesses is discussed in chapter 2. The most important of these are the Cottesloe Declaration (1961), the "Message to the People of South Africa" (1968), and the Ottawa decision on apartheid as *status confessionis* (1982). For a detailed analysis of the relationship between Belhar and antecedent witnesses, see Piet J. Naudé, "The theological coherence between the Belhar Confession and some antecedent church witnesses in the period 1948-1982," *Verbum et ecclesia* 42, no. 1 (2003): 156-79.

The rejections of the Belhar Confession

Now that a broad picture of the theologies that shaped Afrikaner civil religion has been painted, the rejections of Belhar can be read in its light. It needs to be emphasized that Belhar speaks far beyond the specific theological situation of South Africa in the period leading up to 1980. That situation was the original impulse for the confession, however, which a sound reading of Belhar requires us to keep in mind.

Regarding the unity of the church

> Therefore, we reject any doctrine which absolutizes either natural diversity or the sinful separation of people in such a way that this absolutization hinders or breaks the visible and active unity of the Church, or even leads to the establishment of a separate church formation.

Belhar does not deny the reality of "natural diversity" among people. To do so would be to deny actual empirical realities. Contrary to Afrikaner civil religion, which absolutizes diversity to the point of making separation a principle of creation and the gospel, this diversity of background, culture, and convictions is seen from the perspective of reconciliation in Christ. It is Christ who turns diversity and pluralities from threatening divisions into opportunities for reciprocal service and enrichment within the one visible people of God. The establishment of separate churches for different races is a denial of Christ's reconciliation and therefore a sinful practice.

> ... which professes that this spiritual unity is truly being maintained in the bond of peace whilst believers of the same confession are in effect alienated from one another for the sake of diversity and in despair of reconciliation;

Belhar clearly witnesses against the inadequacy of merely a spiritual unity. Unity in and among churches is obviously of a spiritual nature, but when people share the same confession in the same country, their "bond of peace" requires a visible unity. If one goes the route of separation here, one makes diversity an aim in itself and shows oneself to be in despair of Christ's reconciliation.

45

... which denies that a refusal earnestly to pursue this visible unity as a priceless gift is sin;

If an ecclesiology is built on the assumed God-willed differentiation in creation and a view of the church as cultural prolongation of this separation, there will be no need or urgency to pursue unity. Unity in the church is a priceless gift from God that is to be embraced. Any doctrine that teaches otherwise is sin.

... which explicitly or implicitly maintains that descent or any other human or social factor should be a consideration in determining membership of the Church.

The "weakness of some" (in the language of the synod of 1857) not to receive Holy Communion with new converts from a different background, language, and culture, as well as the missiological practice and method of converting people as an ethnic entity, became the principle used to justify separate church formation. Once this ethnic or cultural principle comes to determine actual membership of the church, a false requirement beyond faith in Christ is set down. This doctrine is to be rejected as a false vision of the church in which human and social factors supersede our being in Christ.

Regarding reconciliation in society

Therefore, we reject any doctrine which, in such a situation, sanctions in the name of the gospel or of the will of God the forced separation of people on the grounds of race and colour and thereby in advance obstructs and weakens the ministry and experience of reconciliation in Christ.

Article 3 of the Belhar Confession moves from the unity of the church to reconciliation in society. It is perhaps the most directly contextual of all the articles. The rejection clause refers to "such a situation" and draws on the earlier statement of forced racial separation in a country that claims to be Christian. Note that Belhar does not make any reference to apartheid as a political system. Belhar remains at the level of Christian doctrine. If the Bible teaches that the message of reconciliation is entrusted to the church, and if a new doctrine is professed that sanctions enmity and forced racial separation as being the will of God or even the good news of Christ, such a teaching should be rejected as heresy and ideology. Such a false teaching takes as its assumption that people from different racial groups are in principle not to be reconciled but only to be physically and spatially separated. In this way, the very possibility to minister and actually experience reconciliation in Christ is obstructed in advance.

Regarding social and economic justice

> Therefore, we reject any ideology which would legitimate forms of injustice and any doctrine which is unwilling to resist such an ideology in the name of the gospel.

Article 4 builds on unity and reconciliation to proclaim justice to the poor, to those who suffer, and to those who are treated unjustly. In this particular case Belhar rejects both an ideology and a false doctrine. It is not the task of a confession to write definitions. With some certainty, though, we can infer what "ideology" refers to here — namely, a belief system that legitimates and upholds a socioeconomic framework that works for the unjust advantage of some and the exclusion from basic life necessities of others.

Belhar obviously addresses the specific situation of South Africa in the 1980s. At that point the bitter irony of Afrikaner history had already emerged. Those who were poor and downtrodden under British rule and who built themselves up with enormous effort, those who drew on great piety from the spiritual resources of being an elect people of God in a country where they were predestined to proclaim the gospel — those very same people became oppressors themselves. Those who were in their own self-understanding "slaves in Egypt" used their newly gained political power after 1948 to intensify racial privileges through numerous laws that excluded black people from the land, the education system, and the economy of South Africa. Like Israel, whom they sought to emulate, the former "slaves" became masters of new slaves. The false doctrine in this case was to see such injustice as the will of God. How do good Christian people turn injustice into "justice"? Keeping in mind our discussion above, this was possible on three interconnected bases.

First, there was the understanding that white people were called by

God to be guardians of the "lesser" black people and therefore should decide for them. Second, the sense of justice that Afrikaners held, which they believed found best expression in equal rights and exercised in territorial separation, so that blacks were not dominated by whites but could actually develop to their full capacities. Third, the universal problem that theological convictions are, but for the grace of God, to a considerable degree shaped by socioeconomic and other nontheological factors. The same theology that lifted Afrikaners up was, in a strange psychology of both sympathy and fear, used to keep black South Africans marginalized.[73] The isolation of apartheid meant that Afrikaners were not exposed to the spirit of the Enlightenment, which promoted democracy and was based on universal human rights. In fact, when the rest of the free world accepted that view formally in 1948 in the U.N. Universal Declaration of Human Rights, the grand project of apartheid moved directly in the opposite direction.

If God reveals himself to be in a special way the God of those who suffer, and if the church is called to stand where God stands, then a doctrine that legitimizes separation and unjust privilege, as well as a gospel that is unwilling to resist such injustice, is a heresy.

73. See the Beyers Naudé Centre, *The legacy of Beyers Naudé*, Beyers Naudé Centre Series on Public Theology (Stellenbosch: SUN Press, 2005), pp. 55-62, for an incisive and moving account of Beyers Naudé from 1967 on why Afrikaners held the racial beliefs they did.

Chapter 2

The relation between Belhar and some antecedent church witnesses in the period 1948-1982

A creed without a preceding, serious theological history can never be other than horribly dull, unoriginal, second-hand.

— Karl Barth, *Church and society*[1]

Normally, a confession of faith is not carefully planned like a systematic theology or a catechism. The very nature of a confession — which "the Church can say only when all its other possibilities are exhausted"; that is, "when reduced to silence it can say nothing else but Credo"[2] — renders it

1. Karl Barth, "The desirability and possibility of a universal Reformed creed," in *Theology and the Church: Shorter writings, 1920-1928,* p. 130 (London: SCM Press, 1962).
2. Karl Barth, *Church dogmatics,* I/2: *The revelation of God* (Edinburgh: T. & T. Clark, 1956), p. 624. Barth's famous definition and subsequent discussion of a confession in his *Church dogmatics,* I/2, pp. 620-60, will be discussed in more detail in chapter 3. The definition includes an inherent contextuality in a number of ways. A confession is a proclamation of the church in a specific situation that requires the interpretation of a specific location (geographic) at a specific moment (reading the signs of the times) about a specific issue (focused on the content of the confession), thus placing the confession in the midst of the political, cultural, and economic realities of society (see pp. 625-26). For broader views on Barth and confessions, see Dirk J. Smit, "Social transformation and confessing the faith? Karl Barth's views on confession revisited," *Scriptura* 72 (2000): 67-85; and Georg Plasger,

This chapter is based on Piet J. Naudé, "The theological coherence between the Belhar Confession and some antecedent church witnesses in the period 1948-1982," *Verbum et ecclesia* 42, no. 1 (2003): 156-79.

highly contextual and time-bound, though obviously not without wider significance beyond its own time. Nevertheless, this kairos characteristic of a confession does not detract from the fact that confessions do not "fall from the sky" without significant antecedent developments.[3]

The people involved in formulating and accepting a confession bring with them their own histories and convictions. The biblical and theological roots of a Christian confession are in place long before the confession itself arises, drawing from the canon, the tradition (including earlier confessions), and continued reinterpretations thereof. In fact, the confession is a confession not because it wants to declare an unknown secret or spring a surprise on the church but exactly because it aims at a renewed interpretation of what is known but is presently lost or concealed.[4] The social, economic, and political developments that precede and inform a confession are mostly not neutral and, because of their theological interpretation by the confession itself, are themselves at stake in the act of confession.

This is true also for the Confession of Belhar, adopted in its draft form by the DRMC in October 1982 and finally as a fourth confession in 1986. I believe that part of Belhar's power resides in its ability to constantly keep in mind the context and the preceding tradition from which it grew. In the same way that responsible biblical hermeneutics requires some understanding of the world "behind the text" (as well as the possible layers in the text and in its formation), it would be wise to investigate some of the important historical texts underlying the Belhar Confession.

There are, historically speaking, three confession-making periods to choose comparative documents from. First, the early church, when faith consensus was reached in the creeds of Nicea and Athanasius and in the Apostles' Creed. The relation between Nicea and Belhar is discussed in more detail in chapter 4. Second, the Reformation period and beyond,

---

Die relative Autorität des Bekenntnisses bei Karl Barth (Neukirchen: Neukirchener Verlag, 2000).

3. "Kairos," a Greek word meaning "time," has the sense of an opportune or God-appointed moment (e.g., as used in Mark 1:15). In the confessional tradition of the twentieth century, it refers to a crisis time that calls for a prophetic word from God to be spoken. The South African Kairos Document (1985) is an example of such a prophetic witness.

4. John W. de Gruchy, in reference to J. C. Wand, *The four great heresies* (1955), indicates that the first trait of a heresy is that it brings something novel into the church; see John W. de Gruchy, "Towards a confessing church," in de Gruchy and Villa-Vicencio, *Apartheid is a heresy*, p. 83. Willie Jonker, my dogmatics professor at Stellenbosch, used to remark: "If one day you say something completely new in the church, you are probably erring."

with numerous catechetical and confessional writings, including the Three Formulae of Unity (Belgic Confession, Heidelberg Catechism, Canons of Dort), which formed the confessional base of the DRMC until 1986. References to the Three Formulae are frequently made in the exposition of Belhar throughout this book. Third, the twentieth century, which brought us the Barmen Declaration in Germany and the growing resistance against apartheid in South Africa and elsewhere in the ecumenical church.[5]

The documents drawn on for this chapter represent a selection of church or ecumenical statements critical of apartheid in the period from 1948 to 1982, when the draft version of Belhar was prepared. This chapter is not the first to address this theme, as *Apartheid is a heresy* (1983),[6] *Bonhoeffer and South Africa* (1984),[7] and *Between Christ and Caesar* (1986)[8] have already listed and discussed historically important documents that were directed against apartheid. Apart from adding a small but significant earlier document to the lists available, I hope to show a theological coherence in these documents and to relate them to the Belhar text. This effort will complement the earlier literature on the theological resistance against apartheid and, it is hoped, heighten interest in the continued theological appropriation of Belhar itself.

The assumption is obviously not that Belhar is the summary of other documents, like a kind of "final conclusion," where everything declared earlier is presented in some form of balanced overview. A confession is not a report. Neither should one look for mere verbal agreements or corresponding phrases that might be important, as in ancient text-comparisons and text-critical work on the Bible. My proposal is that we attempt to find some theological coherence between Belhar and a selection of documents critical of apartheid preceding the confession. This is not merely an exercise in examining interesting church history; rather, it is a legitimate requirement for the interpretation of the Belhar text.

---

5. For a specific discussion of Barmen, see Dirk J. Smit, "Barmen and Belhar in conversation — a South African perspective," *Nederduitse Gereformeerde Teologiese Tydskrif* 47, nos. 1-2 (2006): 291-302.

6. De Gruchy and Villa-Vicencio, *Apartheid is a heresy*.

7. John W. de Gruchy, *Bonhoeffer and South Africa: Theology in dialogue* (Grand Rapids: Eerdmans, 1984).

8. Readers are referred to this book by Villa-Vicencio for most of the texts. See Charles Villa-Vicencio, *Between Christ and Caesar: Classic and contemporary texts on church and state* (Cape Town: David Philip; Grand Rapids: Eerdmans, 1986). I will quote from the texts, using their internal numbering where available.

I list the following documents — remarkably representing Catholic, Lutheran, ecumenical, and Reformed views on apartheid — in chronological order:

- Dutch Reformed Mission Church: Circuit of Wynberg decision on apartheid (1948)[9]
- Southern African Catholic Bishops' Conference (SACBC): *Statement on apartheid* (1957)[10]
- Cottesloe Declaration (1961)
- South African Council of Churches (SACC): *A Message to the People of South Africa* (June 1968)
- Lutheran World Federation (LWF): "Southern Africa: Confessional Integrity" (Sixth Assembly, Dar es Salaam, 1977)
- Alliance of Black Reformed Christians in Southern Africa (ABRECSA): *Charter and Declaration* (October 1981)
- Open letter by 123 DRC pastors and theologians (March 1982)[11]

9. Since this decision is relatively unknown and fairly short, I quote it here in full (my translation). This is a remarkable statement from September 1948, the year in which the National Party came to power: "The circuit of Wynberg [situated in the southern suburbs of Cape Town] of the DRMC in South Africa accepts the following motion with regard to the policy of apartheid in our country: 1. The circuit declares that it finds no grounds in Holy Scripture for color-based apartheid. 2. This body objects to the proposed apartheid laws and makes an earnest appeal to the government not to apply any 'forced' apartheid laws. 3. The circuit also requests in a friendly manner that the government will accept as a principle always to consult representative colored leaders regarding proposed legislation affecting coloreds, and that the cooperation of the coloreds be a condition for policy implementation. 4. The circuit confirms that the Christians from the area of this circuit will pray that the government will be led to deal with all colored groups in our country in a Christian manner."

10. For a full list of statements and pastoral letters issued by the bishops between 1952 and 1982, see Andrew Prior, ed., *Catholics in apartheid society* (Cape Town: David Philip, 1982), pp. 167-95. The choice of one such statement is clearly not representative of the views of all South African Catholics in this period, but it does provide some insight into the stance of the Catholic Church around 1957.

11. The dissenting voices from within the DRC are mostly described in terms of powerful individuals like Bennie Keet, Ben Engelbrecht, and Beyers Naudé. There were more such voices, however, of which Willie Jonker was, theologically speaking, the most influential inside the DRC. (His legacy still needs to be made available to a broader English readership.) By the 1980s these individual voices assumed a wider base among ordinary dominees (i.e., Afrikaner Church ministers) within the DRC. Two of the most significant protests were the Hervormingsdaggetuienis (Reformation Day Witness) on October 31, 1980, by eight leading academics, and the Open Letter, signed by 123 people (formulated by March 1982; first published on June 9, 1982, in *Die Kerkbode* and later discussed in *Perspektief op*

• World Alliance of Reformed Churches (WARC): "Racism and South Africa" (Twenty-first General Council, August 1982)

After reading the documents carefully, I constructed a theological profile under four headings that emerged from the material. They will form the outline of this chapter, with each being considered in relation to the Belhar text itself: (1) a confessional interpretation of the situation in South Africa, (2) the biblical and theological sources cited in support of such an interpretation, (3) core theological themes relevant to the South African situation, and (4) a vision of social change in South Africa.

A confessional interpretation of the situation in South Africa

Dietrich Bonhoeffer once remarked: "Seeing the world *sub specie Christi* is the paramount theological activity for Christians."[12] One could say that different ways of "seeing" was exactly the core issue at stake during the South African church struggle. There are obviously many perspectives on a situation like the one that was emerging in South Africa after 1948. These may vary across the disciplines, such as history, politics, economics, sociology, and theology, and vary among different schools of thought within these disciplines. The contrasting theological views in support of and against apartheid have been well documented and discussed. All the statements listed above, in one way or another, express a view on the situation as interpreted by the compilers at the time of their proclamation.

It is interesting to note the development from language with strong theological disapproval to a more technical language suited to a confessional interpretation of the situation.[13] One would not expect, for exam-

---

die Ope Brief, ed. David Bosch, A. König, and Willem Nicol [Cape Town: Human & Rousseau, 1982]). For the sake of our analysis, I will include the Open Letter, which, because of its wider base, could assume at least some legitimacy, although, unlike the others, it was never accepted as an official church document. Dissent from the Gereformeerde Kerk in this period is evident from the Koinonia Declaration (1977), in which apartheid and its attempts to construct a Christian justification were rejected.

12. Dietrich Bonhoeffer, *Creation and fall* (London: SCM Press, 1959), pp. 7-8.

13. For an excellent treatment of *status confessionis*, see Dirk J. Smit, "What does *status confessionis* mean?" in *A moment of truth: The confession of the Dutch Reformed Mission Church, 1982*, ed. G. D. Cloete and Dirk J. Smit, pp. 7-32 (Grand Rapids: Eerdmans, 1984). It is interesting to note that in 1980 the WCC's Central Committee requested members "to de-

ple, to find "confessionalist" language in a Catholic document. The 1957 SACBC statement, however, alludes twice to the spirit of a confessional interpretation. First, it declares "the principle of apartheid as something *intrinsically evil*" and notes the innumerable offenses against charity and justice flowing from "this *fundamental evil* of apartheid" (my emphases). Toward the end of their statement the bishops direct an earnest plea to white South Africans "to consider carefully what apartheid means: *its evil and anti-Christian character*" (my emphasis). It clearly is no mere condemnation of apartheid's effects or its application only (as was later argued by some in the DRC) but of the principle in toto, using theological language ("evil" and "anti-Christian") that signals strong disapproval and rejection.

Second, the bishops' statement charges that "the white man makes himself an agent of God's will and the interpreter of God's providence in assigning the range and determining the bounds of non-white development. One trembles at the *blasphemy* of thus attributing to God the offences against charity and justice that are apartheid's necessary accompaniment" (my emphasis). This is very strong theological language and unambiguous in its confessional intent. Blasphemy as used here in its ethical sense ("offences against charity and justice") is no less theological in its depiction of false prophecies ("agent of God's will and interpreter of God's providence"), with the added dimension of racist supremacy, where some "play God" over the lives of others, thereby inadvertently falling into idolatry.

The question about the formation of a confessing church arose after the Sharpeville killings and when the results of Cottesloe (1961) were rejected by the DRC's regional synods.[14] This thinking emerged in the first years after the Rivonia trial,[15] with the heightened security after the ban-

---

clare as a fundamental matter of faith that the doctrine and practice of apartheid is a perversion of the Christian Gospel," asking members to express this through a confession of faith, a covenant, a *status confessionis,* or an equivalent commitment (see Ans van der Bent, ed., *Breaking down the walls: WCC statements and actions on racism, 1948-1985* [Geneva: WCC, 1986], p. 71).

14. Sharpeville refers to the place where 69 black South Africans were shot dead and 186 wounded by apartheid police on March 21, 1960. The protestors had publicly burned their compulsory passes (ID books), which were used to administer influx control of black people into so-called white areas. The WCC called for an urgent consultation in South Africa to discuss the churches' response to these events. This important meeting of South African churches affiliated with the SACC, which became known as the Cottesloe consultation, took place in Johannesburg December 7-14, 1960.

15. Rivonia is a suburb near Johannesburg where a number of African National Congress (ANC) leaders were arrested on Liliesleaf Farm on July 11, 1963. The so-called Rivonia

ning of the Communist Party and the ANC. The now well-known Rev. Beyers Naudé had in the meantime set up the Christian Institute. In a number of articles in *Pro Veritate* between July and December 1965, he spelled out his views on why the time had arrived for a confessing church.[16]

This confessional theme arose and was shown with greater clarity in the 1968 SACC *Message to the People of South Africa* (hereafter referred to as *Message*). The very first line sets the tone: "We are under an obligation to confess anew our commitment to the universal faith of Christians, the eternal Gospel of salvation and security in Christ Jesus alone." For the first time we hear an official South African church meeting to depict the political policy of racial separation in terms of doctrine, making it an issue of faith. In clear language, the statement reads: "We believe that this doctrine of separation is *a false faith, a novel gospel*" (my emphasis), and its concluding paragraphs demand a clear choice between a commitment to an ethnic group and a commitment to Christ.

In subsequent years, the debate widened to include contributions from the Netherlands and Germany, notably by Eberhard Bethge, who, after a visit to South Africa in 1973, wrote that "in many quarters the view now is that a *status confessionis* now exists, and some individual Christians sacrifice themselves to draw public attention to this fact."[17] This ecumenical awareness informed the LWF meeting in Dar es Salaam in 1977. Addressed by Bishop Manas Buthelezi from South Africa on the issue of a *status confessionis*, the ensuing statement is clearly a confessional declaration. It begins: "The Lutheran Churches are confessional Churches." This is motivated with a reference to Scripture and the Augsburg Confession and the need for "concrete manifestations" of this confession. Well aware of their own German past, the Lutherans note that "political and social systems may become so perverted and oppressive that it is consistent with the confession to reject them." They then appeal to the white member churches in South-

---

trial refers to the high court case of a multiracial group of nineteen ANC leaders (including Nelson Mandela) on the charge of treason for promoting terrorism and plotting the violent overthrow of the state. The trial ran from November 1963 to June 1964. Those found guilty received a variety of sentences, including life sentences, which were mainly served on Robben Island, near Cape Town.

16. See John W. de Gruchy, "Towards a confessing church," in de Gruchy and Villa-Vicencio, *Apartheid is a heresy,* pp. 76-77. Naudé took his understanding of the confessing church from the German context. It includes being and living as alternative community.

17. See de Gruchy, "Confessing church," p. 77, and original reference on p. 91, n. 9.

ern Africa "to recognize that *the situation in Southern Africa constitutes a status confessionis*" (my emphasis). The implication is that "churches would publicly and unequivocally reject the existing apartheid system."

In this statement the threshold between adiaphora (neutral matters) and confession had decidedly been crossed. The scene was set for the South African churches to take this up.[18] And one could hardly ask for a more appropriate church than the Mission Church — itself the product of church separation and its members suffering under apartheid — to take the baton further. Under the charismatic, theologically informed, and strategic leadership of Allan Boesak, the road was paved toward a confessing church. The founding charter of ABRECSA, in 1981, took the same line as the Lutheran statement: "We . . . unequivocally declare apartheid *a sin*, and that the moral and theological justification of it is a *travesty of the Gospel*, a betrayal of the Reformed tradition, and *a heresy*" (my emphases). With this statement the theological initiative in the DRC family shifted toward its black members and toward one of its daughter churches.[19] Although the technical term *status confessionis* is not used by ABRECSA, the confessional interpretation of the political situation is clearly upheld.

A year later, in 1982, Allan Boesak was elected president of the World Alliance of Reformed Churches, meeting in Ottawa. His opening speech was printed as the first chapter in *Apartheid is a heresy* and was a powerful call for the alliance to take a strong stance against racism as such ("it is a sin, and a form of idolatry") and against apartheid in particular: "In South Africa . . . apartheid is not just a political ideology. Its very existence as a political party has depended and still depends on the theological justification of certain member churches of WARC. For Reformed churches, this situation should constitute a *status confessionis*. This means that churches should recognize that apartheid is heresy, contrary to the gospel and inconsistent with the Reformed tradition, and consequently reject it as such."[20] It is now history that such a decision was indeed taken, resulting, inter alia, in the suspension of the two white Reformed Churches in South Africa.

18. The Open Letter of 1980 (see Bosch, König, and Nicol, *Perspektief op die Ope Brief*) does not use technical confessional terms but clearly states: "The church will always witness that no societal order may proceed from the fundamental irreconcilability of people or groups of people and set up a societal order based on such a principle" (2.1.2, my translation).

19. Allan Boesak's book *Black and Reformed: Apartheid, liberation, and the Calvinist tradition* (Maryknoll, N.Y.: Orbis Books, 1984) remains an important milestone in the development of an indigenous Reformed theology in South Africa.

20. De Gruchy and Villa-Vicencio, *Apartheid is a heresy*, p. 8.

The refusal to share the Lord's Table in Ottawa with representatives of the white churches was an ironic twist in the long history of table exclusion started by the now-notorious decision of the Cape DRC in 1857. Feedback from Ottawa was delivered to a packed audience in the seminary at Stellenbosch. When asked by the dean to thank the speakers, Professor Willie Jonker made a short unprepared speech, concluding with: "It may be painful, but the voice of Ottawa is the voice of the Holy Spirit from the ecumenical church to the DRC."

In September 1982 the General Synod of the DRMC met, with Izak Mentoor as moderator and Boesak as assessor, and formulated "A statement on apartheid and a confession of faith." In it the church clarified that it had already taken a stance in 1978 and that the Ottawa decision was a consequence of this, and that (after confirming Ottawa) "we can do no other than with the deepest regret accuse the DRC of theological heresy and idolatry."[21]

At the synod it was felt that the clarity of the "no" should be matched by an equal clarity of the "yes."[22] The dramatic moment of moving to actual confession is discussed in more detail in chapter 3. A small commission was tasked to draw up a draft confession that was accepted, widely circulated in the Mission Church, and formally adopted four years later as the Confession of Belhar.[23]

As one would expect, Belhar continues faithfully in the tradition of the Confessing Church. Although the Accompanying Letter does not refer to the *status confessionis* as a technical term, the letter puts itself and the ensuing confession in the ambit of the *status confessionis*: "We are deeply conscious that moments of such seriousness can arise in the life of the Church that it may feel the need to confess its faith anew in the light of a specific

21. At that point I had just completed my seminary studies and was privileged to be present at the synod at Belhar as an unofficial visitor. The decision on heresy and idolatry, accepted by a vast majority, was preceded by an emotional appeal by some speakers on behalf of the mother church, "who taught us the gospel of Jesus Christ. How can we now call her heretical?" Not seeing the structural, systemic nature of apartheid, many ministers of the DRC with a heart for mission and evangelization expressed the same sentiment. The late Mike Smuts, a well-loved evangelical, remarked to me, "I give up my holidays to preach in the Mission Church over Christmas. Am I now a heretic?"

22. See Barth, *Church dogmatics*, I/2, p. 629.

23. Although certain specific individuals drafted the document, the Belhar Confession has always been presented as being authored by the church. See interesting examples of these "shifted"-author documents in Karl Barth, *Church dogmatics, I/2: The revelation of God* (Edinburgh: T. & T. Clark, 1956) (henceforth Barth, *Revelation*), pp. 637-38.

situation" (par. 1). In paragraph 3 it speaks further of "this objectionable doctrine" and "such a false doctrine." In Belhar itself, as discussed in chapter 1, all three rejection clauses in articles 2 to 4 begin with the words "Therefore, we reject any *doctrine . . .*" (my emphasis, note slight wording difference in art. 4), thereby clearly confirming the pattern established by antecedent church declarations concerning the understanding of the sociopolitical situation from a confessional perspective.

If we accept that the institution of an apartheid state after 1948 was not possible without theological legitimization, or that the system could not be maintained against considerable political and economic odds without religious and moral justification, then we begin to understand the significance of a *status confessionis*. It destroyed apartheid's Christian canopy, and it took less than a decade (but still at a tremendous human cost) to formally dismantle the system itself.

The biblical and theological sources cited in support of a confessional interpretation

In this section we consider the genre of church declarations. They are normally the outcome of careful deliberation from a consensus-seeking community. A certain hermeneutical framework is therefore implicitly taken for granted, and one would not normally expect detailed references, such as required in a synodical report or a theological treatise. It needs to be examined how these statements were argued from Scripture and tradition, and whether there is a link between these arguments and Belhar.

In 1957 the Catholic bishops focused on the two criteria of *charity* and *justice.* These are cited twice as complementary virtues, with the significant implication that charity (love), without restorative justice in society, is rendered meaningless.[24] They derive their content and application from Christ's teaching and "the change of heart and practice that the *law of Christ* demands" (my emphasis). In this way, the bishops' statement takes

---

24. See the devastating analysis and critique offered by Johann Kinghorn, ed., *Die N. G. Kerk en apartheid* (Johannesburg: Macmillan, 1986), pp. 169-74, especially regarding the ethics of *gun aan ander* (grant to others), which was frequently used to support separate development. For an interesting view of the relationship between reconciliation, justice, and peace from a covenantal theological perspective, see Adrio König, "Is versoening (te) goedkoop?" in *Koninkryk, kerk en kosmos,* ed. P. F. Theron and Johann Kinghorn, pp. 130-43 (Bloemfontein: Pro-Christo, 1989).

its legitimacy from Scripture and from clear, biblically aligned criteria as they make their social-ethical evaluation of the South African situation at that time.

The Cottesloe Declaration, with its surprisingly detailed and wide-ranging social commentary (see below, "A Vision of Social Change"), takes a decisive stand in its first section: "In its social witness the Church must take cognizance of all attitudes, forces, policies and laws which affect the life of a people; but the Church must proclaim that *the final criterion of all social and political action is the principles of Scripture* regarding the realization of all men of a life worthy of their God-given vocation" (my emphasis).

The *Message* (1968) presents its proclamation in much more powerful and emphatic language. After the confessional opening line referred to above, a sevenfold annunciation of "The Gospel of Jesus Christ . . ." follows like the Beatitudes, making absolutely clear wherein lies the authority and content of the message. The very title of the statement as a "message" already foretells what is to follow — namely, the gospel, the will of God for South Africa today.

Part of ABRECSA's significance lies in the fact that it provided a platform and stimulus for black people of Reformed conviction to challenge the white face of Reformed theology (both English and Afrikaans), with its exclusive origin from and orientation toward Europe. More important, however, it aimed at reclaiming the inner thrust of the Reformed tradition — inextricably linked to apartheid in South Africa — for the cause of justice. The crucial question was: "What does it mean to be black and Reformed in Southern Africa today?"[25]

In the light of this Reformed confessional orientation, we are not surprised to read in the first statement of the theological basis, "The Word of God is the supreme authority and guiding principle revealing all we need to know about God's will for the whole existence of human beings. It is this Word that gives life and offers liberation that is total and complete." Herein lies the classic Reformed belief about the *claritas* and *perspecuitas* of the Scriptures linked to its liberative intentions. The actual ABRECSA statement sets up a rhetorically powerful antithesis between a false and a true interpretation of the Reformed tradition.[26] Hence, ABRECSA rejects

25. See charter motivation 2.4.

26. One can see this from the corresponding, but antithetical, sections in points 4 and 5, which are already precursors to a confessional style — that is, statements of faith followed by statements of rejection.

an interpretation of the Reformed tradition where "the Word of God [is] subjected and made subservient to the claims of cultural and racist ideology" (point 4.1).

Apart from an insistence on the supremacy of the Word, there is an almost defiant and proud reclamation of the tradition to ensure "a truer understanding" thereof (point 6). This is accomplished by: "declaring unequivocally that apartheid is a sin . . . and a betrayal of the Reformed tradition" (point 7), followed by a specific reference to the Belgic Confession (point 8), with a terse conclusion: "This is our tradition. This we will fight for" (point 9).

This Word-tradition argument is typical of Reformed theology,[27] where Scripture is the ultimate authority and tradition is always under Scripture, but held authoritatively because of a confession's correspondence with Scripture (the *quia* view).[28] This was carried forth into the Ottawa meeting of WARC the following year (1982), and even the wording indicates that Ottawa took its cue from ABRECSA. After declaring that the situation constituted a *status confessionis,* the meeting stated: "We declare with black Reformed Christians of South Africa that apartheid . . . is a sin, and that the moral and theological justification of it is a travesty of the gospel, and in its persistent disobedience to the word of God, a theological heresy" (see ABRECSA, declaration point 7). This was again confirmed at the DRMC synod later that year, in the very same format, namely a declaration of *status confessionis,* then a judgment of apartheid as a sin, and any defense thereof a theological heresy. At this point, the principled stance, the specific view of the situation, slowly and carefully emerged from the witness of the local and ecumenical churches over two decades, giving rise to the actual act of confessing itself. Belhar was born.

There is a marked difference between Belhar and the preceding docu-

---

27. The Open Letter reflects the same spirit: it contains a number of direct and indirect scriptural references and bases its prophetic witness on the assumption that a Christian state, along with the church, would listen to the Word of God (2.2.1). As confessional bases, the Apostles' and Nicene Creeds are mentioned as testifying to the normative unity of the church (1.1.5), whereas article 27 of the Belgic Confession is used to argue that no criterion other than faith may be used for membership of the church (1.2.2). Churches in the DRC family with the same confessional basis therefore need to express their unity in a visible form (1.2.3).

28. The *quia* (Lat. "because") view is that confessions are true *because* they are in accordance with Scripture, whereas the *quatenus* (Lat. "insofar as") view holds that confessions are true *insofar as* they are in accordance with Scripture. The latter is a weaker form of confessionalism than the former.

ments with regard to its claim to be nothing more than a scriptural confession in line with the ancient and Reformed confessional tradition. Even a cursory look at Belhar reveals the differences. Each of the three middle articles (2, 3, and 4) is provided with lists of supporting biblical texts and pericopes. Belhar's aim is clearly not to present an exegesis of each text. It does, however, wish to demonstrate that it carries forth the main themes of unity, reconciliation, and justice as found in Scripture, whence it claims its authority. Belhar is much more attentive to demonstrate beyond any doubt its correspondence to Scripture and the church's confessional tradition. A short discussion of actual scriptural references will follow in chapter 3, where the confessional character of Belhar is set out in dialogue with Karl Barth.

Core theological themes relevant to the South African situation

A contextual interpretation of the gospel usually has a "closure effect," restricting the multidimensional and many possible meanings of the Word to one or two focused interpretations. This is true of the canon itself and is part of the church's continued interpretation of the gospel for its own time. This is particularly evident from great events like the Reformation, the rise of various liberation theologies (political, feminist, womanist, black, and ecological), and the insight that all theologies are in fact "local," despite the power and dominance of Western theology, with its purported universalist character.[29] This is even more the case regarding confessions, with their implicit "kairos character" and their clear choice of a specific word from God for now.[30]

The following questions now arise: What were the dominant theological themes, if any, put forward by the church in the years leading up to Belhar? And what impact, if any, did they have on Belhar's final formulation? From my analysis, three clear focal points emerged: the visible unity of church, the lordship of Christ, and a common humanity.

29. Robert Schreiter's *Constructing local theologies* (Maryknoll, N.Y.: Orbis Books, 1985), although somewhat dated, remains one of the best expositions of a "sociology" of theology.

30. See Piet J. Naudé, "Reformed confessions as hermeneutical problem: A case study of the Belhar Confession," in *Reformed theology: Identity and ecumenicity II; Biblical interpretation in the Reformed tradition,* ed. Wallace M. Alston Jr. and Michael Welker, pp. 242-60 (Grand Rapids: Eerdmans, 2007).

Ecclesiology: The visible unity of the church

It is interesting to read the documents and find that the foremost theological issue relates to the church. Strong affirmations for church unity are especially evident in the context of a church that was divided along racial lines, motivated from a particular view on mission and a specific neo-Calvinist-inspired interpretation of Scripture.[31] There was a deep sense that what was at stake was, in the first place, not a new political ethic or theory of social change. In line with the confessional view of the situation, and in the context of a de facto *corpus Christianum*,[32] there was no doubt that if the church could find a true unity in itself, changes in society would be inevitable.[33] This assumption, clearly underlying all the statements, is a necessary condition for the bold witness to the unity of the church. In fact, it places this witness in a specific frame, namely, that unity is itself the best that the church can offer a society in need of hope, and that black and white people can indeed reconcile.

The clear statement from the Cottesloe consultation encapsulates this "order" and is a summary of what would return as themes in the ensuing years: unity that supersedes diversity; no exclusion from the body on racial grounds; and spiritual unity expressed in visible forms. Let us look at Cottesloe, part 2, points 3-6 in more detail.

> 3. The Church has a duty to bear witness to the hope which is in Christianity both to white South Africans in their uncertainty and to non-white South Africans in their frustration.
>
> 4. In a period of rapid social change the Church has a special responsibility for fearless witness within society.

Points 5 and 6 then spell out what this witness would be:

---

31. See Kinghorn, *Die N. G. Kerk en apartheid*, p. 100.

32. Note Etienne de Villiers's exposition of the theocratic ideal underlying the Reformed tradition generally and the support for the apartheid state specifically. See his article "The influence on the DRC on public policy during the late 80s and 90s," *Scriptura* 76 (2001): 51-61. It will be shown below that both supporters and adversaries of apartheid assumed a close church-state-society interaction that is no longer possible in South Africa today.

33. See Piet J. Naudé, "The Dutch Reformed Church's role in the context of transition in South Africa: Main streams of academic research," *Scriptura* 76 (2001): 88-90.

5. The Church as the body of Christ is a unity and within this unity *the natural diversity among men is not annulled but sanctified.*

6. No one who believes in Jesus Christ may be excluded from any Church on grounds of his colour or race. The *spiritual unity* among all men who are in Christ must find *visible expression* in acts of common worship and witness, and in fellowship and consultation on matters of common concern.[34] (my emphases)

The same formulation is found in the ABRECSA charter, although it is more inclusive of sex and language differences. In the motivation provided, it takes up the painful question of history, identity, and theological self-expression by so-called mission churches, as the following demonstrates: "Being 'mission churches,' they have been divided into separate denominations by the 'mother' missionary societies even though they share the same confessional base, and these divisions are not of their own making" (2.2). In the series of rejections found in the declaration, the ecclesiology against which ABRECSA sets itself up is clear: "The heresy that the unity of the Church is a mystical one,[35] where ethnicity and culture in fact become a mark of the Church" (4.5).

In the Open Letter the visible unity of the church is seen as a direct result of God's reconciling work in Christ. Coming from the heart of the DRC, this letter clearly deals with the issue of unity and diversity. Unity is of primary importance and a matter for confession; diversity is secondary and serves as reciprocal enrichment and not disunity in the church: "The church will therefore struggle against factors threatening its unity" (1.1.3).

At the WARC Ottawa meeting, this ecclesiology assumes a greater urgency and is laid down as the dividing line between authentic and inauthentic forms of church. The suspension of the two white South African Reformed churches from WARC in Ottawa must be seen in the light of the Nairobi meeting of WARC in 1970, which had already declared: "The Church that by doctrine and/or practice affirms segregation of peoples . . . as a law for its life cannot be regarded as an authentic member of the body of Christ."[36] Furthermore, Ottawa declared that, as apartheid in fact "con-

34. In the interest of historical accuracy here and elsewhere in quotations, I retain the sexist language of the original.

35. I am not sure whether the use of "mystical" instead of the usual "spiritual" was deliberate, as the former is theologically related to Reformed-Catholic differences about conceptions of the church. The overall point nevertheless remains clear.

36. The emphasis on "law and order" was linked to the protection of the state's security

tradicts the very nature of the Church and obscures the gospel from the world," these two churches were to be suspended. However, they would be "warmly welcomed back once more" on condition that black Christians were no longer excluded from worship and especially Holy Communion, when concrete support was given to sufferers under apartheid, and when the synod unequivocally rejected apartheid and committed itself to the dismantling of the system in both the church and in politics (see sec. 2.4.a-c).

In 1978 the DRMC had already referred to the fact that apartheid takes irreconcilability as a point of departure. Then in 1982 it affirmed that this view stood in direct contrast to "the main artery of the Christian Gospel," which is also the main artery of the Church's existence. From this it follows that "the visible effect of reconciliation between God and man is the existence of the Church as a reconciled *community of people,* a unified community" (original emphasis, my translation).

The biblical defense of an apartheid ecclesiology is based, inter alia, on a link between the Babel and Pentecost events interpreted as though God indeed wills and affirms the plurality of distinct nations. Only the SACC's *Message* (1968) directly opposed such an exegesis, and it is the only document of those discussed here with an explicit link between the Spirit and the church. It affirms "the truth proclaimed by the first Christians, who discovered that God was creating a new community in which differences of race, language, nation, culture, and tradition no longer had power to separate man from man." The *Message* emphasizes that apartheid, in contrast, "insists that we find our identity in disassociation and in distinction from each other. . . . It reinforces distinctions which the Holy Spirit is calling the people of God to overcome. This policy is, therefore, a form of resistance to the Holy Spirit." How do these sentiments relate to Belhar?

This preeminence of ecclesiology, in the forefront of church witnesses over many years, is reflected in the very structure of Belhar. One could rightly say that the heart of the Belhar Confession lies in its view of the church. Belhar is, in other words, fundamentally an ecclesiological statement.

The expression of belief in the triune God in article 1 does not stand alone but is intrinsically linked to this God "who gathers, protects, and cares for his Church." Article 2 confesses that the visible unity of the

---

and, as emerged from the TRC hearings, was used as a basis for persecuting other-minded church leaders. See *Truth and Reconciliation Commission of South Africa Report,* vol. 4 (Cape Town: The Commission, 1998), p. 66, chap. 3.

church, followed by reconciliation (art. 3) and justice (art. 4), is established through the church. Here we find confirmation of the pattern seen earlier. There is a movement from the church to the world on the assumption that intra-ecclesial realities have a direct and profound impact on social realities outside the church. Article 5 concludes the confession with a call to the church "to confess and to do all these things" in obedience to Jesus Christ.

Christology: The lordship of Jesus Christ

The lordship of Christ, perhaps the oldest confessional phrase of the early church, is witnessed to in relation both to its ecclesiological and to its broader historical significance. Christ as Lord is able to reconcile people and bring them together in one body. This is the christological foundation for the ecclesiological vision described above. The witness to Christ's lordship, with its "bifocal" vision of church and world, also reinforces the assumption of an intrinsic link between church and society, creating the opportunity to chart the way not only for the nature of the church but also for the relationship between church and state, where the lordship of Christ is set against earthly rulers.

The last point is very important, as the apartheid state found part of its authority in its self-proclaimed Christian foundation, while at the same time persecuting those who "mix religion and politics" for revolutionary purposes.[37] The clearest formulations for this second focal point — Christ's lordship versus state authority — are found in the *Message* and in the ABRECSA charter. The *Message* states: "The Gospel of Jesus Christ declares that Christ is our master, and that to him all authority is given." This implies that the highest loyalty and primary commitment is due to him alone, and not to either "one group or tradition" or "the demands of the South African state," which must be clearly distinguished from "the demands of Christian discipleship." The last two paragraphs of the *Message* reinforce this twofold vision that Christ is master of the church, on the one hand, and that, on the other, Christ is Lord of the world (and "South Africa is part of his world"). The final call is to be committed to Christ alone.

The Open Letter's very structure testifies to its stance on the lordship

---

37. The most elaborate statement on church-state relations from a Reformed perspective at that time is found in "A theological rationale and call to prayer for the end to unjust rule," issued in 1985. See Villa-Vicencio, *Between Christ and Caesar*, p. 246.

of Christ over the whole of life, though it is couched in terms of reconciliation. The church can make a contribution to reconciliation by uniting itself (first part), but equally so by its prophetic witness in society (second part): "We therefore reject any notion that the church may occupy itself only with 'spiritual issues' and may further retreat from other spheres of society" (beginning of point 2, my translation). "Reconciliation is a prophetic witness to the whole of society, and therefore the church may not remain silent on issues like moral decay, family disintegration, and discrimination" (2.1.1, my translation).

The ABRECSA charter takes the lordship of Christ in all of life, "even in those situations where his lordship is not readily recognized," as one of its theological basis points, rendering an eschatological significance to this lordship. In light of this lordship, Christians are responsible for the re-formation of the world as an integral part of discipleship, and "obedience to earthly authorities is only obedience *in God*" (original emphasis; see points b-d).[38] ABRECSA therefore rejects an interpretation of the Reformed tradition that would accept "the demand of paying uncritical allegiance to the State, which is regarded as divinely instituted" (see statement 4.4). The following reference to the Belgic Confession shows the deep belief that the cause of the faithful, "which is now condemned by many judges and magistrates as heretical and impious, will then be known to be the cause of the Son of God" (statement 8).

In the Ottawa statement, faithful allegiance to Jesus Christ is set over against "the claims of an unjust or oppressive government," and "Christians who aid and abet the oppressor" are denounced (sec. 1). The theological rationale for this is supported by the fact that apartheid is based on a fundamental irreconcilability of human beings, "thus rendering ineffective the reconciling and uniting power of our Lord Jesus Christ" (2.1a).

It is now instructive to note that the Belhar Confession follows the same order, going from Christ's reconciling work in the church (art. 2) to his reconciling work in the world (art. 3), as well as linking the latter with the issue of church-state relations. One should therefore read: "We believe that Christ's work of reconciliation is made manifest in the Church . . ." (art. 2.2) in close relation to "reconciliation in and through Jesus Christ"

---

38. For a critical analysis of the exegesis, see J. A. Loubser, *The apartheid Bible* (Cape Town: Tafelberg, 1987); and recently Louis C. Jonker, "Israel en die nasies. 'n Kritiese nadenke oor die dokument *Ras, Volk en Nasie*," *Scriptura* 2 (2001): 165-84. For the theology underlying such an exegesis, see Kinghorn, *Die N. G. Kerk en apartheid*.

(art. 3.1), where reconciliation in this article is linked to the church's role as the salt, light, and peacemaker in the world.

The inclusion of a witness to the state is couched in strictly theological language. Belhar's judgment is that the "credibility" of the message is seriously affected "in a land which professes to be Christian" but is in fact built on enforced separation (art. 3.3). The rejection clause of article 3 is also not aimed at the state as such but at *the doctrine* that sanctions forced separation in the name of the gospel. The theme of commitment to Christ alone in the face of state violence (so evident in the *Message* and ABRECSA) is clearly spelled out in article 5: "We believe that, in obedience to Jesus Christ, its only Head [note the lordship language], the Church is called to confess and to do all these things, *even though the authorities and human laws might forbid them* and punishment and suffering be the consequence" (my emphasis).

In this way, Belhar's Christology remains true to the content and structure of preceding church witnesses. The rule of Christ extends over both church and society and is professed from the former to the latter. Where the church follows Christ in obedience to his rule but is resisted by the state, the higher commitment to Christ will prevail.

Anthropology: The search for a common humanity

From a theological perspective, the struggle against apartheid was indeed, as shown so far, a struggle for the nature of the church and the lordship of Jesus Christ. At the grassroots level, however, there was a struggle for humanity and the human dignity of each person, irrespective of his or her race. My conclusion, from the documents under discussion, is that this theme is not independently developed but is subsumed under the first two theological views. The church is the one body of Christ, where only faith is required for membership; Christ is Lord in society, and in his kingdom there is no place for forced separation based on race. We saw in chapter 1 that the dehumanization caused by apartheid was made possible by a combination of neo-Calvinist theology and the precarious socioeconomic position of Afrikaners. The issue of the human person and his or her status in creation therefore became a crucial theme that needed to be addressed. The cue for the significance of Belhar today, which is discussed in the last part of this book (chaps. 7-9), is taken from the theme of a new humanity.

Apartheid theology did not deny the unity of humanity stemming

from the one Adam. However, it used the creaturely differentiation between man and woman, heaven and earth, and light and darkness to argue
for a God-willed differentiation that, as far as the proponents of apartheid
theology were concerned, was confirmed in the Babel events, where God is
understood to side against uniformity in favor of the pluriformity of nations, each with its own language and territory.[39]

This is the subtext of the *Message,* which is sensitive to this kind of interpretation: "The most important features of a man are not the details of
his racial group, but *the nature which he has in common with all men* and
also *the gifts and abilities which are given to him as a unique individual* by
the grace of God; to insist that racial characteristics are more important
than these is to reject what is *most significant about our own humanity* as
well as the humanity of others" (my emphases). And two paragraphs later,
the *Message* makes a telling remark: "Where different groups of people are
hostile to each other, this is due to human sin, *not to the plan of the Creator*" (my emphasis).

The *Message* herewith contradicts the assumed apartheid anthropology in three ways.[40] First, there is a common humanity among all people
because of their being created by God. Second, people are indeed different,
but this is due to God's gracious gifts to individual people. Third, where
enmity arises among different groups, this should be seen, not as the result
of God's providence (and a reason for legally enforced separation), but
rather as arising from sin, which was overcome by Christ's reconciling
work. This amounts to the direct inversion of an apartheid anthropology
that was constructed on a differentiated creation order; this order re-
mained normative, despite the re-creation brought by the work of Christ
and exemplified in the church.

The reference in the ABRECSA charter to the indivisibility of the body
of Christ, which demands that the barriers of race, culture, ethnicity, language, and gender be transcended, is a surprisingly inclusivist phrase. It is
not explicitly grounded in anthropology, however, but in Christology. In
Ottawa the WARC stated that apartheid incurred "the anger and sorrow of
God *in whose image all human beings are created*" (my emphasis) without

39. Quoted in the Ottawa 1982 "Resolution on Racism and South Africa," 1.5.
40. See Kinghorn's contribution to Jonker's Festschrift, in which he develops the outline of various anthropological types, namely, liberal, racist, and nationalist (Johann
Kinghorn, "Teologie en sosiaal-antropologie," in Theron and Kinghorn, *Koninkryk, kerk en
kosmos,* pp. 112-29).

further clarification, thereby drawing on the strong *imago Dei* tradition in Christian theology and ethics.

I have earlier remarked that Belhar is primarily an ecclesiological document. One would therefore expect to find a strong focus, not so much on our common *creaturely* humanity, but on the *re-created* humanity as exemplified in the church. In this new community, matters of creation such as different languages and cultures serve as enrichment and no longer disunity. Article 1 refers to the triune God's gathering of the church; article 2 focuses on this communion of saints, where unity is manifested as the people of God pursue community with one another and are built up in the new humanity. In article 3 the possibility of reconciliation outside the church is seen as being fostered by the life of the obedient church, "which can open new possibilities of life for society and the world" (art. 3.2). The rejection clauses of article 3 (against forced separation on racial grounds) and article 4 (against any ideology that legitimizes injustices) are both advanced on ecclesiological grounds (re-creation), not on the idea of a common humanity based in creation as such, or creation in the image of God.

There is no doubt that this "narrower" focus of Belhar effectively rejects any trace of enforced separateness based on creaturely features. One might, though, observe two weaknesses in Belhar when read today. The first is its assumption of a seamless unity between church and society and the expectation (rightly so at that time) that changes in the church would lead inevitably to changes in society. Second, because Belhar was specifically fighting a form of natural theology based on creation, it nowhere sought recourse to a common humanity based on creation that is constructed apart from the new humanity of the faith community. These specific focal points of the Belhar Confession must be seen from the context in which the confession arose. One should, however, take into account that South Africa and sub-Saharan Africa are presently much more influenced by the forces of modernity and the culture of human rights than was the case in the early 1980s.[41] This will be pursued in the last part of the book, where we consider Belhar's significance for today.

---

41. For a discussion of the ambiguous relationship between Christian faith and human rights, see Piet J. Naudé, "Between humility and boldness: Explicating human rights from a Christian perspective," *Nederduitse Gereformeerde Teologiese Tydskrif* 48, nos. 1-2 (2007): 139-49.

A vision of social change in South Africa

Apartheid was a pervasive system that permeated every aspect of the individual and society. At the height of apartheid, the numerous laws regulated where people could live, whom they could marry, which school they could attend, what type of work they were allowed to do, and ultimately even what they should think. This situation was justified on biblical and theological grounds to the extent that some apartheid measures were actually put in place by the National Party government at the request of white Reformed churches, for example, the Immorality Act, which forbade sexual relations between people of different races.

We have already seen that alternative church witnesses interpreted the situation from a radically different perspective, to the point of declaring the South African social order a matter of confession. Pro-apartheid theology made clear prescriptive social regulations possible. The question now arises: would alternative witnesses also hold forth a social vision with clear social regulations? In other words, would one find not only *two theologies* at work but also *two social visions* of change in South African society? Ultimately, what would Belhar confess in this regard?

The early Wynberg decision of the DRMC did not deal with any specific legislation. At that stage, which was the same year that the National Party came to power, a number of apartheid measures had not yet been implemented, but the philosophy and direction of the government were clear enough. The circuit therefore stated that it "objects against proposed apartheid laws" and put forward the democratic principle of consultation with the people affected and the request for their consent before any policies were implemented.

The Catholic bishops spoke out in 1957, when apartheid had already been firmly instituted, and fiercely defended what the Nationalist government saw as a revolutionary, Communist onslaught. The bishops followed a firm but very cautious approach to social change. On the one hand, they believed that "all social change must be gradual if it is not to be disastrous." Differential legislation was supported, as long as it aimed at providing services for the less advanced sections of the population.

> A gradual change it must be: gradual, for no other kind of change is compatible with the maintenance of order, without which there is no society, no government, no justice, no common good. But a change must come, for otherwise our country faces a disastrous future. That

change could be initiated immediately. . . . The time is short. The need is urgent. Those penalized by apartheid must be given concrete evidence of the change before it is too late.

On the other hand, a word is addressed to those "who suffer under the sting of apartheid. They are embittered and frustrated and take recourse to revolutionary slogans that require immediate and radical change." A word of warning follows: "They do not stop to contemplate . . . the complete dissolution of society and perhaps their own rapid destruction in the holocaust. This is particularly true of those who find atheistic communism the inspiration of their present striving and their hope for the future."

Despite these very cautious remarks, the bishops, as seen earlier, do not hesitate to call apartheid evil and anti-Christian, and they "deeply regret that it is still thought necessary to add to the volume of restrictive and oppressive legislation in order to reduce contact between various groups to an inhuman and unnatural minimum."

The events at Sharpeville, in 1960, injected a sense of urgency with regard to the need for social change into the Cottesloe consultation. Cottesloe is therefore remarkable for its enormously concrete social commentary, with unambiguous views on a number of contentious issues in South Africa at the time, including direct representation in Parliament, land ownership, job reservation, mixed marriages, fair wages, freedom of worship, fair judicial processes, and migrant labor (see secs. 2 and 3). There is no doubt that Cottesloe not only provided an alternative theological view of the situation but in fact expressed a concrete social vision, spelling out the details for a completely different South Africa (realized some thirty years later) in the same way that apartheid theology involved itself in concrete social arrangements.[42]

By 1968 the *Message* did not refer to specific details concerning the apartheid system but stated in general that "many features of our social order will have to pass away if the lordship of Christ is to be truly acknowledged and if the peace of Christ is to be revealed as the destroyer of our fear." This shift toward a "totalized" view, with fewer and fewer concrete

---

42. This concreteness perhaps explains the strong political backlash against Cottesloe — among others, by the prime minister himself, Dr. Hendrik Verwoerd, who discredited the Cottesloe Declaration in his 1961 New Year radio address. He made it clear that the synods of the DRC themselves still had to speak on these matters — knowing full well what could be expected! Politicians have a keen sense of their enemies and a cunning ability to use religion in their favor.

details, is evident from the Lutheran Church statement of 1977, which referred to "the situation in South Africa" and rejected "the existing apartheid system."

Concrete, specific references are reflected again in the Open Letter (1982) from within the DRC twenty years after Cottesloe. The generic descriptive phrase used by the Open Letter to judge apartheid is "an ordering of society based on the fundamental irreconcilability of people and groups of people" (2.1.2). It follows through with some concrete examples by referring to "laws that became symbols of alienation," such as those dealing with mixed marriages, race classification, and group areas (see 2.2.4). In its discussion of justice, the concreteness of a social view is retained, as migrant labor, underresourcing of black education, poor housing, and low wages are all mentioned (2.2.5) and are linked to the broader political system as such: "all people who consider South Africa as their fatherland should be involved in designing a new societal order" (2.2.6). It states that society should be built on justice, which reflects not so much "law and order" but "order and peace," where all people are treated equally and are afforded equal opportunities (2.2.7). The significance of this concrete social-democratic view lies in the fact that it arose from the Afrikaner community itself, in a way not heard of before.

The ABRECSA charter starts off with an inclusive definition of what is meant by "black" and then depicts the South African social order in strong socioeconomic terms (oppressor and oppressed). Their declaration sketches the situation in general terms, mentioning "political oppression, economic exploitation, unbridled capitalism, social discrimination and the total disregard for human dignity" (see point 2). Ottawa mentions "the apartheid system" and makes a few concrete references to "exclusive privileges" for whites and "large-scale deportation causing havoc to family life" (2.1).

The lack of specificity in the later ecumenical documents may be explained from two perspectives. First, as apartheid became settled as an ideological system, it made no sense to protest against it in piecemeal fashion.[43] Second, as explained earlier, there was a clear assumption that if the theological (ecclesiological) battle was won, the social order, kept intact by a religious worldview, would inevitably collapse.

A vision for a different social order is once again reflected in the Belhar Confession. This new order is mediated through a vision of the new

---

43. However, one should not underestimate the moral effect on the system as a whole of the unambiguous rejection by DRC ethicists in the early 1980s of the Immorality Act.

humanity, made possible by Christ in the church. The negative judgment of the societal situation is described in terms such as "enforced separation of people on a racial basis" (art. 3.3). This is followed by references to "all the powerful and privileged who selfishly seek their own interests and thus control and harm others" (art. 4.3), as well as "any ideology which would legitimate forms of injustice" (art. 4, rejection). Over and against such a society stands the new humanity, the church, which witnesses and stands by those who suffer, with hope for a new social order built on justice.

In Belhar, however, the "generalist" language serves the powerful purpose of both exposing the South African social system and at the same time transcending it. There is no reference in Belhar to apartheid or to the DRC or to South Africa specifically.[44] The theological judgment and rejections clearly aim much wider to "any doctrine" (arts. 2, 3, and 4) or "any ideology" (art. 4), wherever it may be found. Belhar thus shares the tendency of the preceding church witnesses toward a "totalist" evaluation of the situation and does not focus on specific legislation or apartheid practices. However, it gains significantly from its clear, history-transcending theological formulations, sharing the core trait of a genuine confession to speak to all times by speaking to its own time.[45]

Conclusion

The theological interpretation of Belhar is an ongoing task, and much still needs to be done. This chapter attempts to show that Belhar, in some sig-

---

44. The Accompanying Letter is more direct at this point: "In our judgment, the present church and political situation in our country, and particularly within the Dutch Reformed Church family, calls for such a decision [to confess the faith anew]" (par. 1). The letter explains, however, that the ensuing confession itself "is not aimed at specific people or groups of people or a church or churches. We proclaim it against a false doctrine" (par. 3). On the basis of official correspondence and decisions, I have argued elsewhere that the DRC initially saw Belhar as an attack on itself (Piet J. Naudé, "Die Belharstryd in ekumeniese perspektief," *Nederduitse Gereformeerde Teologiese Tydskrif* 38, no. 3 [1997]: 226-43). The interaction between Belhar and the DRC will be included as a case study in chapter 5, where the reception of Belhar after 1986 is discussed.

45. There are already signs that some (white) people who feel themselves marginalized by measures like affirmative action in the new dispensation look to Belhar as a pastoral source of faith and hope — which goes way beyond the historical intentions of Belhar itself. One may feel uneasy about such appropriation, but it underlines the multiperspectival hermeneutics that are possible in this case.

nificant ways, reflects the theological focal points and assumptions of antecedent church witnesses. The core assumption of making statements, or confessing in general, is that of a direct link between ecclesiology and sociology. Changes in the church itself, as well as changes witnessed to and struggled for by the church, will, according to this thinking, inevitably lead to changes in society. That this was indeed true of South Africa up to the early 1990s is clear from our history of transformation, which would not have occurred without the church's varied and sustained witness. The impact of modernity and a liberal constitution (adopted in 1996) changed this core assumption and currently raises serious questions about the church's confessing in the public sphere.

Part 2

CONFESSION

Chapter 3

The confessional character of the Belhar Confession

We cannot confess because we would like to confess in the belief that confession is a good thing. We can confess only if we must confess.

— Karl Barth, *Church dogmatics*[1]

It would be impossible to omit the influence of Karl Barth from any discussion of the Belhar Confession. Such a discussion is led by a number of considerations. The first relates to the history of Belhar in both a broad and a more immediate sense of the word. Broadly speaking, one could depict the theological struggle in South Africa in the twentieth century in terms of the contrasting influences of Afrikaner neo-Calvinism, colored with a dash of Pietism, on the one hand, and, on the other, the tradition of the confessing church that stems from the work of Karl Barth and Dietrich Bonhoeffer.

There is no room to fully develop the intriguing and complex reception of (the equally complex) Karl Barth within South African theology. An important collection of essays dealing with this issue was edited by Charles Villa-Vicencio, entitled *On reading Karl Barth in South Africa*.[2] In

1. Karl Barth, *Church dogmatics,* I/2: *The revelation of God* (Edinburgh: T. & T. Clark, 1956) (henceforth Barth, *Revelation*), p. 624.
2. Charles Villa-Vicencio, ed., *On reading Karl Barth in South Africa* (Grand Rapids: Eerdmans, 1988).

This chapter is an expanded version of Piet J. Naudé, "Would Barth sign the Belhar Confession?" *Journal of Theology for Southern Africa* 129 (2007): 4-22.

the DRC family specifically, the extended encounters with Barth in the Afrikaans dogmatic series by Jaap Durand and Willie Jonker are especially relevant. For the sake of this chapter, the fundamental issue in Barth's relationship to DRC theology is not so much differences in views regarding revelation, Scripture, election, and universalism as it is the critical element introduced against all forms of natural theology in its religious, anthropocentric, and humanistic formations.

Jaap Durand's well-known view is worth repeating. He argues that Afrikaner civil religion was formed and sustained both by Scottish evangelicalism and by Kuyperian neo-Calvinism. Kuyper's cosmology and emphasis on the order of creation, though not as crude as German *Ordnungstheologie,*

> combined with orthodox Reformed Christology in such a way that any effort to subject theology to a Christological criticism was defused from the start. As a result the dominant natural theology was never recognized for what it was.[3] One of the great tragedies in the development of Afrikaner Reformed theology in the three decisive decades of its evolvement (1930-60) was that Karl Barth's criticism of religion and natural theology was never really heard or given the opportunity to be heard in those Kuyperian circles that needed it most.[4]

Unlike some other South African churches,[5] there also was not a DRC reception of the "socialist" and "political" Barth as introduced by Marquardt and Gollwitzer.[6] The "public" and "social" value of Barth for the DRC resided in his ability to (1) dismantle the natural theological elements

3. Because of elements of natural theology and nationalism in his theology, Johan Heyns, well-known church leader in the DRC and professor of dogmatics in Pretoria, could not really set forth and appreciate the critical element in Barth's theology. See his *Die kerk* (Pretoria: N. G. Kerkboekhandel, 1977), pp. 126-27; *Dogmatiek* (Pretoria: N. G. Kerkboekhandel, 1978), p. 379; and "Burgerlike ongehoorsaamheid," *Skrif en Kerk* 12, no. 1 (1991): 36-53. See also comments by Willie D. Jonker in his "In gesprek met Johan Heyns," *Skrif en Kerk* 15, no. 1 (1994): 13-26, and *Selfs die kerk kan verander* (Cape Town: Tafelberg, 1998), pp. 133-34.

4. Jaap Durand, "Afrikaner piety and dissent," in *Resistance and hope*, ed. Charles Villa-Vicencio and John W. de Gruchy, p. 40 (Cape Town: David Philip, 1985); and "Church and state in South Africa: Karl Barth vs Abraham Kuyper," in Villa-Vicencio, *On reading Karl Barth*, pp. 121-38.

5. See Villa-Vicencio, *On reading Karl Barth*.

6. See the few comments by Pieter Verster, "Politiek en teologie. Oos-Europa 1990 — Barth agterhaal?" *Nederduitse Gereformeerde Teologiese Tydskrif* 32 (1991): 614-21.

78

in neo-Calvinism, which provided the theological basis for apartheid, and (2) expose the anthropocentric tendencies of Pietism as an inner-focused religion.[7]

In his Barth centenary lecture, Willie Jonker summed it up as follows: "The complacency of the church, the self-satisfaction of some forms of neo-Calvinist theology with which we were acquainted, the shallow moralism of Christianity as a whole, the self-deception of pietistic, Arminian and Methodist preoccupation with personal holiness and perfection with which we were perpetually confronted within our circles — these were the things for which Barth opened our eyes."[8]

Indirectly, Barth's theology loomed over the erosion of apartheid's theological foundation (negative) and provided the thrust for a confessing church (positive) exemplified in the *status confessionis* (1982) and the Belhar Confession (1986). The mainstream DRC thinking was not ready for the reception of Barth at that time because of the theological and hermeneutical framework of its self-understanding. However, the "confessing" Barth was received by the DRMC/URCSA (Uniting Reformed Church in South Africa) and had a tremendous impact on them. This enabled the retrieval of a critical Reformed theology that in the end destroyed the theological respectability of the apartheid system and that enriched the Reformed tradition with a dynamic new confession.

The immediate historical context of Belhar also requires us to take a careful look at Barth. After the acceptance of a *status confessionis* at the October 1982 Mission Church synod, Prof. Gustav Bam made a short speech in which he made a passionate appeal for the act of actual confessing. An extract from that dramatic speech (my translation from the original Afrikaans) speaks for itself:

7. One should not easily bundle Pietism or Evangelicalism together as purely inner-focused forms of Christianity. A case could be made that someone like Beyers Naudé came from an evangelical background and translated the passion for mission into a social vision for South Africa (see Durand, "Afrikaner piety," p. 48).

8. Willie D. Jonker, "Some remarks on the interpretation of Karl Barth," *Nederduitse Gereformeerde Teologiese Tydskrif* 29 (1988): 30-31. The value of Jonker's contribution lies in his argument that Barth should be interpreted as a modern theologian who responded to the Enlightenment challenge in a unique manner. In Jonker's view, Barth's response to the challenges of freedom, rationality, and autonomy was more adequate than Bultmann's hermeneutical theology or political theologies that have developed in Europe and Latin America since the 1960s. For a brilliant exposition of Barth in the context of the Enlightenment, see Willie D. Jonker's recently (posthumously) published book *Die relevansë van die kerk* (Wellington: Lux Verbi, 2008).

The meeting just took a decision of great significance. This is a holy moment. With the proclamation of a *status confessionis,* the synod says: I have reached a point where — on account of both the church and the state — I understand and experience the rules of apartheid over my life as a consequence of presuppositions and convictions that directly conflict with the gospel of Jesus Christ, as I understand it. I experience this conflict of beliefs so strongly that it compels me to confess and to reject the false teaching that threatens me. I find myself in a situation where I must either confront the powers that threaten to neutralize and weaken my faith confession or be silent and come to nothing.

Status confessionis is not brought about by the severity of poverty or even by the intensity of the pain of injustice but only by the specific threat against the faith.

There is, however, a second element. When I find myself in a *status confessionis,* the words spoken from this position should exhibit the status and character of confession. This is not merely a decision I take or a policy declaration I proclaim or an administrative and procedural arrangement I make in my negotiation with others. This is a confession on the same level as the other confessions of the church.

The ancient Christians said in the *status confessionis:* "Jesus Christ is Lord." In this way they confessed against the Roman decree "Caesar is lord." The Apostles' Creed and the classic ecumenical symbols have partially grown from this confession. Even if this was not formally the case, in essence it came down to this.

The Canons of Dort developed from a *status confessionis.* Faith is clearly confessed, and false doctrine that contradicts this faith is clearly condemned. The declaration in 1934 by the Confessing Synod of Barmen is the most recent confession that developed from such a situation. I read to you the first article of this confession.

"I am the way, and the truth, and the life. No one comes to the Father except through me." (John 14:6). "Very truly, I tell you, anyone who does not enter the sheepfold by the gate but climbs in by another way is a thief and a bandit. . . . I am the gate. Whoever enters by me will be saved" (John 10:1, 9). Jesus Christ, as he is attested for us in Holy Scripture, is the one Word of God, whom we are to hear and whom we are to trust and obey in life and in death. We reject the false doctrine that the church can and must acknowledge yet other events and powers, figures and truths as God's revelation apart from and besides this one Word of God, as a source of its proclamation.

In this I clearly hear the language of confession. This is the language we use on Sunday mornings: I believe in God the Father, the Almighty, Creator of heaven and earth.

Neither Ottawa nor the Temporary Ecumenical Commission moved toward the confession and rejection of the false doctrines. For Ottawa this was not required. The WARC is not a church. But the *status confessionis* asks the church to confess clearly and to reject clearly. A symbol must be created as part of the confession of the church by which the church explains itself here and now, a confession over against which the false teaching could be recognized.

Therefore, brother chairman, I would like to put a friendly request that the Synod appoints an ad hoc commission to write such a confession and bring it before this Synod for approval.

Karl Barth, one of the composers of the Barmen Declaration, says in his *Church dogmatics* that such a confession should comply with four criteria:

1. The confession should never be motivated by any ulterior motive. I may therefore never confess because I hope to make some kind of profit or to destroy some kind of political system. The sole purpose should be the glory of God and nothing — yes, nothing — else.
2. Confession is not the expression of an opinion or a firm conviction. It is the protest of the faith when this faith is confronted and questioned by life. A confession cuts through the clichés of the day and cuts to the bone. Therefore, a *status confessionis* does not just go back to old confessions but creates a new confession.
3. Confession is no lyrical effusion or emotional discharge. It is a deed of daring and conflict.
4. Confession is a free deed, under compulsion of the Holy Spirit, seized by the Word of God, and only that. Confession does not happen under the instigation of a worldly opinion. Confessing is not something to play with, because it is like fire. Let us engage with this as we should with holy things.

Thereafter a motion was submitted by the co-ministers of Beaufort-Wes Dos, namely: "As a consequence of the *status confessionis* against apartheid, the honorable synod appoints an ad hoc commission to prepare a confession for this synod to consider." This motion was adopted unanimously, and it was ruled that the Moderature (the senior body in the synod) appoint this commission.

The members of this ad hoc commission were Prof. Gustav Bam (chair), Prof. Jaap Durand, Dr. Dirkie Smit, Rev. Isak Mentor, and Dr. Allan Boesak. After the meeting of that day, Durand and Smit met at the University of the Western Cape, close to the Belhar church, and discussed the structure of a possible confession around the themes of unity, reconciliation, and justice. Smit wrote a draft that very evening, and he and Durand discussed this draft early the next morning. It was then discussed by the whole commission. Boesak suggested minor changes to the introductory section, and after a few further editorial changes, the document was submitted to the synod. On Wednesday morning, October 6, 1982, the synod accepted the confession without any changes as a draft confession for discussion in congregations. It was formally accepted four years later at the DRMC synod of 1986. These dramatic events clearly point to the direct Barthian influence on the actual process that led to the writing and adoption of the Belhar Confession.

The first consideration when approaching the work of Karl Barth in its relation to Belhar is historical. The second consideration is theological, in the systematic sense of the word. Many people in the DRC family of churches (and elsewhere, I suppose) may broadly agree with the content of Belhar but do not see the document as an actual confession with the status accorded to, for example, the Three Formulae of Unity. For them, Belhar is an important statement against a political system, which reminds us of important themes, but its status is that of a contextual and time-bound proclamation, of secondary importance to the creeds and earlier Reformed confessions. This chapter is an argument for the actual confessional qualities of the Belhar document. There is a clear apologetic intent here that must be understood from the struggle to receive Belhar into the DRC family.

If one asks hypothetically, for example, whether Barth would sign the Belhar Confession, one obviously does not express a historical possibility. It is rather an investigation of the confessional status of Belhar in the light of important and highly influential work undertaken by Barth on the topic. The method I follow is quite simple. I present Barth's own criteria for a Reformed confession, rearrange them slightly, and then subject the Belhar Confession to those criteria. If Belhar passes the test on the most salient points, I assume that Barth would have been delighted to support it as the will of God for our time. This is the manner in which Barth himself evaluated older confessions and determined their status.[9] It is then hoped that others would be convinced that Belhar is indeed a confession to be taken up in the tradition of the Reformed churches.

The third consideration in the relation between Barth and Belhar is a hermeneutical one. In fact, this book could be construed as a reading of Belhar from different angles. Each angle — history, earlier creeds, reception, current significance — opens another view on Belhar. In this chapter, Belhar is interpreted from the criteria or marks of confessions. Issues such as its biblical foundation, its contextuality, and its embodiment in the life of the church are therefore discussed. In this manner, the cumulative insights gained from an interaction with Barth not only defend Belhar's confessional status but actually highlight its meaning as well.

Three primary texts from Barth may guide us here.[10] In historical order, they are "The desirability and possibility of a universal Reformed creed" (1925);[11] the section on the nature of confession as discussed in Holy Scripture and authority in the church in *Church dogmatics, I/2: The revelation of God;*[12] and the elaboration on witness and the *status*

---

9. Barth refers a few times to *Bedingungen* (conditions) that must be fulfilled in order to distinguish between confessions (*Revelation,* pp. 627, 647, 660). Some may indeed be "second-class and of doubtful status," like the Swiss Formula of Consent of 1675 (and others). We must emphasize that Barth's "conditions" are not meant to be a list of abstract postulates; according to him, he is merely describing a reality in the life of the church!

10. I will undertake a close reading of these three texts without the almost unbearable weight of Barthian scholarship from secondary sources. To keep the engagement with Barth "uncluttered," references to the many South African sources on the history of theological developments up to 1986 will also be limited. For a detailed and instructive discussion of Barth and the social context of these writings on confession, see Dirk J. Smit, "Social transformation and confessing the faith? Karl Barth's views on confession revisited," *Scriptura 72* (2000): 67-85.

11. Karl Barth, "The desirability and possibility of a universal Reformed creed," in *Theology and Church: Shorter writings, 1920-1928,* with an introduction by T. F. Torrance (London: SCM Press, 1962) (henceforth Barth, "Creed"), pp. 112-35. This is Barth's address in June 1925 to the World Council of the Alliance of Reformed Churches (WCARC) holding the Presbyterian System, in Cardiff, Wales, and repeated to the General Assembly of the Reformed Association of Germany, Duisburg-Meidenrich, in the same month and year. The question facing the alliance was whether the principle of a universal Reformed creed is desirable and whether the conditions exist that would make that possible. As will be intimated below, Barth argues persuasively against such ideas.

12. Barth, *Revelation,* pp. 620-60. This piece, which reflects the dramatic experiences of 1933-34 (the ascendance of Hitler and the adoption of the Barmen Confession), was written

confessionis in *Church dogmatics,* III/4: *The doctrine of creation.*[13]

These texts clearly relate and speak to one another. For the sake of simplicity, I use the 1925 text ("Creed") as my point of departure. There is an important historical reason for considering this text as a primary reference point. Barth was not naive about the situation in Germany after World War I, as he refers explicitly to a rising "fascist, racialist *nationalism.*"[14] His insights at that point, however, were not yet influenced by the dramatic events that led to the formulation of the Barmen Confession in 1934, in which he played a crucial role that so clearly affected his later work on *status confessionis* and confessions. In fact, he forcefully argued in his address before the World Council of the Alliance of Reformed Churches (WCARC) that the situation was not ready for a new creed and that a creed was neither desirable nor possible. In that situation, judged by Barth as not providing the historical and theological preliminaries for a confession, his criteria might be most useful. I am not suggesting that Barth later changed his mind, only that his ideas of 1925 were not expressed under the urgent conditions of a few years later, and not formulated after the actual act of confessing in 1934.

Let us cite the full definition with which Barth begins his address: "A Reformed Creed is the statement, spontaneously and publicly formulated by a Christian community within a geographically limited area, which, until further action, defines its character to outsiders; and which, until further action, gives guidance for its own doctrine and life; it is a formulation of the insight currently given to the whole Christian Church by the revelation of God in Jesus Christ, witnessed to by the Holy Scriptures alone."[15] Below are

---

in the summer of 1937 and published in German in 1948 as part of the *Kirchliche Dogmatik.* The English version appeared in 1956.

13. Karl Barth, *Church dogmatics,* III/4: *The doctrine of creation* (Edinburgh: T. & T. Clark, 1961; German original published 1951) (henceforth Barth, *Creation*), pp. 73-86. It is instructive to note that this section falls under Barth's discussion of special ethics. For him ethics flows from the doctrine of creation as the command of the Creator, to which humans — saved by grace — freely respond. This response constitutes "special ethics" and, broadly speaking, assumes two forms: a response to God, and a response to our fellow human beings. The response to God occurs in the keeping of the Sabbath, readiness to witness to God in confession (our focus passage here), and prayer. See further discussion on ethics on pp. 96-98 below.

14. Barth, "Creed," p. 133 (original emphasis).

15. In Barth's 1937 discussion, he writes a slightly different version: "A church confession is a formulation and proclamation of the insight which the Church has been given in certain directions into the revelation attested by Scripture, reached on the basis of common deliberation and decision" (Barth, *Revelation,* p. 620).

my divisions, representing a slight rearrangement of Barth's definition and not following his own subsections as numbered in the original text.

A confession witnesses to the revelation of God

Barth's typical christological concentration is evident in the definition and elsewhere in his theology. In his discussion on witnessing as a response to God, Barth reiterates: "Christian confession will be confession of truths, facts and principles only as and to the extent that it is first and decisively confession of Jesus Christ."[16] He makes clear that the earliest biblical confessions all had a christological focus (e.g., "Jesus is Lord"). Reading carefully, however, one can see a clear trinitarian intent in his exposition. A creed is derived from the revelation of *God* as occurred in *Jesus Christ* and must be "plainly given and revealed from heaven through the *Holy Spirit*."[17] Where will knowledge about this revelation be found? The answer is clear: in the witness of the Holy Scriptures.

Behind these apparently simple formulations lie important theological decisions. Reformed creeds derive their authority from their correspondence to Scripture, as Scripture is both the basis of a creed's certainty and its judge.[18] This stands in opposition to Catholic notions, according to which two other authorities — church tradition and doctrinal papal teaching — are also authoritative sources of God's revelation.[19] Furthermore, the temptation yielded to by modern Protestantism (as interpreted by Barth at the end of the nineteenth century) is to grant to history, or "significant historical events,"[20] a character of revelation not fundamentally, but only qualitatively, different from the Bible.

To say that a creed should make a statement about God immediately calls forth the question of source and authority. The source is God as revealed in Christ and witnessed to in the Scriptures, through the work of the Spirit, and not cherished human opinions, even when they are called "expressions of faith."[21] In a very strong pneumatological formulation,

16. Barth, *Creation*, p. 84.
17. Barth, "Creed," p. 113, with a reference to Luther.
18. Barth, *Revelation*, pp. 625, 638.
19. Barth speaks of "Roman Catholic immanentism in which Church and revelation are equated" (Barth, *Revelation*, p. 653).
20. Barth, "Creed," p. 113.
21. Barth, "Creed," p. 113.

Barth insists that one confesses "precisely what the Spirit of Jesus Christ, the Spirit of Scripture, the Spirit of the community, allows and commands."[22] Creedal authority is therefore a *derived* authority, based on clear consonance with Scripture (the *quia* view), the only canonical witness to God's revelation.

Let us take up these points and make three remarks about Belhar with regard to its view of God, its source of revelation, and its consonance with Scripture.

God

Belhar is fundamentally an ecclesiological confession, born out of a long preceding church struggle. In a direct allusion to the Heidelberg Catechism, it understands the church as being gathered, protected, and cared for by the triune God, Father, Son, and Holy Spirit (art. 1). The three middle articles on unity, reconciliation, and justice are all deeply embedded in trinitarian convictions.

Belhar confesses the unity of the church as it consists of the people of *God* reconciled in *Christ*, and it maintains that, through the work of the *Spirit*, unity is a binding force. We have one God and Father, we are filled with one Spirit, and we are obedient to one Lord.

The message of reconciliation has been entrusted to the church by *God* in and through *Jesus Christ* and is based on the conquering of sin and death by the lifegiving *Spirit*, who enables a new obedience.

Article 4, on justice, commences with a statement about *God's* revelation in justice and true peace. It then quotes extensively from the Lukan announcement of *Jesus'* coming that he, because he is filled with the *Spirit*, will bring freedom and healing to the captives and the sick.

The confession ends with a reference to the triune God in doxological language, creating a circular construction, where the God who gathers the church (art. 1) is now praised and glorified (art. 5). The whole text is therefore a statement about God, as revealed in the Father, Son, and Holy Spirit.[23]

---

22. Barth, *Creation*, p. 86.

23. One is acutely aware of the gender bias of these traditional formulations. Belhar must be read in its own historical context and from the perspective of its primary concern with race, and not so much gender. For an attempt to read both Nicea and Belhar from the insights of feminist critique, see Piet J. Naudé, "Can our creeds speak a gendered truth? A femi-

Revelation

Concerning the source of revelation, Belhar was clearly not born out of a Catholic-Reformed dispute as to whether Scripture is the only true source of knowledge about God. A major issue, however, was related to Barth's concern about the relationship between revelation and history. In the light of the German Christian movement, Barth is particularly sensitive about history as a supplementary form of revelation. A confession, he writes, "does not confess God in history or God in nature, as individuals, and it may be many individuals, in the Church think they see him. It confesses Jesus Christ, and Jesus Christ as attested by the prophets and apostles."[24] Hence, Belhar spoke against a theological interpretation of specific historical events since the Dutch settlement in 1652 and the couching of these events in the language of revelation. This kind of interpretation made possible a pious reconstruction of events as "God's hand in our history,"[25] based on a neo-Calvinist understanding of predestination and general grace. What made this view so difficult to refute was the fact that it was supported by a specific hermeneutic, a specific reading of Scripture that declared historical events as the will of God and as evidence of his gracious divine providence. In this manner, a strong Christian edifice was constructed in which a system of racial separation and pluriformity in church and society could be both called for, and from which it could be defended as God's revealed will.[26]

In simple language, and related to one of the strong thrusts in Barth's own theology, Belhar's deep theological struggle was against a specific form of natural theology presenting itself as salvation history; against a Christian faith that turned into idolatrous religion.

---

nist reading of the Nicene Creed and the Belhar Confession," *Scriptura* 86 (2004): 201-9. See also the discussion below in chapter 8, and the later inclusive versions of the Belhar text.

24. Barth, *Revelation*, p. 621. See the opening paragraph of Barmen in this regard.

25. There are many well-known sources on the history and structure of "apartheid theology." One of the most recent books is the detailed analysis of the theologies of F. J. M. Potgieter and Ben J. Marais in Hans Engdahl, *Theology in conflict: Readings in Afrikaner Theology* (Frankfurt: Peter Lang, 2006).

26. See Engdahl, *Theology in conflict*, pp. 136-37.

Scripture

A crucial question is whether Belhar is a statement that corresponds to the witness of the Holy Scriptures. Barth makes clear that "it is definitely not the case that confession must always be made in biblical words or in the language of Zion. . . . It often may and must choose wholly secular language. . . . If only it proceeds from hearing the Word of God. . . ."[27] In the Reformed tradition there is a healthy tension between the conviction that confessions are commentaries on Scripture and that they always stand under and not next to Scripture, but that they indeed correspond to Scripture *(quia)* and hence are authoritative and true.[28] There is a specific hierarchy in Barth's thinking here. In line with the Protestant tradition, Scripture stands uniquely as the only canonical witness. Then follow the confessions as "a first commentary," occupying "first place among all the witnesses," being "the leader of the chorus" among the many voices (e.g., exegesis, preaching) that testify to God's revelation in Scripture. Confessions therefore require from us "a privileged hearing."[29]

There are two limitations with regard to the relationship between confession and Scripture. First, a confession inevitably reflects the status of biblical scholarship at the time of its adoption (e.g., disputed text references in the Belgic Confession). Second, because of its tendentious character, not all the themes of Scripture are reflected, but only those relevant to the subject matter of the confession. Confessions are highly selective and limited,[30] and they must be judged on whether their intent and message are in consonance with Scripture, not whether the whole of Scripture is represented.

Belhar does not quote a text for each statement. Its use of Scripture is rich in its thematic references to unity, reconciliation, and justice, drawing on relevant pericopes and even whole chapters.[31] New Testament passages

27. Barth, *Creation,* p. 86.

28. Barth, *Revelation,* pp. 620, 625.

29. Barth, *Revelation,* pp. 649-50. In my view, this point is rarely acknowledged by biblical scholars.

30. See the discussion below of the temporal, spatial, and material limitations of a confession.

31. Apart from the elaborate and detailed defense of the much-debated article 4 of Belhar by Dirk J. Smit, "In a special way the God of the destitute, the poor, and the wronged," in *A moment of truth: The confession of the Dutch Reformed Mission Church, 1982,* ed. G. D. Cloete and Dirk J. Smit, pp. 53-65 (Grand Rapids: Eerdmans, 1984), one finds some exegetical

(forty-four in total) abound in articles 2, 3 and 4, and it is noteworthy that the four Old Testament references in the confession are all cited in article 4, on justice (with strong links to the Gospel of Luke and the Letter of James). Even critics of Belhar who did not accept it as a confession concede that it is a biblical statement.[32]

Thus far the only noteworthy criticism has been against the formulation of article 4: "that in a world full of injustice and enmity, he [God] is in a special way the God of the destitute, the poor, and the wronged." Even before the official adoption of Belhar, this formulation was objected to. The exegetical and theological explanation by Dirk J. Smit in his 1984 essay[33] remains an adequate response to those who have attempted to tarnish the confession by implying that it is aligned with the Marxist notion of class struggle and that it promotes the tenets of liberation theology that subscribe to a partisan view of God not found in Scriptures.[34]

The overwhelming exegetical and ecumenical consensus supports the Belhar view on this point.[35] The Reformed tradition has taught us an important hermeneutical lesson in the judging of confessions. They must not later be judged on what is now construed as ambiguous, but on the directions in which they lead us. Barth reinforces this point in his discussion of the critical reception of confessions: "We can be loyal to its direction and still think that in detail and even as a whole, as our confession, we would rather have it put otherwise."[36] The important point is that we keep moving in the direction the confession indicates.

---

work on Belhar's use of Scripture in A. C. J. van Niekerk, "Moet ons die belydenis van Belhar (1986) as 'n nuwe belydenisskrif aanvaar?" *Skrif en Kerk* 12, no. 2 (1996): 443-55 (especially his point 4). See also Andries Daniels, "Bybelgebruik in die Belharbelydenis se artikel oor 'eenheid,'" *Scriptura* 77 (2001): 193-209 (on Belhar art. 2); and E. E. Meyer, "Interpreting Luke with the confession of Belhar," *Scriptura* 72 (2000): 113-20 (on Belhar and Luke).

32. Up to now, this has been the view, for example, of the Dutch Reformed Church, the "mother" church in the DRC family.

33. Smit, "God of the destitute," pp. 53-65.

34. The South African context of the 1980s was not very conducive to the reception of a document linked to either liberation theology or Communist ideas. See the refutation in Afrikaans of charges about liberation theology by Naudé in Johan Botha and Piet J. Naudé, *Op pad met Belhar. Goeie nuus vir gister, vandag en more* (Pretoria: Van Schaik, 1998), pp. 62-64.

35. One of the best expositions and analyses of the option for the poor from historical, exegetical, ecumenical, and philosophical perspectives is Heinrich Bedford-Strohm, *Vorrang für die Armen. Auf dem weg zu einer theologischen Theorie der Gerechtigkeit* (Gütersloh: Gütersloher Verlaghaus, 1993).

36. Barth, *Revelation*, p. 650.

It is instructive to hear Barth in relation to article 4 and read his words in the historical context of the "colored" DRMC around 1982: "Also today if the Confession be genuine, it must come from the boundaries. It must be the Creed of those who are forsaken by God and who, as the forsaken, are visited by God; of those who are lost and who, as the lost, are rescued."[37] In words very close to the actual text of article 4, he states that the great reward of a confession "consists in our being allowed[38] to stand on the right side, on God's side. . . . If in confession a man stands on God's side, this has the sober and liberating implication . . . that God stands on his side."[39]

A confession gives insight into God's revelation for the moment

One could speak here of the temporal limitation of a confession. A confession is a prophetic word whose truthfulness often lies in fusing the horizons of Scripture and our judging of history as a kairos moment.

Apart from securing the unique and incomparable position of Scripture, Barth's polemic at this point is against the Lutheran claim in the Formula of Concord (1577) that the Augsburg Confession is the authority for the correct interpretation of Scripture *ad omnem posteritatem* (for all posterity).[40] This says too much, he argues, and it denies the provisional, fragmentary, and changeable character of a confession, which is subject to both the limitations of its humanity and the proviso stemming from our eschatological expectations.[41]

For Barth, the temporal limitation relates to the original meaning of *dogma,* which is insight given by God for the time but always open for new receptions and better understandings in the recurring renewal of our faith

---

37. Barth, "Creed," p. 129.

38. Note the use of the passive here!

39. Barth, *Creation,* pp. 85-86. This quotation is derived from the context of Barth's discussion that a confession does not seek results and that those who bear witness to it should be free from fear and anxiety. They stand on God's side and step into God's freedom.

40. Barth, "Creed," p. 115. For Barth, the Lutheran position is equal to lifting the confession to the level of a second source of revelation, which is reminiscent of the Catholic position (*Revelation,* p. 658).

41. One must understand this from the doxological character of confessions. The infallible, final, and unalterable praise to God will happen only at the end of time. Everything before that is provisional (see Barth, *Revelation,* p. 657).

statements in the light of Scripture. These statements are human and therefore fallible declarations; they may be superseded later, but the confessors are confident that what is spoken is the truth, *here and now*.

For Barth, this *hic et nunc* character of confessions also stems from the simple insight that a *status confessionis* is not a permanent position but is related to a special occurrence of being confronted or questioned about the truth of the gospel. "If a man tries to be a permanent martyr, he can never be one at all, because he obviously does not see that martyrdom or witness is an act which can be realised only on the basis of a special summons in a special situation."[42] He laments the reality that the church usually realizes this summons too late. The confession is often a word spoken when "the great wasting of the Church has already taken place."[43] In a beautiful metaphor on this page Barth says that a confession is an attempt to cover the well when some children have already drowned. "Better late than never," he tellingly adds.

There is no doubt that Belhar was both historically and theologically the result of a *status confessionis*.[44] This means "that Christians, or a church, feel that a 'moment of truth' has arrived, that a situation has developed in which the gospel itself is at stake."[45] There are factors that in theological terms "create the circumstances in which a declaration of a confession is rendered understandable and justifiable — if not inevitable."[46]

The first words of the Accompanying Letter make the situational character of the confession clear: "We are deeply conscious that *moments of such seriousness* can arise in the life of the church that it may feel the need to confess its faith anew *in the light of a specific situation*. . . . In our judgment, *the present church and political situation* . . . calls for such a decision" (my emphases).

The decision to confess "here and now" is therefore a complex hermeneutical act. It not only involves the reading of Scripture but implies a specific judgment on the historical realities of the time. Those who oppose a confession often do not seek to criticize its biblical base but —

42. Barth, *Creation*, p. 79.

43. Barth, *Revelation*, p. 633.

44. For an in-depth analysis of this concept and its history, see Dirk J. Smit, "What does *status confessionis* mean?" in *A moment of truth*, ed. G. D. Cloete and Dirk J. Smit (Grand Rapids: Eerdmans, 1984), pp. 7-32.

45. Cloete and Smit, *A moment of truth*, p. ix.

46. Jaap F. Durand, "A confession — was it really necessary?" in Cloete and Smit, *A moment of truth*, pp. 33-41 (35).

standing on the other side of history — are unable to see that the situation is so serious that it requires the act of confession. A confession is mostly accepted in spite of its history, writes Barth. And of those who oppose a confession on these grounds, he says: "Men in the Church and the world, if they want to avoid the decision to which a confession summons them, may pretend that they do not see the danger of it. But in reality the fact that they do this shows that they have seen it very well."[47]

Despite this emphasis on the provisional status of confessions, history teaches us that "corrections" to the text of a confession rarely, if ever, occur afterward. If there is serious conflict, the way to deal with "better formulations" (as was done with art. 36 of the Belgic Confession) is for a church to declare a consensus (re-)interpretation of the original text. Although not canonical, the historical integrity of the text should be honored. Barth's distinction between detailed content and broad direction is helpful here. I therefore do not foresee "improvements" to Belhar in a greater united Reformed church, but specific interpretations are a probability, and might even be required.[48]

A confession is a spontaneous statement

A confession, unlike a catechesis or a theological declaration, cannot really be planned in advance. It is neither the work of established synodical commissions nor the lyric expression of religious emotions over a bad situation.[49] Barth makes it abundantly clear that confessions are actions in obedience to the will of God. It is an "unpremeditated witness."[50] There is an urgency and necessity behind confessing. "Confession is bound to neither calendar nor clock. When its hour comes, it may and must occur."[51] Therefore "'I believe' is first to be said after all other possibilities are exhausted. When struck on the mouth, I can say nothing except 'credo.'" Barth con-

47. Barth, *Revelation*, p. 643.

48. The DRC indicated in 1990 that article 4 might be formulated differently without altering the intention (i.e., direction!) of the confession. Now, after more than twenty years, it does not seem feasible to propose such textual improvements. A "common explication" might be the way to reach consensus on this or other points.

49. Barth, "Creed," p. 119.

50. Barth, *Creation*, p. 80.

51. Barth, *Creation*, p. 85. There is also the strong view that "we cannot confess because we would like to confess in the belief that confession is a good thing. We can confess only if we must confess" (Barth, *Revelation*, p. 624).

tinues with typical sharpness: "A Creed of any other kind is a bit of lazy magic and comes from the Devil — even though verbally it be the Apostles' Creed."[52]

For Barth, the spontaneity of a confession is a fundamental theological issue and should not be seen as a psychological description, either of the act of confessing or of the people involved in this act (e.g., "the situation was so electrifying, and they were so enthusiastic, outgoing, and spontaneous").

First, spontaneity relates to the source and true origin of confession, namely, that it is prompted by the Holy Spirit and is insight that is given and not sought. It is like the disciples who are told not to worry over how and what they must say — that it would be given to them at that hour (Matt. 10:19).[53] Second, spontaneity reflects the nature of a confession as free action,[54] the free word of a free man, responding to the free grace of God, who commands him as Creator.[55] Third, spontaneity determines the genre of confession as doxology. "What does it mean to praise God?" asks Barth. "It means to pay him honour by confessing him." This praise "is in some measure the climax of all human action Godwards."[56] Finally, that a confession is "spontaneously" formulated refers to the realities of the situation as well. It is not spontaneous in the sense of utter novelty and total unexpectedness. It is spontaneous in the sense that the church has fought "a hard battle against theological lies and half-truths."[57] Now, under the impression of the kairos, the church says: "We believe." Barth says this plainly: "A creed without a preceding, serious theological history can never be other than horribly dull, unoriginal, second-hand."[58]

The battle against a false doctrine, as it emerged in apartheid theology, was a long and hard one. It has been shown in chapter 2 how various ecumenical bodies between 1948 and 1982 resisted the false gospel of non-

52. Barth, "Creed," pp. 128-29.

53. Barth, *Creation,* pp. 80, 86.

54. One of the toughest questions in the reception of the Belhar Confession is whether its content and confessional status can and must be "forced" on the new reunifying churches in the DRC family. Quite a number of people who would endorse the content of the confession do not see it as more than an important statement, not at the same level as earlier Reformed confessions. If one follows Barth's line of thinking here and elsewhere, Belhar can only challenge, but its content we "cannot and will not force on anyone" (*Revelation,* p. 625).

55. Barth, *Creation,* pp. 77, 78, 85.

56. Barth, *Creation,* p. 74.

57. Barth, "Creed," p. 129.

58. Barth, "Creed," p. 130.

reconciliation.[59] Belhar stands on the shoulders of many brave and prophetic individuals, known and unknown, and stands in the tradition of resistance exemplified by the Barmen Declaration, the Catholic Bishops' conferences, the WCC and SACC, the Christian Institute, ABRECSA, and the WARC, to name but a few.

In the actual situation of the 1982 DRMC synod, the spontaneity of the confessing act testified both to its continuity, with a long tradition, and to a certain discontinuity. Up to that point there were declarations, theological messages, and open letters, but never a confession. Belhar both honored the theological prehistory and radically sharpened the resistance by adding a "yes" to the "no" of the preceding years (see discussion below under the section "A confession expresses an important aspect of the will of God").

A confession is formulated by a concrete Christian community within a geographically limited area

Barth insists that the "subject" of the confessing act must be a concrete Christian community, a local church or a synod, as the commissioned voice of the Reformed community. "The subject of a Church confession is the Church," because "Church confession is a Church event."[60] Barth's insistence on the church here is to avoid confessions that are merely the opinion of individuals or groups within the church; even if the confession starts with a few individuals, they should speak in the name of the whole church and to the whole church.[61] As noted earlier, even where certain specific individuals drafted the confession, the "author" should always be presented as the congregation.[62] Here we stand at the spatial limits of a confession.

In the context of the WARC, Barth's view must have poured cold water on those who hoped for some endorsement for the process of formulating a universal Reformed creed. Just as Barth judged the situation in 1925 as

---

59. Piet J. Naudé, "The theological coherence between the Belhar Confession and some antecedent church witnesses in the period 1948-1982," *Verbum et Ecclesia* 42, no. 1 (2003): 156-79.

60. Barth, *Revelation*, pp. 637, 624.

61. Barth, *Revelation*, p. 623.

62. See the interesting examples Barth gives of this kind of "shifted" authorship (*Revelation*, pp. 637-38).

not requiring the act of confessing,[63] he also judged the meeting of the alliance itself as too ethereal to constitute a *concrete* Christian community. What is at stake is the interaction between the Reformed notion of creed and its concept of church. There is obviously a "universal" church in the historical and geographic sense, but that church is fully visible and realized only in the concrete *coetus particularis* (particular company), gathered into one external body and united through Word, sacrament, and discipline.

"I can *believe*," writes Barth, "with the most distant, with the 'ecumenical company' *(coetus oecumenicus);* I can *confess* my faith . . . only with my neighbors, that is with those known to me as fellow believers."[64] The geography must be limited to the faith community where we really "weep and rejoice together . . . in the muck and misery of this definite earthly place."[65] With an interesting play of words, Barth writes that a world creed (the question before the alliance meeting) will be a worldly creed, "one of those mixtures of resolutions . . . by which in the *world* men summon one another to great matters, which are proclaimed and listened to, but which are never, now or hereafter, *believed* by anybody."[66]

This is perhaps a good explanation why the genre of Belhar is different from its predecessors. The Cottesloe Declaration (1961), the *Message* (1968), the statements of the LWF (1977) and WARC (1982), and the Kairos Document (1985) were all very important, *but they lacked the concreteness of the* coetus particularis *to confess.*[67] But gathered in the suburb of Belhar in 1982 was a church community representing the suffering, the grieving, and the misery of forced removals, and the dehumanization experienced in every bus, train, school, beach, or store in South Africa over the previous thirty years. Here is a concrete faith community, crying from the heart: "We believe! And we reject!"

63. Barth, "Creed," p. 131. Barth notes the possibility of a "premature confession" but also warns that this must not be an excuse for not confessing at all! (*Creation*, p. 79).

64. Barth, "Creed," p. 125.

65. Barth, "Creed," pp. 125-26.

66. Barth, "Creed," p. 126, original emphases.

67. In my view, this should make ecumenical bodies cautious about writing and adopting actual confessions (like the Accra Confession, which the WARC issued in 2004 in its General Council meetings in Accra, Ghana). How is such a confession embodied and actually believed afterward?

A confession expresses an important aspect of the will of God

A confession is not a general treatise on God. It does not merely want to repeat in broad terms what we believe. The prior requirements of a spontaneous declaration, emanating from a concrete faith community at a specific moment, find their dogmatic and ethical specificity here. If the church confesses, it must believe it has something true and important and cardinal to say about the counsels of God, and that it has something definite to offer in God's name.[68] There must be a concrete situation related to both doctrine and life that forces the church into the act of confession. The confession will therefore carry the scars from the preceding battle against half-truths and theological lies.[69] It will therefore always be a protest against "unbelief, superstition and heresy," speaking the full truth against "the mass of human error which consists supremely in half and quarter and eighth truths."[70]

I have briefly referred above to the unity between doctrine and ethics in the very structure of Barth's work. Here he speaks unequivocally: A confession must refute theological lies; it must say "no" to half-truths. But it must also offer something positive. It must say "yes," it must speak "Thus says the Lord"; it must include "not only what is essential for doctrine but also what is essential for living . . . in the immediate situation."[71]

This is based on Barth's interpretation of the reason why the Reformed tradition accepted dogma. This acceptance had nothing to do with abstract gnosis. It was "wholly ethical," requiring obedience in the whole of life and society.[72] As long as a confession commits us only to a theoretical position, it is not a confession. One of the strategies to neutralize the pressure of a confession is, according to Barth, the desire that "the confession should be a mere theory," no longer requiring us to make difficult decisions in practice, no longer venturing in the direction that the confession points.[73] It becomes a confession only when the word it speaks implies an action.[74] Barth is of the opinion that Reformed creeds — exactly because

---

68. Barth, "Creed," p. 129. For Barth to write a confession so that "as many as possible can rally under the banner of a very general Yes" can happen only at the price of the "yes."

69. Barth, "Creed," p. 130.

70. Barth, *Creation*, p. 80.

71. Barth, "Creed," p. 132.

72. Barth, "Creed," p. 132.

73. Barth, *Revelation*, p. 645.

74. Barth, *Creation*, p. 84.

they were ethical creeds — sent believers into society, where they positively influenced the social reconstruction of Europe. Let us look briefly at the interplay between doctrine and ethics in the Belhar process and content.

The decisive turning point that undermined the moral legitimacy of the apartheid system was when it was no longer judged as merely an ethical aberration, a practical mistake made by people with good, pious intentions; a system not flawed in principle but only inefficiently applied, with negative consequences for the majority of people in South Africa. The turning point came with the insight that what we have here is a false gospel, half-truths combined into a theological lie, a new doctrine no longer within the ambit of Christian orthodoxy — a heresy![75]

The Accompanying Letter picks up this point: "We make this confession because we are convinced that all sorts of theological arguments have contributed to so disproportionate an emphasis on some aspects of the truth that it has in effect become a lie" (par. 1). The confession is not aimed at specific people or churches: "We proclaim it against a false doctrine, against an ideological distortion that threatens the gospel itself" (par. 3).

This is why Belhar is structured to say "yes" in its five statements, but also to say "no" in the rejection clauses of the three middle articles on unity, reconciliation, and justice.[76] This is discussed in chapter 1. These rejections are clearly theological in the narrow sense of the word: "Therefore, we reject any *doctrine*. . . ."

This doctrinal focus is the explanation why Belhar — like the earlier Barmen Declaration — is so silent on the specifics of the situation. Nowhere is apartheid or the National Party or the white Reformed churches mentioned. The confession was not meant to expose persons, churches, or political parties — it intended to expose false doctrine, wherever confessed and whoever confesses it. Barth insists in his later writing that a confession is always a refutation of a counterdoctrine, a new dogma that has crept into the church and that is now threatening its unity.[77] Far from aiming at or causing schism (an old criticism against confessions), confession of the true doctrine is exactly aimed at *restoring the unity of faith already broken*

---

75. See the essays in de Gruchy and Villa-Vicencio, *Apartheid is a heresy*, published a year after the draft formulation of the Belhar Confession.

76. Barth makes it quite clear that the content of a confession, although it may involve protest, should be far more positive than negative. "For decisively, originally and finally God Himself, whose partisan the confessor may be, says Yes, and only incidentally, relatively and for the sake of the Yes does He say No" (*Creation*, p. 81; see also Barth, *Revelation*, p. 631).

77. Barth, *Revelation*, pp. 628-30.

by the half-truths! (No wonder Belhar witnesses so strongly to unity in its second thesis, bringing us back to the "old" doctrines.)

This in no way diminishes the ethical thrust of the confession. Belhar arose from inhumane sociopolitical realities and an increasingly militarized security state. The ethical situation was what brought the kairos, and not a theoretical, doctrinal issue per se. But once interpreted doctrinally (as argued above), a new urgency arose that prompted the church to draw from its tradition the available tools to address such a situation. This resulted in, for example, the declaration of a *status confessionis,* the prayers for the fall of the government, the call for sanctions, actual confessing, peaceful demonstrations, mass meetings at funerals, and many other displays of opposition to the unethical situation.

Ethics was not only the real-life conditions from which Belhar grew, it was also the confession's deepest intention. A confession without a corresponding practical attitude is already a confutation of the confession.[78] Because of the unity between doctrine and life, because of its character as ethical creed, the confession requires action and implies a radical conversion in church and society.

The Accompanying Letter speaks clearly about this in its third and fourth paragraphs, stating that there are attitudes and conduct that work against the gospel and that require continuous, collective soul-searching. In a prefiguring of the Truth and Reconciliation Commission, which came more than a decade later, the letter says that the confession "demands the pain of repentance, remorse, and confession; the pain of individual and collective renewal and a changed way of life." The prayer is for a new beginning as we walk together on "the road of reconciliation and justice" (par. 4).

The text of the confession itself is about a realized faith: concrete, visible church unity (art. 2); a life of obedience based on reconciliation in Christ (art. 3); and the actual realization of justice as we stand by people in any form of suffering and need (art. 4). Ethics culminates in article 5.1: "the Church is called to confess *and to do* all these things" (my emphasis), even if punishment and suffering would be a consequence.

In summary, Belhar does not bring a new gospel, but it does have "something definite to offer in God's name."[79] It was the bold expression of God's will in a specific situation at a specific time. It exposed an ideo-

---

78. Barth, *Revelation,* p. 645.
79. Barth, "Creed," p. 129.

logical gospel, and it had definite guidelines for what was essential for life and society in the immediate situation. Belhar spoke of "an insight currently given" — until further action.

A confession addresses both outsiders and insiders

Barth makes clear that the creed defines the character of the Christian community to outsiders and gives guidance for the community's own doctrine and life. The implied "method" here is that a confession exerts pressure on the rest of the church and, through the church, on the world.[80] Let us start with these "outsiders."

Barth suggests that the creed "addresses itself to the widest possible public."[81] For him, this is the reason why open letters often accompany creeds and, as at the outset of the Reformation, require major theological work. A creed is not a sectarian, in-house document but a public witness, speaking to whoever is in reach and will listen. The seeking of an "outside" public is no cheap media event to draw attention to the confessing church. The requirement of "publicity" stems from both the basis and the purpose of the confession. Its basis is divine revelation, to which the church is called to witness in the world. Its purpose is to reply to a counterdoctrine that already has a public status.[82] The idea of a private confession makes no theological or practical sense.

In the context of concrete history, the public audience is probably restricted to those within the country or to the churches (both for and against) for which the creed implicitly or explicitly speaks. The geographic limitations mentioned earlier apply here too. But — and this is important — the truth of the creed, though spoken under specific circumstances, is no mere contextual truth limited by time and space. Even if it deals with an aspect of the gospel most urgent in that situation, it is "the insight currently given *to the whole Christian Church*[83] by the revelation of God in Jesus Christ."[84]

---

80. Barth, *Revelation,* p. 642.

81. Barth, "Creed," p. 117.

82. Barth, *Revelation,* p. 639.

83. The whole church refers to "the fathers behind us" and "the brothers beside us" (I keep the gender bias for historical reasons; see Barth, *Revelation,* p. 647). One might add: the whole church includes the future sisters coming after us!

84. Barth, "Creed," p. 112 (my emphasis).

In fact, the local church speaks both *from* the universal church and *to* the universal church, and as such the confession is proceeding from one part and directed to other parts of the church.[85] Therein lies the possibility of current and future receptions beyond the space and time of a creed's origin. Owing to its insight into God's revelation, "it is a document of obedience to the Holy Spirit of the Word of God." Hence, the creed has an enduring power "to continue speaking even at a great distance from its own geographical and temporal and historical place in the Church."[86]

In a sense, the act of confession is a missionary activity of the church.[87] It speaks into a situation where people are "surrounded by a Christianity which [has] fallen into error."[88] This is how the church's task toward outsiders is to be explained. By redefining and reclaiming the true character of the Christian community for outsiders, they are stirred into reflection and hopefully recognize that they are surrounded, or even live by, an error-ridden form of the Christian faith.

This apparently innocuous task of "defining its character" or "helping to make visible the contours of the Christian community"[89] is exactly what was at stake for the DRMC by the end of the 1970s. As explained in chapter 1, this church came from the missionary work of the DRC. At first "colored" or "slave" members were accepted into the church. Because of cultural concerns and "the weakness of some,"[90] it was decided in 1857 by the Cape Synod that, for practical purposes, these members would be accommodated in "mission houses" with their own services and sacraments. By 1881 a separate church that later became the DRMC was established on exactly the same confessional basis and speaking exactly the same language as the "mother" church — the DRC.[91]

85. Barth, *Revelation*, pp. 622-23.

86. Barth, *Revelation*, p. 653.

87. See the interesting reading of Belhar as a missionary document by Jan Mathys de Beer in his recent doctoral thesis, "Die missionêre waarde van die Belhar Belydenis vir die N. G. Kerk. Instrument tot inheemsvording" (University of Pretoria, 2008). His core argument is that Belhar may assist the DRC to become a truly indigenous church if the confession is read in the context of recent missiological theories.

88. Barth, "Creed," p. 118.

89. Barth, *Creation*, p. 84.

90. This is a euphemistic reference to the concern of white congregants who preferred to have separate church services. At that stage, the principle of one church and one communion was still maintained. But over the next thirty years the practical situation overran the theological views.

91. For an account of this event, see the sober church-historical essay by C. J. Botha,

With the rise of apartheid as a theology and as a political system, mother and daughter churches stood and lived on opposite sides of the racial divide. The core theological questions were no doubt ecclesiological: What is the church? How does re-creation relate to creation? What should count as the requirements for membership of the church? Is church unity only invisible, spiritual, and eschatological? The answers to these and other questions were given from two theological paradigms: a neo-Calvinist, pietistic Afrikaner theology that claimed to be Reformed and Christian,[92] and the culmination of truths as expressed in the Belhar Confession, supported by the ecumenical church and claiming to be Reformed and Christian as well.[93]

Belhar was about the redefinition of the character of the church. It was a powerful statement to outsiders[94] (church and world) against (1) using the natural diversity of people as a basis for sinful separation, (2) having spiritual unity with little practical effect, (3) the despair of reconciliation in a country that calls itself Christian, and (4) the use of social factors as a

---

"Belhar — a century-old protest," in Cloete and Smit, *A moment of truth*, pp. 66-80. The birth of the Mission Church was in no way a glorious occasion. It started off with a boycott, as only four of the twelve congregations were represented at the beginning, on October 5, 1881, in Wellington. Later, this very church underwent a schism when the Rev. I. D. Morkel formed the Calvin Protestant Church in 1950, as he believed that the DRMC was actually buying into the apartheid model. (Should this church be part of the reunification process currently under way?)

92. The recent publication of Hans Engdahl's dissertation, *Theology in conflict*, complements the classic analyses of the development of apartheid as a theology by John W. de Gruchy, with Steve de Gruchy, *The church struggle in South Africa* (London: SCM Press, 2004), and the essays edited by Johann Kinghorn, *Die N. G. Kerk en apartheid* (Johannesburg: Macmillan, 1986). Engdahl presents a careful reading of original Afrikaans sources in reconstructing how an Afrikaner theology developed from both neo-Calvinist and practical perspectives. On F. J. M. Potgieter, see pp. 65-142; on Ben Marais, see pp. 143-236.

93. Barth knows this kind of Christian-versus-Christian situation after his Barmen experience. In an illuminating comment he states: "The worst attempts to silence a confession consist in making it impossible on its own ground, the intellectual and spiritual" (*Revelation*, p. 644). In the end, confessing is a very complex hermeneutical struggle involving both the interpretation of Scripture and the interpretation of the situation. It may take years (if then) before one group sees the falsity of its own views.

94. A confession champions the Christian cause especially before those to whom it is alien, says Barth. Peter's confession ("You are the Christ") after the question Jesus asked was, strictly speaking, not an act of confession. Had he witnessed in the courtyard of the high priest before the cock crowed, it would have been confession. After Pentecost, when Peter speaks boldly in the face of opposition from the high priests, he truly confesses (Acts 4:8; 5:29; see Barth, *Creation*, p. 85).

consideration in church membership. The message to other churches and the political order of the day could not be clearer: You are surrounded by and are part of a Christianity that has fallen into error, where heresy and superstition are presented as the truth. The "inside" audience of the confession is obviously the confessing church itself. It is possible to identify four implications for that community.

The foremost implication is that you confess against yourself first. Barth makes it clear that we must be careful not to deceive ourselves. The protest of the confessor is against others *and himself*.[95] In words echoing Barth's view, the Accompanying Letter exudes this awareness: "Along with many, we confess our guilt" (par. 1); "we speak pleadingly rather than accusingly" and "we know that the attitudes and conduct that work against the gospel are present in all of us. . . . It is certainly not intended as an act of self-justification and intolerance, for that would disqualify us in the very act of preaching to others" (par. 3). A confession is a service of love, writes Barth, and an invitation to return to the unity of faith, which is now expressed anew and more accurately.[96] The judgment of the "no" does not come from the confessors but from God, who judges through the truth of Scripture.

As the act of confession is so rare and arises from a theological necessity and compulsion, its second implication is a fairly substantial redefinition of self-understanding and identity. Leaders and members of the DRMC (and later the URCSA) frequently say: "We are Belhar; if you receive us in a reunification process, you receive Belhar." It would not be an overestimation to say that, after a century of protest, humiliation, and self-doubt, Belhar provided the DRMC with a new sense of theological worth, which they were denied by a missionary dispensation based on domination and control.

The third implication is — at least for Reformed churches — a rewriting of church orders to ensure the status and embodiment of the confession in catechesis, liturgy, and interchurch dialogue.[97] This is the guidance of doctrine and has in practice led the DRMC to the acceptance of Belhar as a fourth confession, beyond the traditional Three Formulae inherited from Europe.

95. Barth, *Creation*, p. 82.
96. Barth, *Revelation*, pp. 630-31.
97. Barth refers to the impact of the confession — sometimes not even noticed — on every aspect of the church's life: preaching, worship, instruction, and congregational life (*Revelation*, pp. 629, 645, 651).

The fourth implication is for the life of the church in its witness and service to the world. The witness to and action for unity, reconciliation, and specifically justice are strengthened by Belhar because it gives guidance and helps set the framework for interchurch and government cooperation in the field of social provision and diaconal services. If Belhar is not embodied and lived in the realities of South Africa today, it might have official status, but we are committing "pure treachery" against it. "That there is no venture for the confession means that there is a venture — on the part of the confessors — against the confession."[98]

Conclusion

This chapter has aimed to demonstrate that in many ways Belhar conforms remarkably well with the reasonably strict criteria for a Reformed creed. It clearly adheres to the criteria outlined by Barth under the specific circumstances of his 1925 address to the WCARC in Cardiff. These were further deepened and confirmed by the Barmen events and Barth's subsequent writings on this topic.

It was said at the beginning that a link between Barth and Belhar serves both a hermeneutical and an apologetic purpose. If the reader has grown in his or her understanding of the confession and has been convinced of the formal creedal status and the theological truth of the confession, much would have been achieved. The real test, however, is accepting not merely the status of the document but its reception and implementation amid the realities of the twenty-first century. Treachery is the accepting of Belhar in theory only. Obedience lies in the doing.

98. Barth, *Revelation*, p. 645.

Chapter 4

Confessing the one faith?
Theological resonance between the Creed of Nicea and the Confession of Belhar

Notwithstanding the differences in doctrine among us, we are united in a common Christian faith, which is proclaimed in the Holy Scriptures and is witnessed to and safeguarded in the ecumenical creed . . . , which faith is continuously confirmed in the spiritual experience of the church of Christ.

— First World Conference on Faith and Order (Lausanne 1927)[1]

In the previous chapter, the Belhar Confession was read in the light of general criteria for confessions of the church, as set out by Karl Barth. The aim was, inter alia, to demonstrate Belhar's formal confessional qualities. Many church declarations and ecumenical consensus documents have been and are continually being published. Not all of them are called confessions, as they either do not purport to be confessions, or — where a confessional intent exists — they fail to satisfy theological criteria that

---

1. Resolution 4.8 of the First World Conference on Faith and Order (Lausanne 1927), as cited by Anton Houtepen, "Common confession," in *Dictionary of the ecumenical movement,* pp. 195-96 (Geneva: WCC, 1991).

This is a reworked version of Piet J. Naudé, "Confessing the one faith: Theological resonance between the creed of Nicea (325 A.D.) and the Confession of Belhar (1982 A.D.)," *Scriptura* 85 (2004): 35-53.

have grown with the history of the church, especially in the Reformed family of churches.

Not many churches actually accept confessions. This will be discussed in more detail in chapter 5, where the reception of Belhar is outlined. But one symbol has become the mark of confessional unity in the church across our many divisions. This chapter attempts to establish the confessional status and meaning of Belhar, not from the perspective of formal theological requirements, but from Belhar's consonance with the most ecumenical of all symbols, the Nicene Creed.

The deceptively simple question is: Does Belhar confess the apostolic faith of the ecumenical church through the ages, or is it a mere contextual, time-bound expression of faith with limited reach in time and space?

Introducing the study project:
"Toward the common expression of the one faith today"

The search for some agreement on the "essentials" of the Christian faith has been part of the modern ecumenical movement from its very beginning. The First World Conference on Faith and Order, in Lausanne in 1927, included "the church's common confession of faith" in its agenda and agreed that, despite doctrinal differences, delegates held to a common Christian faith, as taught in Scripture and as witnessed to in the Nicene and Apostles' Creeds.[2] With the formation of the World Council of Churches (WCC) in 1948 in Amsterdam, "the visible unity of the church *in one faith* and in one eucharistic fellowship" was expressed as its primary aim.[3]

The question of what exactly this "one faith" is and the issue of how to reach unity in "eucharistic fellowship" were two themes continuously addressed in subsequent years. The latter was taken up in the well-known BEM project,[4] while the former was developed broadly as follows. The Fourth World Conference on Faith and Order, meeting in Montreal in 1963, addressed the very important question of how Scripture relates to Tradition (capital *T*) and traditions (small *t*), as well as the place of the

2. See Houtepen, "Common confession," pp. 195-96.
3. Constitution 3 (my emphasis).
4. See World Council of Churches, *Baptism, Eucharist, and Ministry, 1982-1990*, Faith and Order Paper 149 (Geneva: WCC, 1990).

creeds in a hermeneutical framework such as this. An intense study of the early church and its councils followed, investigating the possibilities of a genuinely universal council in modern times. But by 1967 the Faith and Order Commission judged that such efforts and studies toward a common confession were premature, and in Louvain (1971) the focus shifted to a contextual pluralism of creedal witnesses and accounts of hope. This culminated in the Bangalore statement "Common account of hope,"[5] which made a number of important affirmations about trinitarian faith, including the requirement for a consensus on the apostolic faith.

The search for such a consensus was outlined in a three-stage study initiated at the Lima Commission in 1982, under the title "Towards the common expression of the apostolic faith today." The three interdependent goals were (1) a recognition of the Nicene Creed (without the *filioque*) as *the* ecumenical creed of the church, (2) an explanation of the creed for the sake of contemporary understanding, and (3) finding ways to express the common faith today. The Sixth Assembly of the WCC, in Vancouver in 1983, affirmed the study project, which included contemporary expressions of faith, as well as a focus on the Nicene Creed as the most striking model of unity in the early church, representing part of a *consensio antiquitatis et universitatis*.[6] The possibility of Nicea as an expression of the common apostolic faith was pursued at a number of theological consultations,[7] which led to the publication of a draft document *Confessing the one faith* approved by the Standing Commission of Faith and Order in Madrid.[8] After considerable reactions and further deliberations around the world, the new revised version was approved in Dunblane, Scotland (1990), and published by the WCC in 1991 as Faith and Order Paper 153 under the title *Confessing the one faith: An ecumenical explication of the apostolic faith as it is confessed in the Nicene-Constantinopolitan Creed (381).*[9]

My interpretation of the common-confession project is that it has re-

---

5. World Council of Churches, *A common account of hope*, Faith and Order Paper 92 (Geneva: WCC, 1978), pp. 243-46.

6. Hermann Josef Sieben, *Die Konzilidee der alten Kirche* (Paderborn: Ferdinand Schöningh, 1979), p. 515.

7. Gennadios Limouris, "Historical background of the apostolic faith today," in *Confessing the one faith*, pp. 108-10 (Geneva: WCC, 1991).

8. This draft document was published as World Council of Churches, *Confessing the one faith*, Faith and Order Paper 140 (Geneva: WCC, 1987).

9. World Council of Churches, *Confessing the one faith*, new revised version, Faith and Order Paper 153 (Geneva: WCC, 1991).

tained a bifocal vision of both recognition and explanation of the Nicene Creed, as well as promoting "new confessions of faith as they are provoked today by situations of persecution, of church union negotiations, or of urgent socio-economic, political or ideological threats."[10] Such modern confessions "could enrich the variety of creedal expressions and ought to be communicated within the ecumenical community as concrete evidence that we are 'listening to what the Spirit has to say to the churches.'"[11] Instead of considering such new expressions of faith as purely contextual reactions to specific circumstances,[12] it should be part and parcel of our theological task to show the coherence between "universally received" symbols (like Nicea or the Apostles' Creed) and such modern expressions, precisely to confirm that our one apostolic faith can find expression in a variety of ways.

At this point it should be noted that the primary expression of the apostolic faith,[13] as "the dynamic reality of the Christian faith,"[14] remains the Holy Scriptures. Different traditions arose in the process of developing confessions in postbiblical times, however, with different but concomitant views on the nature and authority of such confessions. Today the ecumenical church encompasses these views and their numerous internal variations, beginning with the distinct authority of select Ecumenical Councils, followed by historically definitive confessions (e.g., Lutheran), including new confessions in new circumstances (e.g., Reformed), noncreedal churches (e.g., Methodist), and even anticreedal churches (e.g., Pentecostal, charismatic).

---

10. Houtepen, "Common confession," p. 197.

11. Houtepen, "Common confession," p. 197.

12. In his overview of confessions as communicative acts, Edmund Arens, *Bezeugen und Bekennen. Elementäre Handlung des Glaubens* (Düsseldorf: Patmos, 1989), moves from *Lehrendes Bekennen* (teaching confession) in the councils and *Bekenntnisschriften* (confession texts) in the Reformation to what he calls *Situatives Bekennen* (situational confession) to depict twentieth-century documents like Barmen (and, by implication, Belhar). The third type creates the unfortunate impression that the early creeds and confessions were "universal" (in the sense of being acontextual) and not in fact also situation-bound.

13. See George Vandervelde, "The meaning of 'apostolic faith' in World Council of Churches' documents," in *Apostolic faith in America*, ed. Thaddeus Horgan, pp. 20-25 (Grand Rapids: Eerdmans, 1988), with discussion of at least six dimensions of the meaning of "apostolic faith" in the context of the WCC. He indicates that one such dimension (point 5 of his list) relates to the Nicene Creed, which is "the ecumenical symbol par excellence."

14. See the introduction to WCC, *Confessing the one faith,* p. 2, par. 7, which tries to avoid the idea that *apostolic faith* refers to "a single fixed formula" or "a specific moment in Christian history."

For this book, I take the Reformed view of confessions as my point of departure. This is, first, the tradition from which I have been engaging in ecumenical theology; second, it is the context from which the Belhar Confession grew. From a Reformed perspective, three remarks are necessary as a background to this discussion.

First, Scripture retains its position of ultimate criterion, the *norma normans* of faith, so that all subsequent expressions of faith are under Scripture and not next to it. Second, the symbols of the early church, notably the Nicene Creed, the Apostles' Creed, and the credo of Athanasius, are accepted with the confessions arising from the Protestant Reformation[15] as in agreement with Scripture *(quia),* and therefore as authoritative expressions of the apostolic faith. Third, in the light of its understanding of the church's witnessing role to the Word in new circumstances and against new heresies, Reformed churches are open to continued renewal of their confessions of faith, albeit subject to certain broad constraints.[16]

An exploration of the apostolic faith, as found in a new confession like Belhar in relation to earlier expressions of faith like Nicea, finds its inspiration therefore both in the specifics of the *Confessing the one faith* project and in the Reformed habit of testing later expressions of faith in the light of earlier ones (representing an accumulated faith tradition), and ultimately in the light of Scripture. In the spirit of the confessing project,[17] this chapter will take the Nicene text as a point of departure and proceed with a comparative reading of the Belhar text. Similarities and differences will be pointed out, but the overriding question remains: Does Belhar confirm the apostolic faith as expressed in Nicea?

There could obviously be a variety of answers to this question. Belhar could confirm the basic theological convictions of Nicea or deny some of these. Or Belhar could supersede Nicea to confirm aspects of our common faith not testified to in the Nicene Creed. Or possibly these "new elements" are not recognized as belonging to our common faith but are collectively a mere contextual witness in a crisis situation. And so one could continue

15. In the Reformed churches of Dutch origin, the Three Formulae of Unity — the Belgic Confession, Heidelberg Catechism, and Canons of Dort — occupy a preeminent position.

16. See Karl Barth, *Church dogmatics,* I/2: *The revelation of God* [Edinburgh: T. & T. Clark, 1956], pp. 620-60.

17. For a critical view of the confessing project (which perhaps misses the ecumenical spirit), see Piet J. Naudé, "Confessing Nicea today? Critical questions from a South African perspective," *Scriptura* 79 (2002): 47-54.

with various scenarios. The focus of this chapter, which is quite narrow and specific, will chiefly address the issue of consonance between Nicea and Belhar, with the former taken as the point of departure. I take "theological resonance" to mean at least a significant theological convergence, and not merely textual agreements or differences.

The intention of the reading below is twofold. It is a contribution to the explication of Nicea as "confessing the one faith," as demonstrated in subsection 2 of each article. But it is also an effort to communicate to the ecumenical church the faith of Belhar,[18] and in turn to test this faith in the light of the most ecumenically accepted of all symbols. Before we venture into a close reading of the respective texts, it is necessary to make a few interesting, but hermeneutically significant, remarks about Nicea and Belhar,[19] keeping in mind that the readers of this book will be fairly well informed about Nicea, but perhaps less so with regard to Belhar.

Nicea and Belhar: Hermeneutical basis for a text comparison

What's in a name?

Both Nicea and Belhar derive their names from the geographic places where they were formulated. In both cases, there is indeed a great deal of significance in the name!

In the case of Nicea, the full name Nicene-Constantinopolitan Creed

---

18. See Houtepen, "Common Confession," who argues that an ecumenical "Book of Confessions," as "an enriching possibility for dialogue and exchange of spiritual experiences" (p. 197), could and should include Belhar as an ecumenical symbol.

19. For the history and context of Nicea, I have relied on the following very informative secondary sources: Gennadios Limouris, "Nicene Creed," in *Dictionary of the ecumenical movement*, pp. 727-28 (Geneva: WCC, 1991); Wolf-Dieter Hauschild, "Nicäno-Konstantinopolitanisches Glaubensbekenntnis," *Theologische Realensiklopädie* 24 (1994): 444-56 (on the text); Adolf Martin Ritter, "Arianismus," *Theologische Realensiklopädie* 3 (1978): 693-719; Lorenzo Perrone, "Von Nicea (325) nach Chalcedon (451)," in *Geschichte der Konzilien. Vom Niceaum bis zum Vaticanum II,* ed. Alberigo Guiseppe, pp. 22-83 (Düsseldorf: Patmos, 1993) (general history and theology); and the well-known classics by Sieben, *Die Konzilidee der alten Kirche,* and J. N. D. Kelly, *Early Christian creeds* (London: Longman, 1972). The best South African source I know is Willie D. Jonker, *Christus die Middelaar* (Pretoria: N. G. K. Uitgewers, 1977), pp. 12-61. For Belhar fewer formal academic sources are available, although, as this book and its bibliography demonstrate, the list of reflections on Belhar is growing in breadth and depth.

(NC)[20] points to the complexity of its formation over an extended period of time from the first ecumenical council, held in the city of Nicea (May 20–June 19/July 25? 325), and its fuller, altered version as accepted by the second council, meeting in Constantinople (May–July 381), to which we will return to below. At this stage attention is directed to the fact that both councils were called together by Roman emperors[21] — Constantine in the case of Nicea, and Theodosius I with Constantinople.[22] In Nicea the emperor hosted the council in his palace, paid for part of the cost, chaired the meeting, and closed the council with a grand banquet, which doubled as a commemoration of the twentieth year of his rule. In Constantinople the council was called by the emperor but met in a church and was chaired by bishops, first Melitius (who died during the council), followed by Gregory of Nazianzus and later Nectarius of Constantinople. In both cases, the council's decisions were enacted by imperial law, as well as by canon law.[23]

Both councils also bore great political significance in ensuring religious unity for the sake of imperial unity. In the view of the Romans, the ruler carried responsibility for religious matters. "This view of the ruler as *pontifex maximus* was retained in Christianity and determined its view of the kingdom for centuries to come."[24] In this light, it would therefore be seen as the duty of the emperor to participate in and influence ecclesial matters, on the assumption of a unity between church and state, which was questioned and abolished only in modern times. The two names reflected in the Nicene Creed thus point to its close alignment with the political power of the day and the strategic importance of the councils per se as representing the common view of the churches in both the West and the East.[25]

The Confession of Belhar takes its name from a fairly humble, so-

---

20. In this chapter I will follow the custom of referring to the document from the year 381 as the Nicene Creed (or NC) and to the earlier version, from 325, as Nicea.

21. The first emperor's council occurred in Arles in 314 to solve the problem of Bishop Cecilan's election as bishop of Carthage (see Perrone, "Von Nicea," p. 26). Since it was a meeting of bishops in the West only, it does not have the status of an ecumenical council.

22. After he defeated Licinius in 324, Constantine ruled over the whole empire until his death in 337. Theodosius I ruled in the West from 379, but after the murder of Gratian, he also ruled over the whole empire, until 395.

23. See Perrone, "Von Nicea," pp. 33, 56, 71-72.

24. See Perrone, "Von Nicea," p. 27 (my translation).

25. It seems as if Constantine had the city of Ancyra in Galatia in mind for the first council. He changed the venue to Nicea as a gesture of compromise to the Arians, who might have felt wary of the outspoken anti-Arianism of the bishop of Ancyra. See Perrone, "Von Nicea," p. 33.

called colored suburb in Cape Town. Since the advent of colonialism in 1652, political power was represented by Cape Town, the seat of legislative power from where, in the period after 1948, laws were passed that ensured that South African society was segregated in every respect on racial grounds.

Belhar, seen as a spatial entity, was itself a result of the infamous Group Areas Act of 1950, which dispossessed "nonwhites" of land and grouped them in segregated African, Colored, and Indian residential areas and townships (informal settlements). Belhar, constructed as ecclesial space, also represented separation. As we saw in chapter 1, the DRMC, which gathered in its general synod at Belhar from September 22 to October 6, 1982,[26] was formed in 1881 as a result of the establishment of separate churches for different racial groups within the DRC family.[27]

In contrast to Nicea, which spoke from and for the "center" in a situation of political and ecclesial unity, Belhar spoke from the margins and represented both political and ecclesial schism. But this does not imply that Belhar at the time represented weakness or political insignificance. The reasons for this were twofold.

First, although South Africa, after the formation of the Union in 1910, accepted a separation of church and state de jure, the close-knit relationship between party, church, culture, and *volk* in Afrikaner nationalism constituted a de facto *corpus Christianum* after the National Party came to power in 1948. As was discussed in chapter 1, the very idea of apartheid as a political system had part of its roots in a specific brand of neo-Calvinist and missiological thinking, and some of the apartheid laws were actually enacted at the request of the DRC. The whole system of a white-dominated South Africa was solidified with the formation of the Republic in 1961, under Hendrik Verwoerd, constituting a close-knit unity that relied on religion for its moral legitimacy.

Thus, the common and unquestioned assumption of both defenders and opponents of apartheid was that the church really mattered.[28] The

26. The draft confession was accepted on the last day of the synod, Wednesday, October 6, 1982. For a moving account of events at the synod, see Johan Botha's narrative in Johan Botha and Piet J. Naudé, *Op pad met Belhar. Goeie nuus vir gister, vandag en more* (Pretoria: Van Schaik, 1998), pp. 33-37.

27. See n. 2 in the preface above.

28. For a discussion of original South African sources on the church around 1980, see Piet J. Naudé, "The Dutch Reformed Church's role in the context of transition in South Africa: Main streams of academic research," *Scriptura* 76 (2001): 87-106.

sociopolitical system of apartheid was interpreted theologically, and the theological (ecclesiological) struggle was not about interesting theoretical ideas but about liberation or continued oppression. In this sense, the voice of Belhar was of great political significance. Although spoken from Belhar, the words fell right in Cape Town, where the rulers knew that the legitimacy of their system was at stake.

Second, the voice of Belhar was influential and powerful because it was not a voice calling from the wilderness but from the very heart of the ecumenical church. The involvement of the broader church in the South African struggle was highlighted in chapter 2 and need not be repeated here. Belhar's antecedent witnesses showed how Catholic, Lutheran, Black, Reformed, and ecumenical declarations from 1948 to 1982 came together in the draft confession of 1982 as the ultimate form of Christian witness against irreconcilability and for unity in Christ. There was no way that this voice could have been ignored.

What's in a heresy?

From the earliest church, creeds and confessions normally had the dual purpose of being a summary of the true faith for baptismal, or catechetical, purposes and as a counterstatement against heterodoxy in its various forms. In both Nicea and Belhar, the content was deeply influenced by that which they opposed. Although Nicea is a creed and Belhar a confession, therefore belonging to slightly different ecclesial and liturgical genres, both texts are characterized by the structure of "true faith" and "heresy."[29]

In Belhar, this is quite evident from the fact that the three middle articles all end with a "Therefore, we reject . . ." clause, wherein the specific dimension of the false doctrine is clearly exposed in the light of the preceding positive statement of the gospel. This was discussed toward the end of chapter 1. Article 2 rejects any doctrine that would endanger the visible unity of the church; article 3 rejects any doctrine that sanctions forced racial separation in the name of the gospel and therefore denies reconciliation in Christ; and article 4 rejects any ideology that legitimizes societal injustice and any doctrine that would be unwilling to resist such injustices. From these rejections, the middle structure of Belhar — confessing unity,

29. See chapter 1 for a discussion of the rejection clauses in Belhar.

reconciliation, and justice — naturally flows, "encircled" by the articulation of faith in the triune God (art. 1) and the call to obedience (art. 5).

In Nicea the situation is, for historical reasons, more complex. The original text of Nicea (325) is much shorter than the version of NC (381) known to us today.[30] It is interesting to note that the shorter version included as part of its main text a clear rejection clause *(anathema)*,[31] whereas the final version has no explicit rejection clauses but is built on implicit rejections taken up in the main text.[32] Scholars generally accept that Nicea was primarily directed against the Arian heresy,[33] in the context of the early church's search for an adequate expression of trinitarian theology. However, NC was an extension of the earlier text, with the purpose of addressing new heresies that had arisen after Nicea and that required amending, with special emphasis on the eighth article about the Holy Spirit.[34] Read backward from the rejections, it is logical to expect Nicea and NC to deal with the issue of the Trinity. Specific heretical views are denounced in explicating the relationship of the Son to the Father. At a later stage, in the light of the Pneumatomachians,[35] the question of the

30. Nicea has 141 words in the original Greek, which includes the anathema of 42 words, and has no "amen," whereas NC consists of 174 words plus the "amen." For a detailed analysis of the two versions and comparisons, see Hauschild, "Nicäno," pp. 444-56.

31. The rejection clause, which refers explicitly to two quotations drawn from Arian theology, is concerned with the second person of the Trinity: *ēn pote hote ouk ēn* (there was a time that he was not) and *prin gennēthēnai ouk ēn* (before he was born, he was not). The clause ends with *toutous anathematizei hē katholikē kai apostolokē ekklēsia* (these the catholic and apostolic church rejects).

32. For a list of these implicit rejections (without discussion), related to the text of NC (381), see Limouris, "Nicene Creed," p. 727.

33. Arius (260-337?) of Alexandria built his ideas on Hellenistic metaphysics in relation specifically to the Logos concept (found in the Johannine gospel). To retain the absolute unity and transcendence of God, only God can be the *agennētos archē* (unborn source), which means that the Son as Logos must be *ktisma* or *poiēma* (a created thing or something made). The consequence is that the Son cannot be accepted as equally eternal with the Father (like in Origen). Therefore he must be a created being; that is, there was a time when the Son was not. The motive to protect the unity, indivisibility, and transcendence of God led to a subordination of the Son. See Ritter, "Arianismus," pp. 693-719, for a fuller, technical discussion.

34. See Limouris, "Nicene Creed," p. 727; Perrone, "Von Nicea," pp. 27-31; and Hauschild, "Nicäno," pp. 449-54.

35. In the first half of the fourth century, the focus of the Arian discussion was on the relationship between the Father and the Son. Nicea (325) therefore has an extended confession regarding Jesus Christ, mostly retained in NC (381), but with a very short confession about the Spirit: "And [we believe] in the Holy Spirit [*kai eis to hagion pneuma*]." In NC (381) this

divinity of the Spirit was also addressed. On the one hand, NC further shows how the one God could be confessed as a Trinity without compromising the unity of God, and on the other, it confirms the divinity of each of the three persons in the Trinity. How the trinitarian confession of NC and Belhar's five articles relate to one another will be apparent from the textual analysis below.

What lies in reception?

The process of reception of both NC and Belhar is of historical and theological significance. A fuller discussion of Belhar's reception will follow in chapters 5 and 6 below. In the case of NC, the process of reception was in fact constitutive for the final formulation itself.[36] In the period between 325 and 381 the faith of Nicea (325) was carried forth in both the East and the West, and in the end it was found to be an inadequate expression of the faith because it did not address all the important heresies pertaining to the Trinity.

What is even more remarkable is the fact that no documented evidence from the 381 council itself suggests that the NC was formulated and accepted in Constantinople. We have confirmation of this only via the reception of the NC at the next council, the Council of Chalcedon, in A.D. 451, which refers back to the 150 fathers' acceptance of the NC in 381. One further textual change occurred after 381 with the insertion of the *filioque* by the West between the seventh and ninth centuries (which contributed to the eventual split between the East and West).[37] But the creed is attested to in liturgies as early as 488 and is accepted in both the East and West as an

---

article is expanded significantly to address the heresy that the Spirit is not equally divine in relation to the other two persons of the Trinity. This heresy (of the so-called Pneumatomachians, or "Spirit-fighters") is mentioned for the first time in 360 by Athanasius and apparently arose in Egypt with support from Macedonius of Constantinople (therefore sometimes called the Macedonian heresy). See Perrone, "Von Nicea," pp. 66-68.

36. For a discussion of the technical meaning of reception in the ecumenical movement and a comprehensive bibliography up to 1998, see Piet J. Naudé and Dirk J. Smit, "'Reception' — ecumenical crisis or opportunity for South African churches?" *Scriptura* 73 (2000): 175-88.

37. The Habilitationsschrift on the *filioque* by Bernd Oberdorfer, published as *Filioque. Geschichte und Theologie eines ökumenischen Problems* (Göttingen: Vandenhoeck & Ruprecht, 2000), is a comprehensive treatment of the struggle regarding the procession of the Spirit from both the Father and the Son.

expression of true faith. The churches of the Reformation, both Lutheran and Reformed, accepted the NC as a basis for faith, although its liturgical use has been superseded by the Apostles' Creed. The WCC process of "confessing the one faith" therefore rightly builds on the most ecumenical of all Christian symbols.

The Confession of Belhar was accepted as a draft confession at the synod of the DRMC on October 6, 1982. It was subsequently distributed to all congregations of the DRMC for comment and formally accepted as a fourth confession at the synod of 1986. Its reception has since gone through a variety of phases. First, it was accepted internally by the members of the DRMC as an expression of their faith in a situation of oppression that constituted a *status confessionis*.[38] Second, it was accepted as a basis of faith in the unification of the DRMC and the DRCA into the URCSA on April 14, 1994.[39] Third, it was accepted as a provisional confession by the Reformed Church in America (RCA) in 2007, and as a full confession by the Verenigde Protestantse Kerk in Belgium already in 1998. Fourth, Belhar has been under scrutiny as part of the reunification process of the DRC family,[40] with the possibility that it be included in the church orders of the reunited church. In chapter 6 the relationship between the DRC and Belhar is discussed in more detail.

Whereas the URCSA is in principle open to a textual reformulation in the light of "a better understanding of the Word of God,"[41] the chances for this are fairly slim. The period to negotiate Belhar's actual content in the process of the DRC family reunion, in my judgment, has passed. Furthermore, the history of Reformed confessions teaches us that a confession's

38. At the 1986 synod, 10 of the 267 congregations voiced their concerns with Belhar, and 24 of the 498 delegates did not sign the confession at first. See Dirk J. Smit, "Das Bekenntnis von Belhar. Entstehung, Inhalt, Rezeption, Relevanz," in *Das Bekenntnis von Belhar und seine Bedeutung für die reformierten Kirchen in Deutschland*, ed. J. Niemöller, p. 26 (Detmold: Reformierte Bund, 1998).

39. Some congregations of the DRCA did not want reunification, and to this day it remains legally a separate church.

40. For a discussion in Afrikaans of the DRC's reaction to Belhar, see Piet J. Naudé, "Die Belharstryd in ekumeniese perspektief," *Nederduitse Gereformeerde Teologiese Tydskrif* 38, no. 3 (1997): 226-43. The core of this article has been included as a case study on reception in chapter 6 below.

41. This is quoted from the URCSA's church orders, article 2 (my translation). The full sentence reads: "In the future, changed circumstances, as well as a better understanding of God's Word, may lead to the acceptance of new confessions or the alteration of current confessions."

formulation, even if later seen as inadequate or even factually wrong, should be retained, not so much for what it confesses, but for what it intends to confess. In extreme situations, a synod could accept an authoritative explication of such a confession to draw certain hermeneutical boundaries for the understanding of a specific formulation.[42]

Specific text-reception problems

Reception problems regarding the NC text mostly involved two concepts: *homo-ousios* (of one being) and *filioque* (and the Son). The first is not a biblical word and was a neologism to express the unity between Father and Son. The second relates to the long struggle about whether the Spirit processes from the Father only, or from the Father and the Son. These two examples merely illustrate that huge debates may still arise after a creed or confession has been accepted.

Belhar is no exception, and the major internal debate for the DRC family has been article 4.1: "We believe . . . that in a world full of injustice and enmity He is in a special way the God of the destitute, the poor and the wronged."[43] Many saw, and still see, in this formulation of God's revelation a (negative) liberation theology and therefore consider it to be unacceptable as part of a confession.[44] The formal view of the DRC synod of 1990 was that Belhar is, taken by itself, not contradicting the Formulae of Unity, although article 4 could have been formulated differently. But in a letter dated November 8, 1996, the DRC leadership has indicated that — despite debates about article 4 — Belhar cannot be simply dismissed as a document of liberation theology. As Belhar travels across boundaries of time and space, new debates will arise. This should not be seen as unwelcome or

42. For a discussion and concrete examples from church history, see my contribution in Botha and Naudé, *Op pad met Belhar,* pp. 85-86.

43. In reading through Belhar from October to December 2002 with an international group of senior students — representing the North and the South, as well as the East and the West — article 4 created no problems. Rather, it was the second article, on church unity, that drew critical discussion. This illustrates the point that one's reaction is hermeneutically determined by one's context!

44. J. M. Vorster, Reformed South African scholar, argued: "The whole revelation of Scripture describes God as God of all people and in a special way the God of the faithful" ("Die belydenis van Belhar in dogma-historiese perspektief," *In die Skriflig* 32, no. 4 [December 1998]: 478, my translation). See his article for further references to the debate that God indeed cares for the poor but cannot be claimed to be their God in a special way.

strange, as it has been an integral part of confession reception since the very early church! What this chapter pursues is whether Belhar as a whole is in theological consonance with the NC. To this end, article 4 will obviously be included in the discussion below.

Accompanying letters

The issue of reception is made even more interesting if one takes into account that Nicea and NC, as well as Belhar, have all been accompanied by a letter to make their content, intention, and authority clear. This has almost become a mark of creeds and confessions, if one takes into account, for example, the Belgic Confession and the Barmen Declaration.

In the case of Nicea, the text was distributed with a letter to the various synods, as well as by a letter written by Constantine to all churches, in which he expressed his joy over the restored unity in faith and declared the council decisions to be the law of the state. The council of 381 sent a letter to Emperor Theodosius in which they confirmed the Nicene faith and the restoration of Christian unity, and in which they requested him to confirm the canons and decisions through an edict of the emperor (to which he acceded on July 30, 381).

Where Nicea and NC can and have been read and interpreted without these letters, the opposite is the case with Belhar. As discussed above, the Accompanying Letter is part of the hermeneutical key to the confessional text itself. In four paragraphs the synod clarifies the seriousness of an act of confession (par. 1), explicates its motive (par. 2) and the spirit in which the confession is made (par. 3), and spells out the aim of reconciliation and unity (par. 4). The Belhar letter has been and will be an integral part of the reception process itself and should be taken seriously.

A textual and theological comparison

The aim of this section is not to engage in a word-by-word comparison, as such an exercise is rendered inappropriate by the different genres of NC and Belhar. The texts are nevertheless important, as they are the bearers of theological meaning. The original Greek text of the NC and the original Afrikaans text of Belhar will serve as points of departure. For the sake of a wider readership, the discussion will work with authorized English translations.[45] As explained at the outset, the focus is on the possible theological consonance between the NC and Belhar, where the NC serves as a point of departure. In some cases the text itself will be the focal point; in others the thematic content as carried by the text will be emphasized.

"We believe in"

In contrast to the Apostles' Creed *(credo in)*, both the NC and Belhar take the plural as subject of confession: "*We* believe. . . ." Despite the fact that the NC might have been partially built on a baptismal formula for use by individual converts, it chooses to emphasize the community of faith into which the individual is born. There is a reciprocal relationship here: As much as the individual's confession is made in communion with the faith of the whole church, so does the communal confession articulate the faith of the individual believer. In light of the precedence of the Apostles' Creed in the Reformed tradition, one would have expected the first person singular in Belhar. However, the plural is used because the subject of confession is the church, which also acts as first recipient of such a confession.[46]

In the NC "we believe in" *(pisteuomen eis)* is repeated four times with reference to the Trinity (once for each person) and significantly includes the church as the object of confession. In Belhar "we believe in" occurs twice, but the first includes the triune God *as a unity,* without separate articles for each of the three persons, and the second refers to the church. With regard to the latter, Belhar's Afrikaans text follows the Apostles' Creed, where *glo in* is reserved for God, and *glo aan* is used for the article on the church.[47] As a positive explication of the gospel and true to its nature as confession, Belhar includes quite a number of "we believe that" statements that serve as a mirror image of the "we reject" clauses in the three middle articles.[48]

45. For the NC, I follow the text in *Prayers we have in common* (agreed liturgical texts prepared by the International Consultation on English Texts, 1975), as used by WCC, *Confessing the one faith.* For Belhar, I use the DRMC official translations into English and German, published by the Nederduits Gereformeerde Sendingkerk, *Konsepbelydenis van die N. G. Sendingkerk in Suid-Afrika* (Huguenot: Paarl Drukpers, 1982).

46. See Barth, *Church dogmatics,* I/2, pp. 620-21.

47. This Afrikaans distinction between *credere in* and *credere* has no direct parallel in English.

48. "We believe that . . ." is used six times in article 2 (unity), four times in article 3 (reconciliation), three times in article 4 (justice), and once in article 5 (obedience).

Already in the very opening lines we see a double convergence between the NC and Belhar. They both take the confessing church as subject
and both take the triune God and the church as objects of confession. The
question now arises whether this points to a deeper thematic consonance.
For this we first turn to the confession of the Trinity.

Trinitarian theology as basis for ecclesiology

We have already seen above that Nicea and the NC were formulated in the
context of the development of the early church's understanding of the
Trinity. One can therefore expect that the three persons would be confessed both in their own personhood and in their interrelationship to one
another.

The first thing that strikes one is the strong emphasis on unity in the
Nicene Creed: We believe in *one* God, *one* Lord who is of *one being* with the
Father, the Holy Spirit who *with the Father and the Son* is worshipped and
glorified; and we believe in *one* church. The focal point of the unity is the
Trinity as one God (against forms of tritheism), where Father, Son, and
Spirit are equally divine (against forms of subordinationism) and from
whose grace the church as one church is established (against ecclesial divi-
sion because of doctrinal differences).[49]

It is instructive to note that Belhar takes the outcome of the struggle
for the church's trinitarian faith as expressed in the NC as its very starting
point: "We believe in the triune God, Father, Son and Holy Spirit." In this
manner Belhar establishes itself on the ecumenical faith of the church
through the ages. The unity of God, so eloquently expressed in the NC, is
taken up in the very last sentence of Belhar: "To the one and only God, Father, Son and Holy Spirit, be the honour and the glory for ever and ever."
This reminds one strongly of the doxological phrase in the Nicene article
on the Holy Spirit, "Who with the Father and the Son is worshipped and
glorified." In both the NC and Belhar, the trinitarian faith is doxologically
and antithetically expressed.[50] If we read the Belhar phrase in conjunction

---

49. It should again be noted that both Nicea and the NC were called by the emperor to
heal specific doctrinal rifts in the church, although both councils also dealt with church governance, appointments of bishops, and many other issues.

50. There is little doubt that this doxological formulation in the Nicene Creed is crucial
to emphasize the divinity of the Spirit. In Belhar the doxology starts with "Jesus is Lord" and

with the very first line of the confession, it emerges that trinitarianism in fact begins (underlies) and ends (takes forward) the confession itself.

Because of the nature of the heresies of its time, the trinitarian faith is itself expounded and defended in the NC. Belhar assumes this faith and uses it as its starting point in order to shift the focus from the unity of God to the unity of the church. The reason is that the heretical situation against which Belhar witnesses is an ecclesial one of separated churches for people of different racial descent. In Belhar there is therefore a "contraction" of the Nicene Creed so that belief in the triune God is immediately linked to the church in a double movement, each of which confirms the NC in an interesting way.

In article 1, the phrase "We believe in the triune God, Father, Son and Holy Spirit" is followed by "who gathers, protects and cares for his Church by his Word and his Spirit, as He has done since the beginning of the world and will do to the end." This is in line with the structure of both the NC and the Apostles' Creed. But where the NC had to give extensive, detailed formulations on the preexistence of the Son and the Spirit,[51] Belhar links the triune God's "preexistence" ("since the beginning of the world") and "postexistence" ("and will do to the end") not so much to himself as to the establishment and protection of the church. To a certain extent the NC focuses on the immanent Trinity,[52] whereas Belhar focuses on the economic Trinity as manifested in the history of the church.

This is immediately followed by the second movement, in article 2.1, which deals in its entirety with the unity of the church: "We believe in one holy, universal Christian Church, the communion of saints called from the entire human family." In a very delicate way Belhar here draws on both the NC and the Apostles' Creed. For the unity of the church, which is the core focus of article 2, Belhar takes over the NC adjective of *one* church (which is absent from the Apostles' Creed). This is followed by the Apostles' Creed formula (the "apostolic" from the NC is therefore not included), with a

---

is embedded in article 5, where obedience to Jesus Christ is set against obedience to authorities and human laws. See discussion of the lordship of Christ below.

51. This emphasis is evident in the description of the Son as "eternally begotten" *(gennēthenta pro pantōn tōn aiōnōn)* and as "begotten not made" *(gennēthenta ou poiēthenta)* and the Holy Spirit as "Lord" *(kyrios)*, who proceeds *(ekporeuomenon)* from the Father.

52. This distinction is obviously a construction we put on the NC today. Because of the heresies it had to confront, the intratrinitarian confession was necessary, but — as will be seen below — the NC in its Christology is as historically related as any "economic" theology could be.

noncreedal addition derived from the Heidelberg Catechism, namely that the community of saints is "called from the entire human family."

In the light of the heresy against which Belhar confessed, it thus derives the unity of the church in article 2 from the NC and elaborates this unity in the four ensuing paragraphs (unity as gift and obligation; unity as visible; unity as manifested in a variety of ways; unity established in freedom). The reference to the church as a "communion of saints" enables Belhar to implicitly assert a contradiction to a view of community where differentiation is seen as grounds for separation, instead of "opportunities for mutual service and enrichment within the one visible people of God" (art. 2.6). That the church is "called from the entire human family" (art. 2.1) enables Belhar to already implicitly assert the unity of the church against the heresy that "descent or any other human or social factor should be a consideration in determining membership of the Church" (art. 2, rejection 3).

The theological structure of the NC is clearly maintained, but in line with the context and heresy that Belhar is addressing, the trinitarian basis of faith is translated into more elaborate ecclesiological terms. Hence, the unity of the triune God becomes motivation for and is reflected in the unity of the community of saints. In this way, articles 1 and 2 of Belhar, as well as the closing section of article 5, are in full consonance with the apostolic faith expressed in the NC.

Christology

In the light of the Arian heresy, the NC had to give detailed attention to the divinity of the Son. This was accomplished in eight expressions from "one Lord" to "through him all things were made." After the Godhead of Christ is firmly established, the NC proceeds to confess the incarnated humanity of the Son, starting with "he came down from heaven" and ending in "he ascended into heaven . . ." in a series of expressions later closely followed by the Apostles' Creed. This twofold christological structure is present in Belhar but interpreted in a particular way commensurate with the aim of the confession.

The divinity of Christ: His lordship

The oldest confession of Christ's divine status, already present in the New Testament (e.g., Rom. 1:3; 1 Cor. 8:6; 12:3), is that "Jesus is Lord." The NC is clear and simple: "We believe in one Lord, Jesus Christ." The *one* Lord is in line with the NC's emphasis on the unity of God; the one *Lord* expresses the ultimate rule and authority of Christ, whose "kingdom will have no end." Where this confession was a case of life and death in early Christianity (because of its challenge to the emperor), the Nicene Creed was formulated under political conditions where this would be accepted by the Roman authorities and therefore expressed in relative freedom.

The lordship of Christ emerges in Belhar under conditions reminiscent of early Christianity. After the confession of unity, reconciliation, and justice, article 5 expresses a challenge and a conviction: "We believe that, in obedience to Jesus Christ, its only Head, the Church is called to confess and to do all these things, even though the authorities and human laws might forbid them and punishment and suffering be the consequence" (art. 5.1). Then follows: "Jesus is Lord" (art. 5.2), after which there appears the trinitarian doxology discussed above.

In chapter 2 it was shown that Belhar's confession of Christ's lordship exhibits the same bifocal vision of antecedent church witnesses. Christ is first Lord of the church, but also Lord of history and society. This is beautifully formulated in article 5, where the headship of the church and lordship over human authorities are juxtaposed in calling the church "to confess and to do all these things." Where the church follows its only head in obedience to his rule but is resisted by authorities and human laws, the higher commitment to the Lord will prevail.

The humanity of Christ: His incarnation

The connection between the NC and Belhar concerning the humanity of Christ is evident from three crucial phrases that put the whole of Christ's earthly work in a strong *pro nobis* framework: "*For us all* and *for our salvation* he came down from heaven" is followed a few lines later by "*for our sake* he was crucified under Pontius Pilate." In a unique way the NC makes clear that Christ's work was directed at humans and their salvation and should therefore be interpreted in such a way as to honor the reality of this salvation. Although the NC does not provide us with a specific salvation-historical theology, it would be fair to suggest that this salvation is epitomized by incarnation-as-reconciliation. Christ was crucified "for our sake" in the sense that he took our sins upon himself and was crucified in our place. And this he did "for us all," reconciling humankind to God (Col. 1:15-20). The first fruit of this vicarious suffering is the church, namely those reconciled to God and one another, because they accept Christ's work as "for our sake."

In this manner the transition from unity to reconciliation, so central to articles 2 and 3 in Belhar, is made within the framework of the NC itself. In article 2 Belhar confesses that "Christ's work of reconciliation is made manifest in the Church as the community of believers who have been reconciled with God and with one another" (art. 2.2). Christ's "work of reconciliation" is a theological summary of the incarnated Christ, and the *pro nobis* character is reflected in the church as a community of reconciled people, in the same way that the NC links the church to the work of the Trinity. Belhar therefore rests fully on the basis of the incarnate Christ as confessed in the NC and, under threat of a serious defilement of the gospel, expands the NC to spell out what the concrete implications of Christ's work "for our salvation" and "for our sake" are.

Belhar's concern is therefore with the *visibility* of our salvation and therefore substantially confesses the manifest *unity of the church* in article 2 and *reconciliation among people in the world* as fruit of this "beneficial work" in the whole of article 3. Making salvation concrete is thus for Belhar an ecclesiological matter because "we believe that God has entrusted to his Church the message of reconciliation in and through Jesus Christ" (art. 3.1). In this way both the christological and the ecclesiological implications of the NC are made explicit in the context from which Belhar was proclaimed.

Pneumatology: The Spirit as giver of life and prophecy

As indicated earlier, text comparisons show that most of the additions of the NC (381) to the original Nicea text (325) relate to the article on the Spirit. For our purposes, two of these additions are of great importance: The Spirit is confessed in the NC as "the giver of life" and as the one "who has spoken through the Prophets." These must be read in the context of the time, where certain people denied the divinity of the Spirit.

The first formulation, which relates to John 6:63 ("the Spirit gives life," NIV), Romans 8:2 ("the law of the Spirit of life"), and 2 Corinthians 3:6

("the letter kills, but the Spirit gives life"), emphasizes the lifegiving work of the Spirit, where life is understood in both physical (see the context of bread in John 6) and spiritual terms. The second formulation relates to 2 Peter 1:21 and brings a unity between the Spirit and the Word of God spoken through the prophets. The intention of the NC is clear: Only God gives life, and it is God who speaks through the prophets; therefore the Spirit is equally part of the Godhead and should be worshipped and glorified with the Father and the Son.

In Belhar the work of the Spirit is shown as "lifegiver" and "Word-giver." These two characteristics are intimately related to one another, especially in a trinitarian context, and they are also externally related to four other realities: the establishment of the church (art. 1), the unity in the church (art. 2), reconciliation in society and the world (art. 3), and ultimately justice for the destitute, the poor, and the wronged (art. 4). Let us cite these references to the work of the Spirit to demonstrate how closely Belhar follows the NC:

Article 1: "We believe in the triune God, Father, Son and Holy Spirit, who gathers, protects and cares for his Church *by his Word and his Spirit.*" The manner in which the triune God establishes and leads the church through history is via the Word-giving and lifegiving Spirit.

In article 2.3 it is confessed that the unity established by Christ's reconciliation "through the working of God's Spirit . . . is a binding force"; that believers "are filled with one Spirit" (art. 2.5); and that "the variety of spiritual gifts . . . as well as the various languages and cultures, are by virtue of the reconciliation in Christ opportunities for mutual service" (art. 2.6).

In article 3 we find a much more direct link to the Nicene text. After confessing that God has entrusted the message of reconciliation to the church, Belhar follows with a twofold repetition of the Nicene phrase referred to above: "We believe that God *by his lifegiving Word and Spirit* has conquered the powers of sin and death, and therefore also of irreconciliation and hatred, bitterness and enmity; that God *by his lifegiving Word and Spirit* will enable his people to live in a new obedience which can open new possibilities of life for society and the world." This powerful formulation gives a distinct cosmic and social interpretation of the Word-giving and life-giving Spirit because God (negatively) conquers social irreconciliation and (positively) opens "new possibilities of life for society and the world" (art. 3.2).

This enables Belhar to make the third and last transition from unity and reconciliation to justice in article 4.1: "We believe that God has revealed himself as the One who wishes to bring about justice and true peace among men; that in a world full of injustice and enmity He is in a special way the God of the destitute, the poor and the wronged and that He calls his Church to follow Him in this."

Belhar commences its fourth article with an important theological statement about the manner of God's revelation to the world. God is known to us via Jesus Christ and the Spirit. And the NC already confessed that the incarnation of Christ occurred by the power of the Spirit. What Belhar does is to link Jesus' incarnation via the Spirit (i.e., his revelation of God), not only to his birth from the Virgin Mary, as well as his crucifixion, death, burial, and resurrection, but to the manner of his ministry in the world. The crucial "markers" of Christ's humiliation and humanity — so well known from both the NC and the Apostles' Creed — are "filled in" with the markers of his self-giving ministry in the world as clearly attested to in the Gospels.[53]

After news of the incarnation, the very same Mary, filled with the Spirit, sings a song of praise to God, who will be revealed as the One who cares for the hungry and who lifts up the downtrodden (Luke 1:46-55). The angels sing praise to God as the One who brings peace on earth (Luke 2:14). And the young Jesus reads from the prophet Isaiah and claims that the Spirit is upon him to proclaim the good news to the poor (Word-giver and lifegiver!), to give freedom to those in prison, and to restore sight to the blind (Luke 4:16-19). The Sermon on the Mount begins with the well-known beatitude "Blessed are you who are poor, for yours is the kingdom of God" (Luke 6:20), whereas the parable of the rich man and Lazarus inverts the order of material and social status in favor of the poor (Luke 16:19-31).

On this basis, Belhar can formulate in revelatory language: "We believe that God has revealed himself as the One who wishes to bring about justice and true peace" (art. 4.1). This is the same God who in Christ "for us all and for our salvation" came down from heaven (NC) to establish reconciliation, peace, and justice on earth (Belhar). Belhar gives a further concrete explication of the Incarnated One and, in a situation of structural injustice and of human oppression, confesses that Christ's ministry "for us all" became a ministry focused on the destitute, the poor, and the wronged, because in God there is no injustice. This is the apostolic faith of the ecumenical church today, says the WCC report. For people who suffer, the

---

53. Unlike in the NC, we find lists of scriptural references throughout Belhar. Here I follow the Lukan line of exploring Jesus' ministry, as suggested in Belhar article 4.

message is clear: "God's solidarity enables them to *struggle* against suffering and death in all its manifestations. In the particular case of human oppression, the victim is assured that God is never on the side of the oppressor, the bringer of death, but will, in his justice, protect the rights and lives of the victims" (par. 157).[54]

"We acknowledge one baptism for the forgiveness of sins"

If one remembers that the NC arose from the baptismal faith of the early church, the link between baptism and forgiveness of sins is a logical one.[55] Baptism was the sign of the forgiveness of sins through the blood of Christ and served as a sign of the individual's incorporation into the body of Christ.

In Belhar this meaning of baptism and sin is assumed and retained, but it is interpreted in the direction of the confession's own intention. In the article on the unity of the church, the reference to the one baptism from Ephesians 4 (art. 2.5) does not so much emphasize introduction into the church as a call to focus on the fact that those believers, now divided by human measures, "are baptised with the one baptism . . . and together fight against all which may threaten or hinder this unity." Baptism is the entrance into a new communion where human divisions of culture, class, and gender are transcended because we are all children of God (Gal. 3:26-29). We are one church in Christ, and we already share one baptism, therefore we cannot give up the precious visible unity of the people of God. In other words, Belhar — arising from a painfully divided church — is concerned about the "entrance" into visible unity, which is based on the already achieved "entrance" into the church, exactly because we confess *one baptism.*

The NC focuses on the forgiveness of sins (in the plural). This leaves the creed open for interpretation from both an individual and a communal perspective, as well as from the perspective of the ongoing forgiveness of sins through a reappropriation of baptism. This social dimension of sin as a singular expression of the negative power in the world is overtly present in Belhar.

Article 2.4 states that: "separation, enmity and hatred between people

---

54. See WCC, *Confessing the one faith* (1991), par. 120, 153-61, 277.

55. The use of *homologoumen* (we confess) and *prosdokoumen* (we await) in the last two articles of the NC is to indicate the qualitative difference with *pisteuomen* (we believe), which is reserved for the Trinity and for the church.

and groups *is sin* which Christ has already conquered." Article 3.2 refers to the belief that God "has conquered *the powers of sin and death,* and therefore also of irreconciliation and hatred, bitterness and enmity." These social-structural descriptions of sin (separation, hatred between people) are in both instances embedded in the confession that sin, in whatever form, has already been conquered by God in Christ (art. 2.4) and the Spirit (art. 3.2). The Scriptures are clear: we have been freed from the power of sin through baptism as a sign that we have been buried with Christ, but also resurrected with him who conquered all authorities and powers (Col. 2:6-15). This includes the irreconciliation enforced by law among peoples and groups "in a land which professes to be Christian" (art. 3.3).

It is interesting to note that the confession of one baptism has never featured strongly in the struggle for church reunification. The divisions at the table of the Lord in 1857 and again in Ottawa 1982 were dramatic and sad reminders of our enmity and divisions. Perhaps the NC and Belhar point us back toward our one baptism, the very basis of our unity in Christ, urging us forward to meet one another as reconciled, justified sinners at the Lord's Table.

"We look for the resurrection of the dead and the life of the age to come"

The NC ends with an encompassing eschatological vision that includes both the personal hope of resurrection and the cosmic hope of a new creation. Against Gnostic or Manichaean ideas of a purely spiritual future, the creed, on the basis of Christ's resurrection, attests to the future of believers as an all-inclusive personal future in God's presence. And from God's purpose to set all things in heaven and on earth under Christ (Eph. 1:10) springs the hope for all of creation to be transformed as God's kingdom reaches its fulfillment in a new heaven and a new earth (Isa. 65:17; Rev. 21). This hope, testifies the ecumenical church, finds expression in the church as a communion of hope,[56] and as "a sign of God's future for the renewal of humanity."[57]

Belhar, so deeply aware of the contingencies of history, is an equally strong eschatological confession. As already shown above, article 1 confesses God's work in the church since the beginning of the world and "to

56. See World Council of Churches, *A common account of hope,* sec. 5, "The church: A communion of hope."

57. World Council of Churches, *Confessing the one faith,* new revised version, par. 272.

the end." The doxology in article 5, with which Belhar ends, professes honor and glory "for ever and ever," opening history in the forward movement of the church, which is taken up in praise of God. These two eschatological confessions relate to history in its relativity, but both Belhar and the ecumenical explication of the NC also take history seriously in its concrete reality here and now. The interpretation of *Confessing the one faith* reads: "We are impelled by our hope *to work for a more humane and just world.* Our pursuit of justice and peace *within history* cannot bring about the kingdom, but our work is done in the trust that nothing of what we have done in expectation of the Holy City is in vain."[58]

Belhar expresses its hope in history in the clear tone of an already realized and realizable eschatology: "We believe . . . that the Church is witness both by word and by deed to the new heaven and the new earth in which righteousness dwells" (art. 3.1). Where the church lives in reconciliation and unity within itself and establishes such reconciliation with words and deeds outside of itself, as salt of the earth, the new heaven and new earth already become visible. In the language of article 4: If the Church follows Jesus in serving the destitute, the poor, and the wronged; and if it stands by people in any form of suffering and need; and if it, as the possession of God, stands where God stands, namely against injustice and with the wronged — there the righteousness of the new earth is already realized. This is exactly a sign of the coming age as confessed in the NC Creed.

Conclusion

This chapter has sought to establish whether a recent confession from Africa confesses the same apostolic faith as the one ecumenical church, universal in time and space. Reading from the twenty-first century, the preceding analysis is, I trust, vindication of the remarkable and enduring significance of a creed stemming from the fourth century after Christ. But it is equally a vindication of a confession from the late twentieth century from a place where few saw any reason for hope and joyful expectation. Nicea and Belhar therefore strengthen our faith as they testify to the ongoing revelation of our one God, who is to be worshipped and glorified forever and ever.

---

58. World Council of Churches, *Confessing the one faith,* par. 275 (first emphasis in the original).

Part 3

RECEPTION

Chapter 5

"A gift from heaven": The reception of the Belhar Confession in the period 1982-2007

Almost thirty years have passed since the DRMC accepted the Confession of Belhar in draft form in October 1982. What has happened to the confession in the meantime? How have other churches inside and outside of South Africa reacted to Belhar? What was the reaction of the DRC specifically? Why is it so difficult to accept a confession that originated elsewhere? Can one accept the content of a confession but not its status as a confession? These are some of the questions addressed in this chapter.

There were huge expectations from those of us who supported Belhar from the beginning. Here was an original African confession. Here the old tidings of the gospel were heard in a fresh language. Here the real issues of our country were addressed from tradition and Scripture. Here was a prophetic message that needed to be heard and was applicable far beyond our borders. Here the kairos and the truth were so evident. In a discussion of Kuyper's legacy (in association with that of Karl Barth), Russel Botman, a well-known church leader in the URCSA, aptly remarked: "Why this first

---

Chapters 5 and 6 are reworked and expanded versions of Piet J. Naudé, "'A gift from heaven' — the reception of the Belhar Confession in the period 1982-2000 and its ecumenical significance today," *Nederduitse Gereformeerde Teologiese Tydskrif* 44, nos. 3-4 (2003): 407-20. The phrase "a gift from heaven" is a translation of *een geschenk uit de hemel*, coined by Marc Loos on the acceptance of Belhar by the Verenigde Protestantse Kerk in België. It is the title of his introductory remarks to *De belijdenis van Belhar en haar betekenis voor ons* (Brussels: Verenigde Protestantse Kerk in België, 2001), p. 5.

Reformed confession conceived on the African soil received so little, if any, attention from Reformed churches internationally, and particularly among Kuyperian and Barthian scholars, remains a mystery."[1]

But we slowly learned that things in the church are never straightforward. Belhar, we saw, had to make its slow journey toward acceptance against many odds. These processes of reception required, and still require, much research and reflection. This chapter begins with a discussion of "reception" as it emerged from dialogues in the ecumenical movement. A short survey is then presented of the actual reception of Belhar over the last three decades, including the most recent events in the Reformed Church in America and the Presbyterian Church in the USA. This is followed by a discussion of why the DRC has, up to now, not accepted Belhar as a confession. This case study is important, not so much for the historical detail about complex and evolving relations in the DRC family, but because one is able to identify generic stumbling blocks in the way of reception that are no doubt applicable elsewhere as well. The partial reception in this case actually teaches us in a strange way quite a lot about reception as such.

What does "reception" actually mean?

One can distinguish at least three phases in the development of "reception" in the church, namely the canonical, the conciliar, and the modern ecumenical phases.

In the New Testament, "reception" is related to Greek words like *lambanein* and *dechesthai,* which are used to depict the "acceptance" of the gospel (Mark 4:20; Acts 2:41) or of Christ himself (John 1:11-12). Paul uses rabbinic terms to describe the "transmission" or "giving over" *(paradidonai* and *paralambanein)* of the Holy Communion tradition (see, e.g., 1 Cor. 11:23). The process of canon formation in the early church, where certain books were accepted as normative for faith, is an example of a complex reception process over a period of three centuries.[2]

---

1. See Russel H. Botman, "Is blood thicker than justice? The legacy of Abraham Kuyper for Southern Africa," in *Religion, pluralism, and public life: Abraham Kuyper's legacy for the twenty-first century,* ed. Luis E. Lugo, p. 347 (Grand Rapids: Eerdmans, 2000).

2. See Ulrich Kuhn, "Reception — an imperative and an opportunity," in *Ecumenical perspectives on the BEM,* ed. Max Thurian, p. 166 (Geneva: WCC, 1983); the discussions by Hartmurt Loewe, "Die Kirchen vor der Aufgabe der Rezeption von Ergebnissen ökume-

In the conciliar phase,[3] "reception" refers to the process whereby local or regional churches use synodical letters to make their decisions known to other churches. Once such decisions are accepted ("received"), the authentic ecumenical mark of the "sending" churches is established. The great councils between Nicea I (325) through Constantinople I (381), Ephesus (431), Chalcedon (451) up to Nicea II in 787 are called ecumenical because their decisions enjoyed authority and acceptance in the wider church. In the words of Catholic ecumenical theologian Anton Houtepen, the councils confirmed that a specific faith position was indeed universal (ecumenical) and diachronically in line with the apostolic faith: "Reception means the recognition of a *consensio antiquitatis et universitatis*."[4]

With the advent of the modern ecumenical movement, there has been a huge increase in bilateral and multilateral church dialogue, as well as numerous church-union discussions. Here we enter the third phase in the development of "reception," and the following description by William Rusch might assist us to understand the shift in meaning: "Ecumenical reception includes all phases and aspects of an ongoing process by which a church under the guidance of God's Spirit makes the results of a bilateral or a multilateral conversation a part of its faith and life because the results are seen to be in conformity with the teachings of Christ and of the apostolic community, that is, the gospel as witnessed to in Scripture."[5]

This definition was not designed to specifically cover the reception process of a confession, but we can nevertheless draw on some important aspects and lessons learned from ecumenical dialogue in general. Five dimensions of reception are highlighted in this description: (1) there is an emphasis on the *process-driven nature* of reception, which may proceed through many

---

nischer Gespräche und Verhandlungen," in *Vernunft des Glaubens. Wissenschaftliche Theologie und kirchliche Lehre*, FS Wolfhart Pannenberg, p. 639 (Göttingen: Vandenhoeck & Ruprecht, 1988); and Lukas Vischer, "The process of 'reception' in the ecumenical movement," *Mid-Stream* 23 (1984): 223.

3. For an excellent discussion of the notion of councils, see Herman Josef Sieben, *Die Konzilidee der alten Kirche* (Paderborn: Ferdinand Schöningh, 1979).

4. Anton Houtepen, "Reception, tradition, communion," in *Ecumenical perspectives*, ed. Max Thurian, p. 145 (Geneva: WCC, 1983).

5. See the discussion of this quotation in William Rusch, *Reception — an ecumenical opportunity* (Philadelphia: Fortress Press, 1988), p. 13. For an analysis of the technical meaning of "reception" as implied here, a discussion in relation to South Africa, and an elaborate bibliography covering the period up to 1998, see Piet J. Naudé and Dirk J. Smit, "'Reception' — ecumenical crisis or opportunity for South African churches?" *Scriptura* 73 (2000): 175-88.

phases before actual legal acceptance by another church; (2) reception has a *dialogical* characteristic, as it is a process arising from and within ongoing conversation between or among churches; (3) reception has a *pneumatological* characteristic as it proceeds under the guidance of the Holy Spirit; (4) reception has a *qualitative* characteristic because there is a requirement that what is "accepted" or "received" should become part of the receptor church's faith and life; and (5) the *critical* characteristic of reception arises from the task to judge whether what is received indeed conforms to the gospel and traditions and can therefore be accepted as the apostolic faith.

It might be useful to link "all phases and aspects of an ongoing process" to the well-known distinction between explication, recognition, and reception. A confession is drafted by one church and is then handed down to other churches. The first task of the receptor churches is to engage in a reading and explication of the confession and to formulate their specific views in their specific contexts. The ideal is a process of common explication, that is, a reading with others, including the sending church, so as to come to a better understanding of the confession. At some point, such explication leads to a situation where the receptor church can say: "This is indeed our faith too. This is indeed the apostolic faith of Scripture and the witness of the church through the ages. We are able to enter into a common recognition of the faith." If a church is able, by its own tradition, to accept new confessions, the third and final phase is a common confession, as formulated in the original or the adapted confession.

This last phase of "full reception" refers to Rusch's idea of making results of conversation "part of . . . faith and life" because the Holy Spirit convinces others that such a confession is "in conformity with the teachings of Christ and of the apostolic community." In the case of a confession, full reception would normally include a juridical act whereby the receptor church includes such a confession as part of its orders, accompanied by wider use in catechetical and liturgical settings, in order to make the confession part of its faith and life.

As we shall see below, "reception" of Belhar therefore does not mean only its formal acceptance as a further confession. Reception in many cases may be possible only in a weaker sense of explication and recognition. However, such explication and recognition are still very important aspects of the ongoing process through which Belhar finds its way into the wider ecumenical church. But the ecumenical church consists of many Christians for whom at this stage full reception of any text, especially in the form of a confessional text, is in principle impossible.

This includes the Roman Catholic Church, as well as the Orthodox family of churches, where only certain ecumenical councils would be accepted as normative. The authority to express the truth in contemporary times is limited to a specific view of the ministry in the church. The Lutheran churches view their particular confessions, stemming from the time of the Protestant Reformation (like the Augsburg Confession and Luther's Small Catechism), as adequate expressions of faith. While further truth-statements or ecumenical treaties, such as the Barmen Declaration, Leuenberg Agreement, and the Charta Oecumenica are supported by certain churches, the notion of confession is both temporally and ecclesially restricted by Lutherans and is thus not extended to any additional documents like Belhar.

Then there is the large group of nonconfessional churches such as the Methodists, Mennonites, the World Evangelical Fellowship, and African Independent Churches. Formal confessions as such are not part of the heritage of these churches. However, where such churches are part of the ecumenical movement, as represented by the WCC, they would not actively resist a common expression of faith, as is found in, for example, the creeds of the early church. Finally, one may refer to charismatic and Pentecostal church groupings that are not part of the ecumenical movement and who are in some cases explicitly anticreedal. They consider creeds or confessions as unnecessary restrictions on the free work of the Spirit and an unnecessary addition to our authoritative Scriptures.

The conclusion is a sobering one. Belhar's full reception in the sense of being a "common confession" is limited to churches of Reformed convictions. The act of confession, in the formal sense, is a unique feature of the Reformed family of churches, which makes up a relatively small, though significant, part of Christianity in the world. However, Belhar's reception at the first two levels of explication and recognition are wide open to the ecumenical church and need to be actively pursued. Let us now turn to the reception of Belhar in particular.

How was Belhar received in the period 1982-2007?

It is not possible to analyze how Belhar was received in all its different forms around the world. The examples listed here are representative of encouraging signs that Belhar is indeed taken seriously in various parts of the church. Some would argue that there has been a strange reluctance with regards to Belhar that is difficult to explain. The history of the church teaches us that confessions are rare and take quite a long time to move and be received beyond their own contexts. A serious explication of Belhar might have occurred in many settings of which I am not aware. What is at stake is not a mere "informal reading" but some kind of official process whereby the confession is taken seriously within church structures.

One example is the Reformierten Bund and Lippische Landeskirche, in collaboration with the Evangelisch-Reformierte Kirche, in Germany. They commenced a study and explication process in May 1998 in Detmold, Germany, and are particularly interested in the relationship between Barmen (1934) and Belhar, as well as the enduring significance of Belhar for their context today. This is still an ongoing process, the beginning of which is reflected in a publication by the Reformierten Bund, *Das Bekenntnis von Belhar und seine Bedeutung für die reformierten Kirche in Deutschland*.[6]

A second example is the Reformed Ecumenical Council (REC). At its meeting in Harare (1988), it was requested by the DRMC to accept Belhar as a confession. A process of reception, in the sense of official explication, followed among member churches. However, by the time of the next meeting, in Athens (1992), the DRMC had withdrawn from the REC, with the result that the reception process was stalled at the first level of explication.

Examples of *common confession* have, to my knowledge, so far been achieved in the following cases. After the draft confession was accepted at the Mission Church Synod of October 1982, the confession was distributed to every congregation in the DRMC to study and discuss, with a view to report back four years later. At the synod of 1986 the confession was formally adopted as the fourth confession of the DRMC, alongside the Reformation-era Belgic Confession, Heidelberg Catechism, and Canons of Dort. In the reunification process of the DRMC and the DRCA to form the URCSA in April 1994, Belhar was brought into the process by the DRMC and accepted as part of the confessional basis of the newly formed church. Technically, one can thus say that URCSA is the first church, apart from the original DRMC, to formally confess Belhar.

The second full reception of Belhar as a confession occurred outside

---

6. J. Niemöller, ed., *Das Bekenntnis von Belhar und seine Bedeutung für die reformierten Kirchen in Deutschland* (Detmold: Reformierte Bund, 1998). See the excellent contribution to this volume by Dirk J. Smit, "Das Bekenntnis von Belhar. Entstehung, Inhalt, Rezeption, Relevanz," pp. 17-33.

South Africa. The Verenigde Protestantse Kerk in België (VPKB), formed as a union of Protestant churches in Belgium in 1979, has had a partnership with the Belydende Kring, a group of pastors under the leadership of Allan Boesak, since 1988. They also had close ties with the URCSA since its formation in 1994. Through the process of explication and recognition, they finally adopted the Belhar Confession (translated into Dutch and French) at their synod at Pâturages in 1998, describing it as "a gift from heaven."

A third church to confess Belhar was the Reformed Church in America (RCA). Already at the General Synod of 2000, their Commission on Christian Unity was instructed "to commend the Belhar Confession to the church over the next decade for reflection, study, and a response as a means of deepening the RCA's commitment to dealing with racism and strengthening its ecumenical commitment to the Uniting Reformed Church of Southern Africa (URCSA) and other Reformed bodies."[7] After a careful explication and reflection with successive reports to the General Synods between 2002 and 2005, a congregational guide on Belhar, *Unity, reconciliation, and justice,* was introduced in 2006. The groundbreaking proposal to adopt the Belhar Confession provisionally, for two years, testing it in worship and teaching and discerning its theology, was overwhelmingly accepted at the General Synod in Pella, Iowa, in June 2007.[8] It is expected that Belhar will be endorsed as a confession of the RCA at its General Synod of 2010, confirming its message for the North American church.

An almost identical process is playing itself out in the Presbyterian Church in the USA (PCUSA). The Advocacy Committee for Racial Ethnic Concerns recommended to the 218th General Assembly (2008) that a committee be appointed to consider amending the confessional documents of the PCUSA to include Belhar in the *Book of Confessions* for that church. The report is expected in 2010. If such a recommendation is indeed made and accepted, Belhar would enjoy full reception in the PCUSA in 2010, or shortly thereafter. To inform congregants, *A study guide of the Belhar Con-*

7. *Minutes of the General Synod 2007,* p. 230.

8. I was indeed honored to join Russel H. Botman from the URCSA in making an appeal to the RCA synod for Belhar's full reception. Our appeal fell on the fertile ground of many years' preparatory work and earnest prayer to seek the will of God in this regard. See Russel H. Botman, "The confession of Belhar and our common future," and Piet J. Naudé, "For South Africa, North America, and the church worldwide," both appearing in *Perspectives: A Journal of Reformed Thought* 23, no. 5 (May 2008): 14-16 and 17-21.

fession and its accompanying letter was prepared by Eunice T. McGarrahan and published by the Office of Theology and Worship in 2008.[9]

The recognition of Belhar in the Dutch Reformed Church

The recognition of Belhar as confessing the same faith handed down in Scripture and tradition, but without full common confession, has occurred in the context of the DRC. In the light of the long church struggle and the preeminent role of the DRC in South Africa's history, it is worthwhile examining Belhar's reception in more detail. As indicated above, this case study highlights, in a generic fashion, the many stumbling blocks to a greater unity of Christ's body everywhere in the world.

At the time of completing this book, in 2008, the process of reunification within the DRC family was still continuing in strides of both hope and despair. The minute details of how church dialogue toward union developed are not our concern here. In short, one could say that Belhar's intention to bring about unity among the formerly divided churches in many cases led to the exact opposite!

The reunion between the former Mission Church ("colored") and the DRC in Africa ("black") to form the URCSA led to a schism and to high court cases that recognized the right of the DRCA to continue as a separate church. When the DRC accepted church reunification and open membership in 1986, a total of approximately 40,000 politically conservative white members broke away to form the Afrikaanse Protestantse Kerk (APK). At times, the URCSA made the common confession of Belhar a precondition for the continuation of talks, only to soften its stance later. As will be seen below, there has been a clear shift in the DRC from wary recognition to an agreement that Belhar be included as the confession of the reunited church, but on the understanding that not all congregants or ministers have to initially sign the confession. The URCSA finds this position untenable, because for them the idea of a voluntary confession is a contradiction in terms, and a "hierarchy" of confessions is an equally strange theological position. This is then countered by the question whether Belhar is greater than the unity it seeks, and whether a "compulsory confession" is not also

9. Available online at www.pcusa.org/theologyandworship/confession/belharstudyguide .pdf. See also recent developments regarding Belhar in the Christian Reformed Church in North America; see www.crcna.org/pages/osj_belhar.cfm.

a contradiction in terms. Outsiders can see that this is indeed a complex process, although it is one that we cannot give up. The process must continue for the sake of Christ, who gave his body that we may be one.

As a Christian who heard the gospel in the DRC, studied theology under its auspices, and still serves as an ordained pastor under its guidance, I have no intention of casting the DRC in a negative light. The DRC confessed its sin for the theological support for apartheid in no uncertain terms and, time and again since 1986, has expressed its desire for the reunification of the DRC family. The full acceptance of the Belhar Confession by the DRC is, in my view, required as an act of discipleship and as a witness to ourselves and the world. Common confession with our very own brothers and sisters, whose churches originally came forth from us by the grace of God through our mission work, has sadly not happened. Based on the "insider" analysis that follows, a common confession by the DRC itself will, humanly speaking, also not occur outside of the family reunification. Let us proceed in four theses to explain the difficult process of reception. It is hoped that others will learn from our struggle.

Thesis 1: The chances of a common confession are ruined if an intensified hermeneutic of suspicion is at work. The DRC took an official stance on Belhar only at its synod of 1990 via a report of its executive committee. This process and decision are analyzed in detail elsewhere,[10] and here I merely restate the fact that the DRC judged that "the Confession of Belhar is, taken by itself,[11] not in contradiction to the Three Formulae of Unity, and that it need not bring separation between the churches" (point 5 of decision, my translation). Although the DRC did not in fact declare in actual words that Belhar is testifying to the same apostolic faith or to "the gospel as witnessed to in Scripture,"[12] its decision, somewhat ambiguously, actually implies this. This recognition is weakened, but not destroyed, by the later reference that "certain expressions could have been formulated differently" and that its own document *Kerk en Samelewing* (Church and society)

---

10. See Johan Botha and Piet J. Naudé, *Op pad met Belhar. Goeie nuus vir gister, vandag en more* (Pretoria: Van Schaik, 1988), pp. 77-89; Piet J. Naudé, "Die Belharstryd in ekumeniese perspektief," *Nederduitse Gereformeerde Teologiese Tydskrif* 38, no. 3 (1997): 226-43.

11. The phrase "taken by itself" is significant. Positively, it means that the text of the confession is taken as speaking independently. Negatively, it means that the DRC had serious misgivings at that stage about the historical context from which the *status confessionis* and Belhar grew and that it tried to read the text in isolation from its origin.

12. Rusch, *Reception*, p. 31.

makes the biblical views on God's relationship to the poor and oppressed clearer *(suiwerder)* than in Belhar (point 8 of decision, my translation).

The logic behind the argument that the DRC implicitly recognized Belhar, in the technical sense, is as follows. The DRC, as a Reformed church, stands on the *quia* relation between confession and Scripture. If a new confession, despite some textual disagreements, is judged not to contradict the earlier confessions and they themselves are true to Scripture, the later confession must then also be in line with Scripture and therefore be expressing the true faith for our time. Although at that stage reluctantly (and for some unknowingly?), the DRC has thus recognized Belhar in the sense discussed above. The fact that the DRC is willing to enter the reunified church with Belhar as part of the confessional status of that church is a further confirmation of this recognition.

The ultimate power to change the confessional foundation of the DRC lies with the General Synod after a consultative process. None of the regional synods has so far made a positive recommendation in this regard. At the level of congregations the situation is more complex. Whereas some congregations and even circuits have fully endorsed Belhar (obviously without juridical status for the institutional church as such), others have rejected the confession not only as confession but also its content (and thereby accepting less than the implication of the General Synod of 1990). At least one can testify to the wide debate and explication of Belhar in many places all over the country and via *Die Kerkbode,* the official newspaper of the DRC.

The 1990 DRC Synod judged that the Belhar Confession is not in contradiction to the existing confessions and that it should not bring about a separation between the two churches, and it noted only one formulation problem.[13] What functioned more explicitly from the start was a perception by the DRC that the confession and its rejections were aimed at the DRC specifically. That the DRC saw it as an attack on itself is to be understood from the context of the time. White South Africa was under immense international pressure, and the DRC itself was ecumenically isolated. This led the DRC to miss a crucial element in the confession and the

---

13. It relates to the expression in article 4 that God, "in a world full of injustice and enmity," is "in a special way the God of the destitute, the poor and the wronged." This was not the real issue, as is evident from the URCSA's view that the confession is not cast in stone but open to reformulation and better insights from others and from Scripture. My interpretation is that a revised formulation at this stage — after almost thirty years — is unwarranted and only a remote possibility.

letter. The letter states clearly that Belhar is not directed against specific persons or a church or churches and that, in line with Belhar's universal intention, the DRMC that confesses it is itself also an "object" of the confession. The letter in fact warns against political misuse of the confession. In reality, however, the historical and political context played a normative hermeneutical role in the DRC's initial reactions.

This context explains the defensive stance on behalf of the DRC and its document *Kerk en Samelewing* in two of the nine subsections of the General Synod decision of 1990. What lies beneath this problem with the confessional status of the Belhar text? It was not the theological merits of the text but, rather, its origins that were found to be problematic.[14] In its November 1996 letter the DRC Commission wrote that, for those opposed to the confession, the link between the *status confessionis* and the involvement of persons with a political motive were stumbling blocks, as it provided a link between liberation theology and Belhar. Although not mentioned, it is well known that Allan Boesak's role in Ottawa as president of the WARC and as deputy chair of the DRMC synod at Belhar led to the popular belief among DRC members that Belhar was considered to be "Boesak's confession" and that it was a political attack on the DRC.

What occurred in this initial reaction was an intensification of a "hermeneutic of suspicion" as usually understood, namely, that all the readings of Scripture and even the production of the texts within the canon were decisively shaped by power residing in ideological biases.[15] The Belhar Confession (especially because of its specificity in confession and rejection) has been reconstructed by many ministers and laypeople in the DRC to be an expression of a specific political-ideological bias. A minister from Pretoria openly linked Belhar to the United Nations, Bishop Desmond Tutu's plea for sanctions, Communism, and AK-47 rifles, and this minister urged the church, which had been cleansed from these influences, to serve

---

14. Barth observes that there is very rarely a confession with an unproblematic history of origin — including, for example, Dort and Augsburg. He emphatically states that the test of Scripture remains the criterion for judging the authority of the confession. "There is no confession whose authority might not seem endangered by the history of its origination. But there is none whose authority might not have the testimony of the Holy Spirit in spite of that history" (*Church dogmatics,* I/2: *The revelation of God* [Edinburgh: T. & T. Clark, 1956], p. 639).

15. An oft-quoted example in South Africa is Itumeleng Mosala's work on the text as an ideological product: *Biblical hermeneutics and black theology in South Africa* (Grand Rapids: Eerdmans, 1989).

God's kingdom and not let it become a "bullying bag" for those practicing their ecumenical shots.[16] A former moderator wrote as late as April 1998: "I have serious problems with the request from various sources that we should study Belhar in its own right or 'on its own' after DRC members almost everywhere have already said that the 'historical origin' of the confession 'is for them a serious problem,' as well as the manner in which Belhar has been made a political tool."[17]

These examples show the deep suspicion in the DRC, making it impossible to read Belhar "op sigself genome" (taken by itself). The accusation that the confession reflects liberation theology cannot be taken seriously,[18] as Belhar nowhere uses the class struggle as a basis for its social analysis, nor does it confess the preferential option for the poor as advocated by Latin American liberation theologians from their specific context. The tag of liberation theology was a rhetorical device to discredit Belhar in the eyes of the DRC. It was the only so-called theological route open to express the inverted suspicion against Belhar from an ideological counterposition.

Thesis 2: Worship and liturgy have only a limited chance of contributing to common confession if worship itself becomes a theologically contested area. It is well known that liturgy can play an important role in any ecumenical or church unification process. Edmund Schlink has forcefully argued that "members of divided churches find it much easier to pray and witness together than to formulate common dogmatic statements."[19] The same issue has been addressed in a discussion about the notion of *lex orandi, lex credendi* (law of prayer, law of confession) in ecumenical theology,[20] later

---

16. This comment comes from a letter written by Rev. J. A. Greyling, published in *Die Kerkbode*, October 29, 1986, p. 15. The letter was published under the title "Where will Dr. Boesak lead the DRC?" (my translation).

17. *Die Kerkbode*, April 3, 1998, p. 7 (my translation).

18. This has been acknowledged by the DRC General Synodical Commission, but the power of perception proved too strong. See my analysis of the "liberation theology" issue in Botha and Naudé, *Op pad met Belhar*, pp. 86-88.

19. See Edmund Schlink, "Die Struktur der dogmatische Aussage als ökumenisches Problem," written in 1961 and included in his volume *Der kommende Christus und die kirchlichen Traditionen* (Göttingen: Vandenhoeck & Ruprecht, 1961; ET, 1967). See also his magnificent effort to construct a Lutheran ecumenical theology, *Ökumenische Dogmatik. Grundzüge* (Göttingen: Vandenhoeck & Ruprecht, 1983).

20. Geoffrey Wainwright, "Lex orandi, lex credendi," in *Dictionary of the ecumenical movement*, pp. 600-604 (Geneva: WCC, 1991).

appropriately extended to *lex convivendi* (law of life together) by Klaus-Peter Jorns (1998).[21] I have previously argued that any text brought into liturgy is hermeneutically "situated in an extended inter-textual situation" that may contribute significantly to its reception.[22] What has been the case with Belhar?

Although local churches have been asked by the DRC leadership to give "prayerful attention" to the confession, such attention has been limited to official church meetings. The path to experience Belhar in liturgy and life, even unofficially, has therefore been closed, except perhaps on the basis of initiatives by individual pastors. There are two deeper reasons for this, superseding the type of debate about liturgy, which one finds generally in the ecumenical movement.

First, at the Ottawa meeting, where the *status confessionis* was accepted, the DRMC delegation refused to share the Lord's Table with the DRC delegation. This was obviously a very painful experience for both parties, especially the DRC, who saw it as a deliberate act of humiliation. Worship, like the infamous 1867 decision to divide the table of the Lord along color lines, once again became a site of struggle for the truth.

Second, an extensive survey and very careful technical analysis of Afrikaans religious broadcasts (radio and TV) in 1987 by Bethel Müller,[23] who focuses on practical theology, led to the following conclusion: "The public worship of the Afrikaans religious programs of the SABC [South African Broadcast Corporation] was completely separated from church and society, from faith and morals, from doctrine and ethics. It was directed solely at 'religious individuals,' with inner-religious needs only. . . . Christianity, as far as the public media go, had been privatized."[24]

Although one should be careful not to draw a one-to-one correlation between public (i.e., broadcast) worship and ordinary worship, the ten-

21. Klaus-Peter Jorns, *Der Lebensbezug des Gottesdienst. Studien zu seinem kirchlichen und kulturellen Kontext* (Munich: Kaiser, 1998), pp. 12-22.

22. Piet J. Naudé, "Regaining our ritual coherence: The question of textuality and worship in ecumenical reception," *Journal of Ecumenical Studies* 35, no. 2 (1998): 247.

23. The final report to the Human Sciences Research Council was submitted in 1989 under the title '*n Ondersoek na tendense in Afrikaanse godsdienstige uitsendings van die SAUK en na die hermeneutiese en homiletiese beginsels wat ten grondslag daarvan lê* (An investigation of tendencies in Afrikaans religious broadcasts of the South African Broadcast Corporation and of the hermeneutical and homiletical principles underlying these tendencies).

24. Bethel A. Müller and Dirk J. Smit, "Public worship: A tale of two stories," in *The relevance of theology for the 1990s*, ed. Johan Mouton and Bernard Lategan, pp. 397-98 (Pretoria: Human Sciences Research Council, 1994).

dency is clear. Issues like unity, reconciliation, and justice, so explicitly addressed in Belhar in the period 1982-86, were directly in contrast to a worshipping trend among Afrikaans-speaking ministers (obviously not all from the DRC) analyzed in 1987. The year 1987 was part of a traumatic phase in South Africa's history. A state of emergency was in force, internal violence was escalating, the wars in Namibia and Angola with strong South African involvement were still raging, and international pressure was increased. "Yet, in public worship, in what South Africans see as the heart of the Christian church, not a single word is mentioned about any of these."[25]

The distance between a pietistic spirituality and the *status confessionis* underlying Belhar was just too much of a divide. The energizing spirit of *lex orandi* was quenched, and the route to common confession blocked.

Thesis 3: In a church-unification process where dialogue partners operate from contradictory social locations, the reception process is seriously impeded. There is so much in common among members of the DRC family: we share the same Reformed tradition, which came to Africa in 1652; we were one church for about 230 years until 1881, when the DRMC was formed; and until 1986 we held the same confessions. Yet the distance is so vast. The reason for this distance is the many faces of Reformed theology in South Africa and elsewhere.[26] These faces may, inter alia, be explained from the radically opposing social locations and subsequent theological foci and interpretation of reality between white and black people represented by the DRC and the URCSA.[27] This is of crucial importance and is clearly illustrated by the DRC decision on Belhar in 1990: "The General Synodical Commission understands that the Confession of Belhar was discussed and accepted with great sincerity by the DRMC's Synod *and that the content addresses issues that are of particular concern to the DRMC*" (my translation and emphasis).[28]

It can hardly be clearer than this. Confessions like Dort, which addresses Arminian heresies, and the Belgic Confession, which deals with Marcionism, Arianism, Epicureanism, and Pelagianism, are by implication

25. Müller and Smit, "Public worship," p. 399.

26. Dirk J. Smit, "Reformed theology in South Africa: A story of many stories," and Daniel L. Migliore, "Reformed theology in America," *Acta Theologica* 12, no. 1 (1992): 88-110 and 1-9.

27. The kind of North-South conflict in the ecumenical movement is here concentrated into two very closely tied, but still separate, churches.

28. See Botha and Naudé, *Op pad met Belhar,* p. 83.

closer to the heart of the DRC's faith than a contemporary expression in simple language about unity, reconciliation, and justice. The DRC at that point reveals a theological stance in contrast to the continued reformation of the church and a fundamental orientation toward European theology, specifically its antiliberal tradition, where debates "sounded more like the sixteenth — or rather seventeenth — century in Europe, than the twentieth century in Africa."[29]

But most of all — and this is the point made by sociologically inclined theories of interpretation — this reveals an inability to "see" the suffering and destruction of human lives in one's own country because the world is perceived from the upper side of history, or from a different class or social location.[30] Living in physically separate worlds in the same country led to separate social constructions of reality and ultimately to opposing theological judgments about that reality. This was true not only of the DRC, for it is a much broader phenomenon in South Africa and indeed all over the world. The words of the Truth and Reconciliation Commission in South Africa on faith communities ring loud and clear: "Many faith communities mirrored apartheid society, giving the lie to their profession of a loyalty that transcended social divisions."[31]

If a closed or determinist view of social structure is maintained,[32] the chance for an acceptance of the Belhar Confession by the DRC seems remote. By 1990 the very issues of unity, reconciliation, and justice were not perceived as urgent enough to warrant a confession. And urgency, kairos,

29. Smit, "Reformed theology," p. 97.

30. There is no room here to develop a full theory of status and class or to apply social-scientific theories to a contemporary "text," as is so fruitfully applied to the Old Testament (Norman Gottwald) or to New Testament studies; see Holger Szesnat, "The concept of 'class' and social-scientific interpretation of the New Testament," *Nederduitse Gereformeerde Teologiese Tydskrif* 38, nos. 1-2 (1997): 70-84, especially regarding his references to the widely read work of Wayne Meeks and Gerd Theissen — especially Meeks, *The first urban Christians: The social world of the apostle Paul* [New Haven: Yale University Press, 1983], and Theissen, *The social setting of Pauline Christianity: Essays on Corinth* [Edinburgh: T. & T. Clark, 1982] — and specifically the class analysis of ancient Greece by G. E. M. De Ste. Croix, *The class struggle in the ancient Greek world: From the archaic age to the Arab conquests* (Ithaca, N.Y.: Cornell University Press, 1989).

31. *Truth and Reconciliation Commission of South Africa Report*, vol. 4 (Cape Town: The Commission, 1998), p. 65, par. 29.

32. Such a view would be difficult to defend. Apart from the impossibility of an Archimedes point beyond all social classes, there is ample empirical evidence to the contrary (e.g., rich people taking up the cause of the poor) and a theological assumption that conversion is — by the grace of God — always possible.

and a clear "yes" or "no" are fundamental features of Reformed confessions. We saw earlier that Barth states: "Without the No the Yes would obviously not be a Yes."[33] But if, as in the case of the DRC, you cannot see the "no," the credo of the "yes" would remain silent.

Thesis 4: The reception of a confession will be very difficult in cases where dialogue partners understand themselves as ecumenically isolated "denominational" churches. The problem of the acceptance of Belhar does not lie primarily at the level of confessional differences, nor does it derive from major or minor disagreements over the content of its text. There is enough evidence to support what Lukas Vischer has observed in the broader ecumenical movement: "Frequently, confessional positions are not defended by a concern for the purity of their teaching. *The real motive is often simply preservation of one's identity* which has developed over the course of history. . . . These may be matters of language, ethnic identity, national pride, or other things."[34] If we accept with Hauerwas that a faith community is a story-formed community,[35] and with Ritschl that "story," with its implicit axioms, determines our identity,[36] a narrative analysis seems an appropriate method to uncover the identity of faith communities in particular and denominations in general.[37]

The question, then, is, What major factors formed the self-understanding of the DRC in the period around 1980? It is obviously a very complex question that can be properly addressed only by a multiplicity of interdisciplinary studies, including literary criticism, history, sociology, and economics. Chapter 1 addressed the theological formation of neo-

---

33. Barth, *Church dogmatics,* I/2, p. 630.

34. Vischer, "The process of 'reception,'" p. 232 (my emphasis). Although he offers a completely different perspective, Wesley Kort is quite cynical about what is called "Christian identity," as it is a social demand expressed with the need to categorize and be categorized in order to control. The declaration of a Christian identity is therefore not actually Christian pressure (see Wesley Kort, *Bound to differ: The dynamics of theological discourses* [University Park: Pennsylvania State University Press, 1992], pp. 135, 139).

35. Stanley Hauerwas, *A community of character: Toward a constructive Christian social ethic* (Notre Dame, Ind.: University of Notre Dame Press, 1981), p. 1.

36. Dietrich Ritschl and Hugh Jones, *"Story" als Rohmaterial der Theologie* (Munich: Kaiser, 1976); and Dietrich Ritschl, *Zur Logik der Theologie* (Munich: Kaiser, 1984), p. 45.

37. See Richard Niebuhr, *The social sources of denominationalism* (New York: Henry Holt, 1929). A well-known example of the narrative approach in the field of practical theology is that of James Hopewell, *Congregation: Stories and structures* (Worcester: SCM Press, 1987).

Calvinism within the DRC, in tandem with missiological and economic factors. But this picture is abstract and theoretical, and it is enlightening to draw a fuller picture from three South African studies on the self-understanding of the DRC. These studies were based on the concept of myth as a belief held in order to make sense of the world.

In his analysis of DRC sermons in the period 1960-80, Johann Cilliers found a decisive structure in the myth of the *volk* (people), where the over-riding urge for preservation is not only seen as a divine decree but is also intensified by a process of clear delineation between the insiders and the outsiders, the "us" and the "enemy."[38] In their discussion of apartheid as neurotic myth and dominant social source of church formation in South Africa, Adonis and Smit refer to mounting fear and an apocalyptic mind-set in the face of social change.[39] In his analysis of ten congregations from the DRC in the period up to 1990, Jurgens Hendricks notes that the pre-scriptive power of myths (determining a view of the world) results in an astonishing lack of historical consciousness of the context in which the congregations operate, and he notes that they hold a romantic view of the past.[40]

As a (partial) "snapshot" of the DRC, stemming from the period of the *status confessionis* and eventual Confession of Belhar, the conclusions of these studies from different angles nevertheless point in the same direction. For an ecumenically isolated church struggling to preserve its identity in a collapsing sociopolitical world that underpinned its dominant myths, the *status confessionis* and actual confession of Belhar served as counter-myths and counternarratives that could not be accommodated in the identity of the DRC at that stage.[41] In the light of our discussion above, this "narrative closure" by a denominational church is the basis for a definitive

38. J. H. Cilliers, "Die teologiese onderbou van die prediking," *Praktiese teologie in Suid-Afrika,* 1994, pp. 1-13.

39. H. C. Adonis and Dirk J. Smit, "Myth versus myth: Conflicting myths in South African religious discourse on violence," *Apologia,* 1991, pp. 21-38.

40. Jurgens H. Hendricks, ed., *Gemeentes vertel. Verandering in 'n Christelike geloofsgemeenskap* (Cape Town: Lux Verbi, 1992), p. 61. See discussion in Frederick J. Marais and Jurgens H. Hendricks, "What happens when congregations try to change their identity? Lessons from the stories of South African congregations," *Nederduitse Gereformeerde Teologiese Tydskrif* 37 (1996): 146-51.

41. The events since 1994 brought both the pain and the opportunity of a "myths vacuum." Much has changed in the social context since then, and much is changing in the DRC's self-understanding as a pluralistic church with many different faces as it becomes more open to active ecumenical participation.

"hermeneutical closure" that renders a common confession of Belhar extremely difficult.

The cumulative effect of these four factors — an intensified hermeneutic of suspicion, worship as a theologically contested site, radically opposing social locations, and a closed, denominational narrative identity — has led to the nonreception of Belhar as confession by the DRC.

It will require extraordinary leadership, great love and patience among the DRC family members, and the transforming work of the Holy Spirit to lead Southern Africa's Reformed churches into confessional union. For the sake of Christ and the world, we dare not give up on each other!

Conclusion

In this chapter we looked at both the theory of ecumenical reception and its practice in the DRC. Both theory and practice are needed for progress toward greater church unity. At times one needs to stand back so as to reflect on the church unification process, which takes up so much emotional and spiritual energy. This reflection should always lead us back to seek an ever greater common confession of our apostolic faith. Do we not confess Christ, whose own body was "divided" so that we may be one?

Chapter 6

The echoes of Belhar in the ecumenical church

We should no longer look upon other Christian communities as if they orbit around our church like before Copernicus, when planets were understood to orbit around the earth. We should rather acknowledge that we, together with other communities, circle like planets around Christ as the sun and receive light from him.

— Edmund Schlink, *Schriften zu Ökumene und Bekenntnis*[1]

Although the DRMC did not "plan" Belhar in the proper sense of the word, the spontaneous act of confessing could emerge only on the basis of, and in conversation with, earlier witnesses. We saw in chapter 2 that Belhar was embedded in many ecumenical witnesses of the time before 1980. In chapter 4 a close reading of Belhar in relation to the Nicene Creed established the theological consonance between the two texts and confirmed that Belhar indeed witnesses to the same apostolic faith held by the church through the ages. In chapter 5 the reception of Belhar in South Africa and beyond our borders was discussed. The complexity of the reception processes was highlighted, and a number of generic stumbling blocks were identified in the DRC case study. We saw that one must be realistic regarding expectations of a common confession, but also that explication and recognition were indeed possible for the greater part of the ecumenical church.

This chapter does not investigate Belhar's formal reception but, rather,

---

1. Edmund Schlink, *Schriften zu Ökumene und Bekenntnis*, vol. 2: *Ökumenische Dogmatik* (Göttingen: Vandenhoeck & Ruprecht, 2005; orig. pub., 1983), p. 696, my free translation.

examines how its main themes have been echoed in the broader ecumenical church, even if specific bodies (like the WCC) do not overtly refer to Belhar. With the exception of the Accra Confession, discussed at the end of this chapter, I do not argue for the actual influence of Belhar on ecumenical documents beyond 1986. Rather, I argue that Belhar is not a lone, isolated voice. Its message was and is relevant to the wider church, as is evident from the examples below.

In short, whereas earlier chapters attempted to read Belhar against preceding ecumenical efforts, we are here concerned with developments after Belhar. The simple question is: Can we discern the voice of Belhar in subsequent ecumenical endeavors? Are there echoes of Belhar in church statements around the world?

We turn our attention here to the three middle articles of unity, reconciliation, and justice and to how they are related to recent or current efforts in the ecumenical church to witness to the same faith confessed in Belhar. This serves to show how Belhar — like any true prophetic word — spoke for its time and locality, but also how it continues to speak beyond itself in both space and time.

Unity

For Belhar, the visible unity of the church is of utmost importance and forms the structural basis of the three middle articles, which should be read as implicating one another reciprocally. After confessing faith in the Trinity in the first article, Belhar follows the formulation of the Nicene and Apostles' Creeds at the beginning of article 2: "We believe in *one* holy, universal Christian Church, the communion of saints called from the entire human family," followed later in article 2.4 by "[We believe] that this unity must become visible *so that the world may believe*" (my emphases). This formulation is directly related to the bylaws of Faith and Order and the constitution of the WCC, which state that the churches are called to the goal of "visible unity in one faith and in one eucharistic fellowship, expressed in worship and common life in Christ, through witness and service to the world, and to advance towards that unity, *in order that the world may believe*" (my emphases; see John 17:21). The DRMC was itself born as a separate church from the DRC in 1881 and knows the pain of so-called spiritual unity without an outward visible form. This is the backdrop to the strong confessional "no!" expressed in the third rejection clause of article 2: "[Therefore, we reject any doctrine] which denies that a refusal earnestly to pursue this visible unity as a priceless gift is sin."

The modern ecumenical movement brought together Life and Work (which began in 1925) and Faith and Order (1927) to form the WCC (1948), which was in turn joined in 1961 and 1971 respectively by the International Missionary Council (founded in 1910) and the World Council of Christian Education. From the beginning, the movement was built on the assumption of the unity of the church "in one common faith and one eucharistic fellowship." After many efforts, the WCC today includes approximately 350 member churches all over the world. Despite this achievement of bringing churches into closer communion, Michael Kinnamon of the Christian Church (Disciples of Christ), a well-known figure in ecumenical circles, makes an interesting observation about "the narrowness of the ecumenical tent." As neither the Roman Catholic Church nor the fastest growing sectors of Christianity (African Independent and Pentecostal Churches) are part of the WCC, he states: "Within twenty-five years the member churches of the World Council of Churches will represent little more than ten percent of the followers of Christ. To put it bluntly, an ecumenical movement whose primary strength is in the churches of the European Reformation will be increasingly irrelevant — and hardly ecumenical!"[2] Even if Kinnamon is correct, I would argue for sustained efforts toward greater unity based on the christological reality that *we are one in Christ* and need to make this already existing reality visible (a point supported by Kinnamon on p. 36 of his article).

At least in some way the WCC does symbolize a form of organizational unity, though the ideal of true ecclesial (eucharistic) unity is still a long way off. Building trust and unity is a painfully slow and sensitive process, and to retain a vision for unity is not easy. No wonder some refer to a loss of this urge for unity and the entering of a postecumenical phase.[3] Others mention the view of African and Orthodox churches that the ecumenical movement is another variation of Western imperialism, and the feeling that "the churches had assembled [in Harare in 1998] because they were scheduled to do so, not because they were mutually committed . . . to making God's gift of unity visible for the sake of the world God loves."[4]

2. See Michael Kinnamon, "Tough times," *Mid-Stream* 38, no. 3 (July 1999): 38.

3. John W. de Gruchy, "Recovering ecumenical vision and commitment in a postecumenical era," *Journal of Theology for Southern Africa* 102 (1998): 1-12.

4. Kinnamon, "Tough times," pp. 39, 41.

It is not the purpose of this chapter to discuss or evaluate the present state of the WCC. The WCC attempted to do some introspection with a report entitled *Our Ecumenical Vision,* prepared for the Harare meeting. The ecumenical church is obviously much wider than the WCC, but it remains an important council, as it expresses a fellowship of churches on the way toward full koinonia. Some results have indeed been achieved with respect to unity. This emerged largely because of the two processes initiated and guided by the council. One is the unity "in one eucharistic fellowship," relating to the Baptism, Eucharist, and Ministry (BEM) process, and the other is the unity "in one common faith," which found expression in the common-confession project discussed in chapter 4 on the Nicene Creed.

The unity in "one eucharistic fellowship" started in 1982 and reached its fulfillment in 1990, when the member churches accepted the so-called BEM report and the accompanying liturgy.[5] Although stumbling blocks and disagreements on baptism, fellowship in the Eucharist, and the authority of ministries remain, and although new threats to these agreements constantly lurk below the surface, both the process itself and the outcome remain an ecumenical gift of the Spirit to the church in the latter half of the twentieth century. BEM is undoubtedly a testimony to a greater sense of unity among churches.

Belhar's own history and confession relate specifically to the sacramental issues in the BEM process. This is referred to a number of times in this book. The division at the table of the Lord twice emerged as a painful sign of sin and disunity. When converts from indigenous peoples were, in some instances, served the Lord's Supper separately, the Cape Synod of 1857 opened the possibility of sanctioning this practice, which in turn contributed in 1881 to the founding of a separate "Mission Church," the DRMC. In 1982, at the WARC meeting in Ottawa, the delegation of the then DRMC did not see a way open to share the table with those who were supporting doctrinal views that had just been declared a *status confessionis.* Although the division pertaining to Holy Communion in the DRC family is not at the same level as those among the mainline church traditions, it has served as both a painful sign of separation and, at many local occasions where joint communion has been possible, as a joyful sign of growing unity. Belhar does address the issue of table fellowship directly in its reference to 1 Corinthians 11 that we "eat of one bread and drink of one cup," as

5. See World Council of Churches, *Baptism, Eucharist, and Ministry, 1982-1990,* Faith and Order Paper 149 (Geneva: WCC, 1990).

well as testifies, in relation to Ephesians 4, that we "are baptised with one baptism" and "confess one Name" (art. 2.5).

The message is clear: we *are* one, as symbolized and made real by the holy sacraments, and should therefore reflect this fact in visible church unity. Belhar's (historically earlier) vision of visible unity in one baptismal and eucharistic fellowship is closely related to the vision emerging later from the BEM process, which remains a continual gift to and task for the church.

Reconciliation

Belhar's third article centers on reconciliation, which is witnessed to by the church in its own being and action: "We believe that God has entrusted to his Church the message of reconciliation in and through Jesus Christ; . . . that the Church is witness both by word and by deed to the new heaven and the new earth in which righteousness dwells" (art. 3.1); "that any teaching which . . . denies in advance the reconciling power of the gospel, must be considered ideology and false doctrine" (art. 3.4). That the task of reconciliation within and outside the church is an enduring one needs no extensive argumentation. To illustrate this, consider two ecumenical initiatives: the joint declaration on justification between Lutherans and Catholics (October 1999) and the declaration of a decade to overcome violence (December 1999).

Interecclesial reconciliation:
Joint Declaration on the Doctrine of Justification

The numerous efforts at two-way and multilateral consultations between churches of various traditions have become almost a hallmark of the modern ecumenical movement, both within and beyond the boundaries and auspices of the WCC. Since the mid-1960s reports on such consultations have been an ongoing project of Faith and Order, published at regular intervals in the *Ecumenical Review.*[6]

Of particular significance in recent years has been the *Joint Declara-*

---

6. See, for example, the following issues of the *Ecumenical Review:* October 1984, October 1986, April 1989, January 1992, January 1995, April 1997, and January 2000.

tion on the Doctrine of Justification, a consensus declaration signed by the Lutheran World Federation (LWF) and the Roman Catholic Church (RCC) on October 31, 1999, in Augsburg (a very appropriate date and place!).

I include this joint declaration under the rubric of reconciliation (and not church unity) because of the particular depth of ecclesial and political schism, stemming from the time of the Reformation, and the limitations of the declaration in establishing full communion. The schism between the Catholic and Lutheran churches led to the Smalcald War (1546-47) and later to the vicious Thirty Years' War (1618-48), which ended with the Peace of Westphalia. The strong condemnations by Lutherans of what they saw as Catholic heterodoxy, and the doctrinal condemnations by the RCC at the Council of Trent (1545-63), strengthened the theological rift between the churches, despite an evolving political peace. The issue of justification is the "chief article" of the Lutheran faith (Smalcald art. 2.1) and is a crucial part of Luther's Small Catechism and the Augsburg Confession.[7] This issue is obviously for Lutherans a nonnegotiable expression of the heart of the gospel, while both Lutherans and Catholics have grown in their understanding of each other's position since Vatican II.

The issue of justification was therefore included in official Lutheran-RCC dialogue from the start. Between 1972 and 1994 extensive study and bilateral consultations resulted in sufficient consensus on core issues relating to the doctrine of justification.[8] This includes very important matters like the biblical witnesses to justification, the nature of grace, the relationship between grace and justification, the surety of salvation, and good works. In short: "The present *Joint Declaration* has this intention: namely, to show that on the basis of their dialogue the subscribing Lutheran churches and the Roman Catholic Church are now able to articulate a common understanding of our justification by God's grace through faith in Christ" (Declaration, par. 5). The declaration ends with a prayer of thanks to the Lord for such a significant step in overcoming church division. "We give thanks to the Lord for this decisive step forward on the way

7. For the texts of these confessions, see the volume edited by Robert Kolb and Timothy J. Wengert, *The Book of Concord: The Confessions of the Evangelical Lutheran Church* (Minneapolis: Fortress Press, 2000): Augsburg Confession (pp. 27-105), Smalcald Articles (pp. 295-328), and the Small Catechism (pp. 345-75).

8. See extensive literature in the footnotes of the Declaration and its addenda. See *Joint Declaration on the Doctrine of Justification: The Lutheran World Federation and the Roman Catholic Church* (Grand Rapids: Eerdmans, 2000).

to overcoming the division of the church. We ask the Holy Spirit to lead us further toward that visible unity which is Christ's will" (par. 44).

This is but one example of significant interecclesial reconciliation, although the *Joint Declaration* points to the many differences that still remain (see section 5, and specifically par. 43).[9] When the *ecumene* is viewed in its entire breadth, the issue of interecclesial reconciliation — so forcefully witnessed to by Belhar — is a current reality, though it will reach its fullness only as an eschatological reality. To this reality we should commit our continued ecumenical energy, as amply demonstrated in this carefully crafted declaration.

Extraecclesial reconciliation: Decade to Overcome Violence, 2001-2010

Belhar is clear that the church, having been entrusted with the ministry of reconciliation, "is called to be the salt of the earth and the light of the world" (art. 3.1), and "God by his lifegiving Word and Spirit will enable his people to live in a new obedience which can open new possibilities of life for society and the world" (art. 3.2). Opening new possibilities of life for the world, where death, nonreconciliation, hatred, and bitterness hold sway, is the task of the church, which is "called blessed because it is a peacemaker" (art. 3.1).

The Eighth Assembly of the WCC, meeting in Harare in December 1998, decided to declare the Decade to Overcome Violence, 2001-2010: Churches Seeking Reconciliation and Peace.[10] Many factors inspired this decision:

9. For further critical reflection, see Gerhard Sauter's incisive article "Die Rechtfertigungslehre als theologische Dialogregel. Lehrentwicklung als Problemgeschichte?" *Ökumenische Rundschau* 48, no. 3 (1999): 275-95; and volume 38 of the *Journal for Ecumenical Studies* (2000/2001), with contributions representing a variety of confessional perspectives.

10. See Diane Kessler, ed., *Together on the Way: Official Report of the Eighth Assembly of the World Council of Churches* (Geneva: WCC Publications, 1999), for the council's decision. For further discussions, see Fernando Enns, "Impuls zur Gegenbewegung — eine Ökumenische Dekade. Das ÖRK Programm zur Überwindung von Gewalt vor und nach Harare," *Ökumenische Rundschau* 48, no. 2 (1999): 167-75; Enns, ed., *Dekade zur Überwindung von Gewalt, 2001-2010. Impulse* (Frankfurt: Otto Lembeck, 2001); Enns, "Elemente einer Kultur der gewaltfreiheit angesichts des globalisierten Terrorismus," in "Theologie und Gewalt," special issue, *epd-Dokumentation* 6 (February 2002): 5-12; as well as *Ökumenische Rundschau* 48, no. 2 (1999), devoted to this issue.

- The discussion in Harare built on the project Churches in Solidarity with Women (1988-98), which focused on overcoming the continued violence against women and children. This theme had to be taken further in a more encompassing sense of peace and reconciliation.
- The very innovative Peace to the City project (1997-98) included seven cities that were engaged in practical peace efforts. Much could be learned from the project, and new cities were added to the list.[11]
- One should also note the long peace-seeking tradition in the WCC itself,[12] illustrated, among other things, by the groundbreaking decision in the context of the conciliar process for Justice, Peace, and the Integrity of Creation (JPIC) in Dresden (1989). The option for violence-free action had to be seen as the core orientation in any context where peace is threatened.
- Finally, the United Nations declared the International Decade for a Culture of Peace and Non-Violence for the Children of the World, 2001-2010, which obviously allows for some convergence of themes and efforts.

At its meeting in September 1999, the Central Committee of the WCC accepted a framework document and formulated a message that echoes the very confessional phrase in Belhar, namely "that the churches are called to give a clear witness to the world of peace, reconciliation and non-violence grounded in justice."[13] The explicitly formulated aims of the "decade to overcome violence" included a specific call to churches to a "renewed confirmation of a spirituality of reconciliation and active non-violence."[14]

Although Belhar does not historically arise from the peace-church tradition, the confessing movement called for prayer and sanctions as nonviolent methods to end the unjust rule. Belhar's vision for the church as a reconciled and reconciling body is clearly aimed to overcome nonreconciliation and violence so as to "open new possibilities of life for society and

11. See Dafne Plou, *Peace to the cities: Creative models of building community amidst violence* (Geneva: WCC, 1998).

12. See Margot Kässmann, *Overcoming violence: The challenge to the church in all places* (Geneva: WCC, 1998), pp. 1-24; Konrad Raiser, "Gewalt überwinden. Ökumenische Reflexionen zu einer 'Kultur aktiver und lebensfreundlicher Gewaltfreiheit,'" in Enns, *Dekade*, pp. 11-30.

13. Charta Oecumenica, *Ökumenische Rundschau* 49, no. 4 (2000): 471, my translation.

14. Charta Oecumenica, pp. 474-75.

the world" (art. 3.2). In this sense, the theme of reconciliation that forms the axis of the Belhar text is echoed in the peace and reconciliation efforts of the broader ecumenical church.

Justice

Belhar makes clear pronouncements on the issue of justice: "We believe that God has revealed himself as the One who wishes to bring about justice and true peace among men" (art. 4.1), and that "the Church must witness against and strive against any form of injustice, so that justice may roll down like waters, and righteousness like an ever-flowing stream" (art. 4.2).

In Sjollema's judgment, one of the most successful campaigns launched by the WCC has been the Program to Combat Racism. This program ran from 1969 to the early 1990s, with a focus on racial justice and specific attention to the situation in South Africa at that time, though not restricted to South Africa.[15] Earlier, we saw the historical and theological links between many ecumenical efforts to witness for justice and the events that lead to the acceptance of a *status confessionis* and the formulation of Belhar in 1982. The issue of justice has in the meantime acquired a much wider meaning than only racism. This is evident from at least three further ecumenical initiatives. Let us note each of these very briefly.

Charta Oecumenica

The Conference of European Churches (CEC), consisting of most Ortho-dox, Reformed, Anglican, Free Church, and Old Catholic Churches in Europe and the Roman Catholic European Bishops' Conference, signed the Charta Oecumenica on April 22, 2001.[16] Its subtitle reads: "Guidelines for the growing cooperation amongst the churches in Europe"; the charter is clearly aimed at making these guidelines practical in a number of ways referred to below. Both the structure of the document itself and its significance for the issue of justice are relevant in this discussion. The structure

15. See Baldwin Sjollema, "Programme to Combat Racism," in *Dictionary of the ecumenical movement*, pp. 825-27 (Geneva: WCC, 1991).

16. For the text of the Charta Oecumenica, see *Ökumenische Rundschau* 50, no. 4 (2001): 504-14; or see www.cec-kek.org/content/charta.shtml.

shows remarkable correspondence to the Belhar Confession — almost as if Belhar's structure served as a guideline![17] The Charta moves from faith in the triune God to unity, reconciliation, and justice, in exactly that order, but obviously with different examples and not couched in confessional language.

Like Belhar, which commences with a declaration of faith in the triune God, the superscript of the Charta's introductory paragraph is "Glory be to the Father, and to the Son, and to the Holy Spirit." This takes the church's trinitarian faith as a point of reference and departure. The Charta then has three subdivisions; I include the relevant corresponding readings from Belhar in parentheses:

Part 1 deals with the unity of the church (Belhar art. 2) and starts with the Nicene Creed's formulation of faith in one, holy, catholic, and apostolic church (art. 2, first sentence), followed by a reference to the unity passage from Ephesians 4:3-6 (art. 2.4). It makes clear that unity is a gift that must be made visible (art. 2.2).

Part 2 of the Charta, which deals with the practical implications of this visible unity, includes a joint proclamation of the gospel, joint action, prayer, and continued dialogue — all with a view that the unity declared in part 1 be made visible in interecclesial reconciliation, in a willingness to confess to one another, and in a commitment to move toward one another (Charta, part 2, par. 3; see Belhar art. 3.1).

Part 3 then explains "our common responsibility in Europe" and remarkably coincides with Belhar articles 3 and 4. It starts with the beatitude reference that those who make peace will be called children of God (Matt. 5:9), exactly as Belhar confesses "that the Church is called blessed because it is a peacemaker" (art. 3.1). Much more is said in this section than was possible in the short confessional style of Belhar, but Belhar's focus on peace and its relation to justice for the poor (Belhar art. 4.1) is unambiguously present in paragraphs 7-12.

In paragraph 7 reference is made to East-West and North-South relationships, and it is stated: "At the same time we must avoid Eurocentricity and heighten Europe's sense of responsibility for the whole of humanity, particularly for the poor all over the world." Paragraph 8 makes it clear that social justice — especially the gap between rich and poor, and unemploy-

---

17. This makes the Charta suitable for discussion under any one of the three articles of Belhar. Here I will focus on the issue of justice, which means I will obviously lose some of the richer convergences between the two texts.

ment — belongs to reconciliation. Paragraph 9 speaks of global justice in the sense of caring for creation, whereas peaceful relations with other religions (Judaism, Islam, and new religious movements) are addressed in paragraphs 10-12.

In a yet another remarkable correspondence, the Charta closes (like it begins) with a trinitarian confession akin to what appears in Belhar articles 1 and 5. The last paragraph starts (like Belhar) with a confession of the lordship of Christ and his headship of the church. "In his Name we will go further on a joint road in Europe." And it closes with a prayer: "We pray to God for the help of His Holy Spirit." This completes the trinitarian structure, leaving no doubt that the voice and concerns of Belhar are heard in the same manner and on the very same issues, albeit in a different context.

The conciliar process of justice, peace, and the integrity of creation

One of the most encompassing ecumenical endeavors in recent decades has been the well-known Justice, Peace, and the Integrity of Creation (JPIC) program. Initiated at the Vancouver Assembly of the WCC in 1983, with the aim "to engage member churches in a conciliar process of mutual commitment (covenant) to justice, peace and the integrity of creation," the process expanded beyond the members of the WCC and included civil bodies that shared the same vision. At the world convocation on JPIC in Seoul (March 1990), ten convictions were affirmed, and the members entered into an act of covenanting on four practical issues: a just economic order, true security of all nations and a culture of nonviolence, a nurturing of creation, and finally the eradication of all forms of discrimination at all levels, including racism.[18] In this way, the issues of justice, peace, and the integrity of creation were treated as three aspects of one reality, each enriching and qualifying the other. Belhar's article 4 resonates in many of these formulations, which time and again confirm Belhar's theological direction. The following examples demonstrate this common focus.

The second affirmation of Seoul is "God's option for the poor" (a contentious issue in the reception of Belhar art. 4.1), and the third affirmation is "the equal value of all races and peoples" (see Belhar art. 3.3). Belhar's article on justice is particularly, though not exclusively, concerned with eco-

18. D. Preman Niles, "Justice, peace, and the integrity of creation," in *Dictionary of the ecumenical movement*, pp. 557-59 (Geneva: WCC, 1991).

nomic and social injustice. This is borne out by the many formulations in Belhar articles 4.1-3 and the biblical references to Deuteronomy, Amos, and Isaiah and specifically the Lukan tradition in the New Testament. The question of socioeconomic justice has itself brought forth the question of whether the structural injustices of the global economy are not a matter of confession *(processus confessionis)* for the ecumenical church.

Furthermore, it is also significant that "integrity of creation" is understood to refer to "the biblical vision of peace with justice," which includes ecological concerns. Belhar obviously does not explicitly address ecological concerns.[19] But its vision of encompassing peace and its interpretation of Jesus' ministry place the confession in the ambit of cosmological concerns. Neither in the Old Testament nor in Jesus' ministry is a dualistic worldview present where religion is understood as a separate life form over and against other realities.

"The unity of the church and the renewal of human community"

We consider here a third example of justice addressed in the context of the ecumenical church. The Faith and Order study project "The unity of the church and the renewal of human community" does not mention justice explicitly, so a short explanation is necessary. There has always been a tension and even conflict between the issues of Faith and Order, on the one hand (focusing on unity), and, on the other, Life and Work (focusing on witness). The WCC consequently took up the challenge to demonstrate the integration between these two concerns and, at its Lima meeting (1982), initiated a study program with the title as given here. The results of various consultations have been published as Faith and Order Paper 151, under the title *Church and world: The unity of the church and the renewal of human community.*[20]

---

19. A confession arises mostly from what it wishes to deny as a threat to the truth. It is obvious that Belhar was not directing its attention to, for example, the ecological impact of an apartheid doctrine. But it is also part of the ongoing hermeneutical task to explicate creeds and confessions in new contexts, so long as one honors the theological direction of the original. An excellent example is the wide interpretation of the Nicene Creed in *Confessing the one faith* to include, inter alia, matters of ecology and secularization. See chapters 7-9 below for a contemporary interpretation of Belhar.

20. World Council of Churches, *Church and world: The unity of the church and the renewal of human community,* Faith and Order Paper 151 (Geneva: WCC, 1990).

The theological structure of this document is of great significance for a discussion of Belhar. First, it confirms that ecclesiology is the theological and social locus through which the renewal of the human community can be achieved. The greater part of the report thus develops themes like the church as kingdom, as mystery, as sign, and as eschatological community. Second, only in this framework does the study address issues of social concern chosen as examples of how ecclesiology and social ethics go together, namely justice (chap. 4) and the community of men and women (chap. 5).

The detail is not my concern here. The way of argumentation is as follows: Like Belhar, which confesses that God brings about reconciliation and justice in the world through the redeemed social structure of his church as exemplified in the church's unity, this Faith and Order study[21] places the renewal of the human community in the context of the unity of the church. Just as Belhar first confesses unity (based on the trinitarian faith), the study report develops the concept of renewal on the basis of unity, thereby merging the "being" and the "action" of the church into an integrated whole.

The following excerpt is a beautiful example of how ecclesiology (indicated here by "mystery" and "sign") and the renewal of a community go together, and how the report echoes, using almost the exact words, some of the concerns expressed in Belhar's article 4 on justice in society:

> As *mystery,* the church participates in the powerlessness of God revealed in the life and suffering of Jesus Christ and is thus called to be in solidarity with all who are without power. As prophetic *sign*, the church participates in God's action to raise up the meek and lowly and is thus called to advocate a fair distribution of power, and the responsible exercise of power, within the life of the human community.[22]

The Accra Confession. Covenanting for justice in the economy and the earth

Our final example of how Belhar's voice continues to speak in the ecumenical church comes from the WARC. During its Twenty-fourth General Council, held in 2004 in Ghana, Africa, it adopted the Accra Confession (AC), a

21. See how a more recent WCC study, *The nature and purpose of the church*, Faith and Order Paper 181 (Geneva: WCC, 1998), also links the church as koinonia (pp. 24-33) to life in communion (pp. 34-55) and service in the world (pp. 56-58).

22. World Council of Churches, *Church and world*, pp. 47-48 (my emphasis).

more recent stance of faith with a special focus on justice. This confession was the final outcome of a long consultation process that followed the 1997 meeting, in Debrecen, Hungary, where churches were invited to enter a process of recognition, education, and confession *(processus confessionis)* on their way to covenant for justice in the economy and the earth.[23]

The AC itself, which is not the result of purely internal WARC initiatives, must be read in the context of the important focus emanating from the WCC Vancouver Assembly in 1983. This assembly urged member churches to engage "in a conciliar process of mutual commitment (covenant) to justice, peace and the integrity of creation," subsequently leading to the well-known JPIC studies and reflections.[24] The world convocation in Seoul (1990) made strong affirmations on JPIC, and the concrete issue of a just economic order, including liberation from the bondage of foreign debt, was firmly put on the agenda of the following WCC assemblies at Canberra (1991) and Harare.

Apart from its introduction (AC 1-4), the Accra Confession was developed in three sections: "Reading the Signs of the Times" (a form of contextual analysis in AC 5-14), "Confession of Faith in the Face of Economic Injustice and Ecological Destruction" (AC 15-36, with 17-35 normally seen as the actual core of the confession), and "Covenanting for Justice" (AC 37-42), which focuses on the commitment of the churches in the future. There are obviously formal similarities between Belhar and Accra. One is able to construct both documents as conveying a call to discern, confess, and act.

As one reads Belhar, and specifically the Accompanying Letter, a clear "discerning the signs of the times" is evident. In fact, the letter opens with such a contextual interpretation:

23. See World Alliance of Reformed Churches, *The Accra Confession: Covenanting for justice in the economy and the earth* (Geneva: WCC, 2004). The WARC itself is of the view that an assembly of churches cannot adopt a confession in the classic doctrinal sense of the word. That is the task, rather, of local and regional churches. By nevertheless calling the statement a confession, the assembly had in mind a "faith stance" that expresses the necessity and urgency of the situation (AC 15). If one takes the "covenanting" notion into account, one could also speak of a "common recommitment of faith" in the Old Testament sense of a covenant renewal between God and God's people.

24. See various contributions by D. Preman Niles, especially *Resisting the threats to life: Covenanting for justice, peace, and the integrity of creation* (Geneva: WCC, 1989), and his two edited volumes *Between the flood and the rainbow: Essays interpreting the conciliar process of mutual commitment (covenant) to justice, peace, and the integrity of creation* (Geneva: WCC, 1992) and *Justice, peace, and the integrity of creation: Documents from an ecumenical process of commitment* (Geneva: WCC, 1994).

We are deeply conscious that moments of such seriousness can arise in the life of the church that it may feel the need to confess its faith anew in the light of a specific situation. . . . In our judgment, the present church and political situation in our country, and particularly within the Dutch Reformed Church family, calls for such a decision.

Accra states its own background in the introductory four paragraphs and specifically mentions a visit delegates took to the slave dungeons near the city of Accra, which reminded the participants of "the horrors of repression and death" (par. 3). Then, from paragraph 5 onward, it engages in "reading the signs of the times," discerning that "the signs of the times have become more alarming and must be interpreted. . . . We live in a scandalous world that denies God's call to life for all" (par. 6, 7).

From such a discernment, or reading of the signs, follows the content of both the Belhar and Accra confessions. Belhar focuses on unity, reconciliation, and justice, whereas Accra is more sensitive, linking justice and ecological destruction, and clearly speaks from its specific interpretation of the global neoliberal capitalist system. Following the core confessional claims is the call to action expressed in obedience and commitment. Where Belhar confesses that "in obedience to Jesus Christ, . . . the Church is called to confess and to do all these things" (art. 5.1), Accra states: "By confessing our faith together, we covenant in obedience to God's will as an act of faithfulness in mutual solidarity and in accountable relationships" (par. 37).

The deeper relationship between Belhar and Accra lies in the similarities of faith claims — specifically with regard to justice. In fact, there are clear, direct influences from Belhar on the actual Accra formulations. After analyzing the devastating effect of "neoliberal economic globalization" (par. 16), as well as "absolute planned economies" (par. 19), on the poor and the earth, Accra confesses directly in line with Belhar: "We believe that God is a God of justice. In a world of corruption, exploitation, and greed, God is in a special way the God of the destitute, the poor, the exploited, the wronged, and the abused (Ps. 146:7-9). God calls for just relationships with all creation" (par. 24). Compare this wording with Belhar's formulation in article 4.1: "We believe that . . . in a world full of injustice and enmity He is in a special way the God of the destitute, the poor and the wronged."

The same call to take a stand is present in both confessions. Belhar confesses that the church follows God and "must therefore stand by people in any form of suffering and need" (art. 4.2). Accra says: "We believe that God calls us to stand with those who are victims of injustice. We know what the Lord requires of us: to do justice, love kindness, and walk in God's way (Micah 6:8)" (par. 26).

In Accra's rejection clauses — though directed much more toward specific global economic and ecological injustices — we hear similar echoes to Belhar's "rejection" in article 4. Listen to Belhar first: "Therefore, we reject any ideology which would legitimate forms of injustice and any doctrine which is unwilling to resist such an ideology in the name of the gospel." Compare now with Accra: "Therefore we reject any ideology or economic regime that puts profits before people, does not care for all creation, and privatizes those gifts of God meant for all. We reject any teaching which justifies those who support, or fail to resist, such an ideology in the name of the gospel" (par. 25).

A remarkably strong affirmation of the deep connections among the various articles of the Belhar Confession is formulated in Accra, paragraph 31, which follows directly on the confession of reconciliation in Christ: "Therefore we reject any attempt in the life of the church to separate justice and unity."

It is clear that Belhar's original confession of justice in the context of apartheid has been recontextualized by the AC to place justice in both a global and an ecological context. This is an excellent example of how the Spirit continues to lead the church in the truth of the gospel for each generation and for each place.

Conclusion

It is evident that the main confessional and ethical issues addressed in Belhar currently appear to be, and will remain, the most urgent items for the ecumenical church in the twenty-first century. In the last part of this book, we return to some specific applications of Belhar in our contemporary world. Belhar must take its rightful place among confessions from around the world as a legitimate "account of our hope." It must find its way into a possible ecumenical book of confessions foreseen by some in the WCC.[25] It must become the subject of discussion in the study commissions of Faith and Order, which will find in Belhar a richness, depth, and clarity with regard to the many burning issues facing the church today.

25. See Anton Houtepen, "Common confession," in *Dictionary of the ecumenical movement*, pp. 195-97 (Geneva: WCC, 1991).

"Belhar is a gift of God to our churches," said Willie Jonker, Reformed theologian from South Africa. "It is a gift from heaven," echoed our Belgian and American sisters and brothers from different contexts.

The time is ripe to receive this gift into the wider ecumenical church.

Part 4

CONTEMPORARY SIGNIFICANCE

Chapter 7

Unity in freedom

Since the Lord has bound the whole human race by a kind of unity,
the safety of all ought to be considered as intrusted to each.

— John Calvin, *Institutes*[1]

Belhar emanated from a specific historical situation. It spoke from and to the burning issues facing South Africa in the early 1980s. But Belhar also spoke, and continues to speak, beyond its original context. The mere fact that others in Africa, Germany, Belgium, and the United States acknowledge the confession as a message for their specific situation testifies to its global significance. The widespread echoes in the ecumenical church, as we saw in chapter 6, are examples of new interpretations of Belhar's core content for our own time.

Belhar belongs to the whole church. It is therefore our collective task to reinterpret and reappropriate the confession in order to demonstrate the enduring significance of its witness. Like any hermeneutical task, we must dare to go beyond the specific origins of Belhar and situate the text in different contexts, addressing new questions of importance in our day. As we all contribute to this lively conversation with Belhar, we will be surprised at the telling relevance of a thirty-year-old African text for us in the twenty-first century.

The last part of this book is devoted to a rereading of Belhar in the

1. John Calvin, *Institutes of the Christian religion* (Grand Rapids: Eerdmans, 1957), 2.8.39.

light of new questions facing us in a postliberation South Africa.[2] Our questions are not unique. The situation in South Africa is sometimes described as a microcosm of the world. References will therefore also be made to shared global concerns.

The middle articles of Belhar on unity, reconciliation, and justice will be the points of reference. As they testify in unison and should always be read together, the distinctions and subdivisions below are not absolute or "neat." There will also be constant references to the trinitarian foundation of Belhar (art. 1), as well as to the call to obedience in article 5. The ideas presented are not an exhaustive list, but merely examples of how Belhar could be reinterpreted in (South) Africa and beyond.

This chapter first sketches the African context in which a reinterpretation of Belhar is attempted. From this context, the core focus of rereading Belhar is derived. This focus, a restoration of humanity for marginalized people, is consequently spelled out in terms of unity in freedom (chap. 7), reconciliation with respect to gender relations and HIV/AIDS (chap. 8), as well as two forms of justice — restorative and economic justice (chap. 9).

Our African context

A large body of current paleoanthropological research suggests that Africa, and specifically Southern Africa, is the cradle of both hominid evolution and the origin of *Homo sapiens* before they migrated to other parts of the world. The evidence, emerging from the famous Sterkfontein world heritage site, north of Pretoria, as well as the recent findings in sea caves in the Southern Cape, suggest that Africa is probably our common homeland, the geographic matrix of the human species.[3]

The fact that humanity evolved from Africa did not preclude a history of successive "inhumanities" undertaken against Africa and the increasing marginalization of Africans over the last few centuries. During the Atlantic

2. A substantially shorter version of some of the topics discussed below in chapters 7-9 appeared in Piet J. Naudé, "It is your duty to be human: Anthropological questions in a post-liberation South Africa," *Criterion: A Publication of the University of Chicago Divinity School,* Spring/Summer 2008, pp. 6-21.

3. For a detailed discussion of the "out of Africa" hypotheses and other views, see Wentzel van Huyssteen, *Unique in the world? Human uniqueness in science and theology* (Grand Rapids: Eerdmans, 2006), pp. 60-67.

slave trade,[4] over the period 1440-1870 between 10 and 13 million able-bodied persons were exported from Africa.[5] They played an indispensable role in the economic and cultural development of Europe and the Americas.[6] The rapid agricultural progress in these regions would have been very difficult — if not impossible — without enslaved African human capital. The slave trade had devastating demographic and social effects on specifically West African societies that were built primarily on kinship and patriarchy.

The abolition of the slave trade eventually led to a markedly different economic and political relationship between Africa and Europe. New technology meant that Europe no longer needed to control human capital but, rather, needed economic and political control over actual African territories. Territorial colonization was in part prompted by the need to secure trade in goods like gold, ivory, timber, and palm oil, and it was also the result of competitive intra-European rivalries during the period 1870-1945.[7]

Trade in precolonial times was essentially codetermined by Africans and their European counterparts, where Africans (although mostly rulers and the trading elite) had a direct influence on events. With the advent of colonial times, asymmetrical power relations played themselves out on the African continent. Commenting on the nineteenth century, Fage observed: "In any clash between European and African interests or beliefs, Europe now possessed both the material means — steam power, firepower, medical power — to impose its will upon Africa, and the moral strength — the

4. See the informative works by Hugh Thomas, *The slave trade: The history of the Atlantic slave trade, 1440-1870* (London: Macmillan, 1997); and John Thornton, *Africa and Africans in the making of the Atlantic world, 1400-1800* (Cambridge: Cambridge University Press, 1998).

5. See the estimated statistics of the slave trade as cited by Thomas, *The slave trade*, pp. 805-6, in terms of carrier countries (Portugal 4.6 million, Britain 2.6 million), destinations (Brazil 4 million), origins (Congo/Angola 3 million), and type of labor (sugar plantations 5 million).

6. See Thornton, *Africa and Africans*, for his very interesting chapters (5-9) concerning the effect of slaves on the cultures of the so-called New World and how reciprocal transformations occurred.

7. See J. D. Fage, *A history of Africa* (London: Unwin Hyman, 1988). He commences his study with early African societies (part 1) and the impact of Islam (part 2), and — important for this chapter — he discusses European expansion and colonial power in parts 3 and 4. The well-known book by Thomas Pakenham, *The scramble for Africa, 1876-1912* (London: Abacus, 1991), focuses more closely on the colonial period and actual territorial invasion of Africa between 1870 and 1906. Pakenham discusses each region in detail, making clear how complex the process of colonization was.

certainty that European civilization would prevail, and also that it was in the interest of the African peoples to do so."[8]

The proverbial "scramble for Africa"[9] was driven by a powerful combination of economic and political forces and was based on the emerging assumption that European civilization was superior to Africa's and that the latter needed developing toward a societal model based upon European religion and values.[10] Starting in West Africa and spreading over into South, East, and North Africa, the major European countries increased their administrative, economic, and eventually military-political control over Africa. What started at the Berlin Conference of November 1884–February 1885 led to a situation where most of Africa came under foreign control[11] and lost the ability to compete equally in the commercial exploitation of its own natural resources.[12]

The rapid decolonization of Africa started in the late 1940s and occurred, inter alia, because of the rising tide of nationalist liberation movements, political instability, and the acceptance of the Universal Declaration of Human Rights by the members of the newly established United Nations. Postcolonial Africa was ill prepared by its colonial and cultural histories to accept responsibilities for its own affairs. A number of factors contributed to the somber picture of Africa after independence.

Colonial powers neglected to invest in general education or training in political-administrative rule of their African subjects; power transitions

8. Fage, *A history of Africa*, pp. 333 and 352.

9. As indicated above, *The scramble for Africa* is the title of the magnificent account of African colonization by Thomas Pakenham (1991), but the term itself has its origins probably as early as 1884.

10. The link between Christian mission and colonial power is an ambiguous one. Pakenham states unequivocally that the scramble for Africa was led by "the empire-building alliance of God and Mammon" and introduced as "Christianity, commerce, and civilization" by British explorer David Livingstone (Pakenham, *Scramble for Africa*, p. 673). For us in Africa, there is a fourth *c*: conquest.

11. Fage remarked that "Europe and the world had accepted by 1902 that the whole of Africa was the property of one or other of the European colonial powers" (*A history of Africa*, p. 391). See his map of Africa on p. 402.

12. Much has been written about colonization, with its ravaging effect on natural resources and even more vicious effects on human communities and identity. For African and African-American perspectives, see Wole Soyinka, *The Blackman and the veil: A century on; and, Beyond the Berlin Wall* (Accra: SEDCO: W. E. B. du Bois Memorial Centre for Pan-African Culture, 1993); and Cornell West, *Prophesy deliverance! An Afro-American revolutionary Christianity* (Philadelphia: Westminster, 1982), especially pp. 47-68 on the genealogy of modern racism.

were poorly managed; new rulers devised economic policies that could not be sustained and that led to indebtedness; dictatorships emerged because of weak civil societal structures, and corruption and misrule became widespread; tribal wars escalated and in some cases led to genocide; and multiparty democracies were not sustainable because of inadequate levels of preparation for governments of this nature.

There is simply no way we as Africans can escape the failures of leadership in many parts of postcolonial Africa, which have contributed to a general Afro-pessimism. The African Union Commission does mention slavery and imperialism, noting that we should not forget, but "we must learn to put things behind us" and focus on Africa's own responsibilities.[13] The self-judgment is fierce and candid: "Distrust for constituted authority, corruption and impunity coupled with human rights abuses have kept Africa in a situation of conflict, thereby undermining all initiatives towards sustainable development."[14] Coupled with this is the deep and enduring sociopsychological impact of a colonized self-perception and a mind-set that leads to cultural diffidence and a notion that "foreign" must be "better."

The intense processes of economic and cultural globalization coincided roughly with the period when Africa entered its postcolonial period. The current global monetary system developed through three successive stages: the gold standard (formalized in 1878), the Bretton Woods System (BWS, 1944), and the current integrated digital capital markets.[15] A common element in all three monetary systems is that they created and sustained a fundamental differentiation between "center" and "periphery."

The gold standard was managed by the Bank of England in London; the BWS was dependent on dollar policies in Washington; and the current emerging financial system is determined by the triad of New York, London, and Tokyo. The poorer countries of today were for the most part still colonized when these monetary systems took shape, and they played only a marginal role in their origin and current direction. The consequence is that a hierarchical, uneven, and asymmetrical system has emerged,[16] with

13. African Union Commission, *Strategic Plan of the African Union Commission*, 3 vols. (Addis Ababa: AUC, 2004), 1:7.

14. African Union Commission, *Strategic Plan*, 1:14.

15. For a detailed historical account of an evolving monetary system, see Peter Isard, *Globalization and the international financial system* (Cambridge: Cambridge University Press, 2005).

16. David Held, Anthony McGrew, David Goldblatt, and Jonathan Perraton, *Global*

clear democratic deficits in decision-making power and with trade agreements that make the poorest countries worse off.[17] The recent failure of the so-called Doha Development Round of trade negotiations reinforced the deep economic rift between rich and poor countries, thus calling for serious reflection on justice in the world.

The cradle of humanity has been subject to slavery, colonialism, political misrule, and globalization. A common thread in these histories is the deadly combination of dehumanization and marginalization. Wole Soyinka speaks about the violation of dignity in Africa in terms of antihumanism, reduction in self-esteem, humiliation, and "the nullification of human status."[18] Any theology that is sensitive to this history, to contemporary Africa, and to the present global situation must ask questions such as the following. First, how are we to understand the human person, and how can we live together in one human community marked by freedom, amid diversity and difference?[19] This is the core of Belhar's second article, discussed in this chapter. Second, how are we to establish reconciliation that can stem our natural inclination to socially marginalize those who are weak — like women in a patriarchal culture, and people living with HIV and AIDS in a society where youth, health, and the Olympic ideal hold sway?[20] This relates to Belhar's third article and is discussed in chapter 8. Third, how can restorative justice assist us to deal with our divided pasts? How can the world become economically more just, and how can Christian theology contribute to an alternative value-system in place of rampant individualism and crass materialism? This may be related to the theme of Belhar's fourth article and is discussed in chapter 9.[21]

---

transformations: Politics, economics, and culture (Stanford, Calif.: Stanford University Press, 1999), pp. 213, 224.

17. Joseph E. Stiglitz, *Making globalization work* (New York: W. W. Norton, 2006), p. 58.

18. Wole Soyinka, *Climate of fear* (London: Profile Books, 2004), pp. xiii, 6, and 104.

19. The core question in our context is not so much about *human uniqueness* — eloquently addressed by Van Huyssteen in *Unique in the world?* — but rather *human dignity*.

20. As this book was being completed, a new intense debate started about the position of gay people in the church in relation to the message of Belhar. A report to the General Synod of the URCSA (October 2008) recommended the full participation of gay Christians in all ministries of the church. The report claims that the recommendations are based on Scripture and the core message of Belhar. The very fact that this debate is being conducted in the URCSA is significant, for the church that first issued the confession is clearly struggling to reappropriate its content with regard to new issues.

21. There is a remarkable similarity between the theme of humanization raised here and the collection of essays brought together by Clint le Bruyns and Gotlind Ulshöfer in *The*

Toward a Christian rehumanization?

These questions about a restored humanity were recently raised by both South African theologian John de Gruchy[22] and Chicago ethicist William Schweiker[23] in their respective efforts to argue for the notion of Christian or theological humanism. These are important initiatives as they attempt to reestablish the ties between the Christian faith and the impulses behind modern humanism that grew from the European Renaissance. One can also refer to the different models of theological anthropology that take differentiation seriously, as for example outlined by Dwight Hopkins.[24]

Building on the Reformed tradition and the core insights and limitations of the Belhar text, a "new humanity" (art. 2.5) will affirm, defend, and promote human dignity and associated Enlightenment values like justice, freedom, and equality. This may become part of a larger Christian humanist project. Belhar does not speak about interreligious dialogue. Some may even construe Belhar as an expression of religious particularism, while we now urgently need interreligious agreements on peace and ecology. It is imperative for the twenty-first century that the notion of a common humanity includes other religions, as well as secular humanists, bound together by common concerns for promoting human dignity and opposing religious and secular fundamentalism.

However, the contribution of the Christian faith to address concerns of our common humanity and common future lies exactly in its motiva-

---

humanization of globalization: South African and German perspectives (Frankfurt: Haag & Herchen, 2008). There are contributions on the humanization of globalization, human dignity in relation to the global economy, gender justice, and a discussion on humanizing the world of work, education, and leisure.

22. John W. de Gruchy, "Christian humanism: Reclaiming a tradition, affirming an identity," *Reflections: Centre of Theological Inquiry* 8 (Spring 2006): 38-65.

23. See three articles by William Schweiker: "Humanity before God: Theological humanism from a Christian perspective," The Martin Marty Center for the Advanced Study of Religion: The Religion and Culture Web Forum, October 2003, http://divinity.uchicago.edu/martycenter/publications/webforum/102003/commentary.shtml; "We are not on our own: On the possibility of a new Christian humanism," in *Loving God with our minds: The pastor as theologian*, ed. Michael Welker and Cynthia A. Jarvis, pp. 31-49 (Grand Rapids: Eerdmans, 2004); and "Distinctive love: Gratitude for life and theological humanism," in *Humanity before God: Contemporary faces of Jewish, Christian, and Islamic ethics*, ed. William Schweiker, Michael A. Johnson, and Kevin Jung, pp. 91-117 (Minneapolis: Fortress Press, 2006).

24. Dwight N. Hopkins, *Being human: Race, culture, and religion* (Minneapolis: Fortress Press, 2005), pp. 13-52.

tion from the distinctive Christian canon and church tradition. Belhar does not address anthropological questions in a philosophical sense on their own. (This is discussed in more detail in chap. 2.) In the Reformed tradition and in Belhar, human beings are always intrinsically related to theology (with emphasis on Christ, the Second Person of the Trinity) and ecclesiology, that is, humans called by God into a new community.

Calvin states in the opening paragraphs of his *Institutes* that knowledge of self *(cognitio hominis)* is reciprocally rooted in the knowledge of God *(cognitio Dei)*. That knowledge has been implanted in the minds of human persons; it shines forth in the universe; and it is witnessed to in Scripture. Because of sin, however, this knowledge of God and self is only possible in Christ, who as our Redeemer reveals God to us.[25]

In Calvin's view, however, there is a deep unity between being in Christ and serving our neighbor, between our pious fear of God and the practice of justice and mercy, between "confession" and "ethics." In Christ we are no longer our own, because we are known by God and belong to him; we are called to lives of self-denial, searching for justice in our relations with others.

"Our whole life," he writes in his exposition of the law, "must be spent in the cultivation of righteousness. . . . The only legitimate service to [God] is the practice of justice, purity, and holiness. . . . Our Lord means, that in the Law the observance of justice and equity towards men is prescribed as the means which we are to employ in testifying a pious fear of God, if we truly possess it." Since Calvin accepted that "the Lord has bound the whole human race by a kind of unity, the safety of all ought to be considered as intrusted to each."[26] As a refugee pastor among refugees, Calvin understood the importance of rehumanization of those who suffer on the margins of society.

Barth makes clear that it is a caricature of Reformed theology to teach that God is everything and man is nothing. No, "God alone is God but God is not alone. God alone possesses divine glory, but alongside his glory there exists a glory which belongs to the world and to man." The meeting point of

---

25. Calvin, *Institutes*, 1.3, 1.5, 1.6, 2.9.

26. Calvin, *Institutes*, 2.8.2, 2.8.53, and 2.8.39. These quotations are drawn from Calvin's exposition of the Ten Commandments. In light of 2009 as Calvin's five hundredth birthday, we can yet again appropriate the immense importance of Calvin for our present understanding of human, political, and economic rights. I draw here on the instructive article and comprehensive bibliography by Dirk J. Smit, "Views on Calvin's ethics: Reading Calvin in the South African context," *Reformed World* 57, no. 4 (2007): 306-44.

God and man is in God's revelation in Jesus Christ. "The revelation of God in the man Jesus Christ is what alone distinguishes man."[27] God can be understood only in "God's togetherness with humanity" as revealed in Christ.[28]

In Christ, the Word made flesh, we come to know both God and ourselves. Therefore, there is a constitutive link between human questions and the human being, Jesus of Nazareth. *Imitatio Christi* is deeply embedded in the Christian tradition. It requires that we live "according to the mode of the Son," but obviously "in ways appropriate to our own circumstances."[29]

Those who are in Christ are called into the community of believers. The church as communal embodiment of faith consequently plays an essential role in our reflections on what it means to be human and what kind of community we should strive for.[30] Following Bonhoeffer, it is wise to maintain a close interrelationship between Christ, church, and ethics. The link between *Christ,* who lived for others; *the church,* as a "new humanity" that expresses its redeemed nature in being "with-each-other" *(miteinander);* and *ethics,* the being "for-each-other" *(füreinander)* and representative action on behalf of others *(Stellvertretung),* is the core structure of Bonhoeffer's theology.[31] This theology served us well in our own struggle for justice in South Africa and is still worth pursuing as all of us face new questions today. In summary, a Christian humanism is defended where one speaks about human persons and human community in relation to Jesus Christ, the church,[32] and concrete action for the restoration of human dignity.

This is the structure of the Belhar Confession as well. Faith in the triune God, with specific focus on Christ's reconciling work, is the origin and hope for the church (art. 1). This church, itself called a new humanity, is

27. Karl Barth, *The knowledge of God and the service of God* (London: Hodder & Stoughton, 1938), pp. 35, 40.

28. Karl Barth, *The humanity of God* (London: Collins, 1960), p. 44. See how Barth here (in 1956) defends his new emphasis on the humanity of God, in contrast to his earlier focus on God's deity (around 1920).

29. Kathryn Tanner, *Jesus, humanity, and the Trinity: A brief systematic theology* (Minneapolis: Fortress Press, 2001), pp. 68, 74.

30. For the link between anthropology and church, see Christoph Schwöbel and Colin E. Gunton, eds., *Persons, divine and human: King's College essays in theological anthropology* (Edinburgh: T. & T. Clark, 1991), pp. 158-65.

31. Dietrich Bonhoeffer, *Sanctorum communio: A theological study of the sociology of the church* (Minneapolis: Fortress Press, 1998), p. 178.

32. Obviously "the church" can refer to the institutional (denominational) church, the ecumenical church, a local faith community, or believers pursuing their vocation in the world. These different meanings will be apparent for each context below.

called to strive for unity in freedom (art. 2). The church has been entrusted to realize reconciliation by both word and deed (art. 3) and must imitate God in practice by establishing justice (art. 4). The church is called to obedient discipleship and concrete ethics (art. 5) in order to reestablish human dignity and to work tirelessly for "individual and collective renewal and a changed way of life" (Accompanying Letter, par. 4).

Unity in freedom

The logic of apartheid theology, as outlined in chapter 2, was that differences of race and culture were in fact God's way of establishing pluralistic forms in nature and society. According to this theology, differentiation is God's creative will, and the separation of people into different churches and separate political systems is the best way to express love and unity. Unity among Christians is therefore only spiritual, and unity among people of different races will always be unity-in-separation.

The struggle against such a theology had to deal with the relationship between revelation, culture, and unity. Belhar's second article stated explicitly that the unity among the people of God, which was both a gift and an obligation, "must become visible" (2.4) and must be manifested in a variety of practical ways. Then follows a remarkable statement (drawn from Moltmann), namely, that "this unity can be established only in freedom and not under constraint" (2.6). The differences in backgrounds, language, and culture are no longer a basis for separation but "are by virtue of the reconciliation in Christ, opportunities for mutual service and enrichment within the one visible people of God" (2.6). How are these words heard in a democratic South Africa? How do we now construct the relationship between church and culture? How do we now deal with unity in freedom and the reconstruction of identity?

In a recent article, Dwight Hopkins argues strongly for conceptual clarity on the notion of culture, which, with "race" and "self," had previously been considered as constituting theological anthropology. Although he focuses on the variety of black theologies, one could accept "the reality of culture, the centrality of culture and the necessity of culture being a location for revelation" in a more general sense.[33] In this re-

---

33. Dwight N. Hopkins, "Black theology: The notion of culture revisited," *Journal of Theology for Southern Africa* 123 (November 2005): 74-83 (74). Hopkins draws on Randwedzi Nengwekhulu for a three-part description of culture in terms of labor, spirit, and art.

gard, Tinyiko Maluleke made the following incisive observation shortly after South Africa's democratic elections in 1994:

> Issues of culture are again acquiring a new form of prominence in various spheres of South African society. It is as if we can, at last, speak truly and honestly, about our culture. This is due to the widespread feeling that now, more than at any other time, we can be subjects of our own cultural destiny. . . . The reconstruction of structures and physical development alone will not quench our cultural and spiritual thirst. On the contrary, the heavy emphasis on the material and the structural may simply result in the intensification of black frustration. We do not just need jobs and houses, we must recover our own selves.[34]

Miroslav Volf echoed this same sentiment a few years later, but from a different perspective:

> In recent decades the issue of identity has risen to the forefront of discussions in social philosophy. If the liberation movements of the sixties were all about equality — above all gender equality and race equality — major concerns in the nineties seem to be about identity — about the recognition of distinct identities of persons who differ in gender, skin color, or culture.[35]

These three interesting views have a direct bearing on a shift in postliberation South African theology. Whereas black theologies of liberation as "theologies of bread" sought, and are still seeking, to liberate human beings from racism and classism, there is an upsurge in "theologies of being."[36] These theologies serve a quest for identity amid the homogenizing effect of globalization in its cultural form.[37] The combined powers of the mass media and multinational companies represent an intense strug-

34. Maluleke, as quoted in Tony Balcomb, "From liberation to democracy: Theologies of bread and being in the new South Africa," *Missionalia* 26, no. 1 (April 1998): 70.

35. Miroslav Volf, "'The Trinity is our social program': The doctrine of the Trinity and the shape of social engagement," *Modern Theology* 14, no. 3 (July 1998): 403-23 (408).

36. Balcomb, "From liberation to democracy," p. 68.

37. For an analysis and theological evaluation of *cultural* globalization, see Piet J. Naudé, "The challenge of cultural justice under conditions of globalisation: Is the New Testament of any use?" in *The New Testament interpreted: Essays in honour of Bernard C. Lategan,* ed. Cilliers Breytenbach, Johan C. Thom, and Jeremy Punt, pp. 267-87 (Leiden: Brill, 2007).

gle between "global/foreign" and "local" in all spheres of life: food, cloth-
ing, music, art, language, economics, and implicit values.

Whereas the struggle against apartheid necessitated a uniformity of
resistance and was aimed at the right to be "the same," the postapartheid
struggle aims at a restored subjectivity and agency with the right to be different. But this difference is now no longer embedded in a tyrannical separateness but in a celebration of difference within a constitutionally guaran-
teed commitment to unity and equality.

The notion that what Africans need is more development aid and
physical infrastructure, despite being important, is fatally flawed and may,
in practice, "result in the intensification of black frustration." What needs
to be restored and cultivated is a culturally mediated reconstruction of the
self in a personal and collective sense. In political terms, the African Renaissance (an unfortunate project title?) is not only about economic development but also about the restoration of cultural pride and selfhood "to
counter the excesses of European modes of being-in-the-world."[38]

The crucial insight, missed by most Westerners, is that restoration of
being not only precedes economic restoration but, in an African situation,
is also the precondition for economic survival. Bread depends on being,
because in a situation of scarce resources, one needs a view of identity
that resists economic greed and self-referential individualism. What one
requires is a notion of identity, as identity-in-community, which underlies redistribution patterns that in turn guarantee physical and economic
survival.

What is needed is the survival of (the) community, instead of the survival of the fittest. This is a fruitful point where African and Western phi-
losophies can meet. I refer here to the well-known notion of *ubuntu*, in
which the Cartesian *cogito ergo sum* (I think, therefore I am) is critically re-
stated as "I am because we are." This provides an alternative vision for human beings to the one at work in the capitalist myth of "the self-made
man/woman."

In order to understand *ubuntu*, the popular misconception of a dual-
ism between "Euro-individualism" and "African communitarianism"
should be corrected. The latter would hold that *ubuntu* is the denial of individuality and a form of communal totalitarianism, whereas the former

---

38. John L. Comaroff and Jean Comaroff, "On personhood: An anthropological perspective from Africa," in *Die autonome Person — eine europäische Erfindung?* ed. Klaus-Peter
Köpping, Michael Welker, and Reiner Wiehl, pp. 67-82 (80) (Munich: Wilhelm Fink, 2002).

would purport that individuality and freedom are the unique product of Enlightenment philosophy.

However, the Comaroffs, well-known anthropologists working in Southern Africa, argue that personhood is always a social creation, no matter how it is culturally formulated. "Nowhere in Africa were ideas of individuality ever absent. Individualism, another creature entirely, might not have been at home here before the postcolonial age. . . . But, each in its own way, African societies did, in times past, have a place for individuality, personal agency, property, privacy, biography, signature, and authored action upon the world. What differed was their particular substance, the manner of their ontological embeddedness in the social."[39] This insight provides a basis for building a notion of difference, exercised in freedom, while maintaining unity and community.

In his book *God in South Africa*, Catholic liberation theologian Albert Nolan notes that *ubuntu* is the most important African concept to depict the shift from being "objects of" to being "subjects in" society.[40] Malusi Mpumlwana seeks equivalence between *ubuntu* and *imago Dei* because God is reflected in love for the other, especially the practice of social love marked by hospitality and accommodation of the other.[41]

Russel Botman, former leader in the SACC and board member of *Theology Today*, links *ubuntu* to Bonhoeffer's christological definition of community: Christ exists as community. The question: "Who is Jesus Christ for us today?" reveals itself as the question of the very existence of the inquirer. The who-question is "the question about love for one's neighbor. That means that man cannot answer the question 'who?' by himself."[42]

The idea that the who-question cannot be answered in isolation provides a link to *ubuntu*, as a communitarian notion of being-in-community. We are, in the words of William Schweiker, "saturated with otherness."[43] On the one hand, identity is nonreducible, in the sense that persons cannot be translated fully into relationships and simultaneously retain their individuality. On the other hand, identity is not self-enclosed because the other is al-

---

39. Comaroff and Comaroff, "On personhood," p. 78.

40. Albert Nolan, *God in South Africa: The challenge of the gospel* (Cape Town: David Philip, 1988), p. 188.

41. For discussion and reference, see Balcomb, "From liberation to democracy," p. 71.

42. Dietrich Bonhoeffer, *Christology* (London: Collins 1960), pp. 31-32, as quoted in Russel Botman, "Who is 'Jesus Christ as community' for us today?" *Journal of Theology for Southern Africa* 97 (March 1997): 32 (noninclusive language retained).

43. Schweiker, "Humanity before God," p. 7.

ways already present as a transcendental condition for oneself. Not only is the who-question epistemologically dependent on the other, but *ubuntu* assumes a constitutive, ontological relationship between self and others.

What are now the christological and ecclesiological implications for reconstructing personal and communal identity? Faith in Jesus as the Christ has significant "identity" consequences. If "identity" refers, inter alia, to socially constructed self-understanding, conversion is at once an identity-shattering and identity-reconstituting event. Whatever cultural or religious achievements I may count on are considered nothing in order to gain Christ, says Paul (Phil. 3:4-11). I am nothing less than a new creation (2 Cor. 5:17). I am crucified with Jesus Christ, and I myself no longer live, but Christ lives in me (Gal. 2:20). As a redeemed human being, the "accidental" features of my concrete existence (e.g., woman, African, gay, disabled, middle-class) are affirmed in Christ, become sources of joy, and are in the faith community no longer grounds for exclusion and marginalization but exactly seen as rich, diverse gifts, contributing to the building up of the church.

I am in Jesus Christ. In his identity there is no contradiction between either the "catholicity" of the preincarnate Logos/postresurrection Lord or the "particularities" of the man from Nazareth, the *ecce homo* who is the suffering Jesus. Though the notion of the "catholicity of persons" is, in contrast to Catholic and Orthodox traditions, weakly developed in Reformed theology, Scripture declares that the whole Christ dwells in every Christian through the Holy Spirit. Every believer is, in the particularity of his or her concrete existence, also a catholic person, carrying the image of Christ's wholeness. Our catholicity, however, is simultaneously constituted by our relationship to other believers, the communion of saints, the church catholic.[44]

The church as a catholic *ubuntu*-community practices social love and reflects Christ in a redeemed sociality, where cheap grace is denounced for the sake of discipleship (Bonhoeffer) and where individual persons discover that genuine personal identity is possible only in a "community of

44. For an Orthodox perspective, see John Zizioulas, *Communion as being: Studies in personhood and the church* (Crestwood, N.Y.: St. Vladimir's Seminary Press, 1985). Though one might argue that Zizioulas's "catholicity of being" may not do full justice to the particularity of a person, the huge stride toward seeing in each person the fullness of humanity in Christ must not be underestimated. For a discussion of Zizioulas and Ratzinger, see Miroslav Volf, *After our likeness: The church as the image of the Trinity* (Grand Rapids: Eerdmans, 1998).

love."[45] In this manner, faith in Christ and participation in the church can (and indeed do) play a significant role to still "the hunger for identity, meaning and self-worth"[46] — probably the most urgent spiritual and cultural need of the African continent.

In the South African context and for that matter in the global context, the church is therefore called to be an example of a new humanity and new community. This is the place where we can "speak truly and honestly about our culture."[47] This is the one community where I can be what I am without fear of marginalization, prejudice, rejection, or separation because our differences are, by virtue of Christ's reconciliation, "opportunities for mutual service and enrichment" (art. 2.6).

This in no way means that racism and disunity among peoples are no longer an urgent issue. Politically speaking, South Africans might live in a postliberation era, but there are clearly other questions on the agenda that determine a realization of freedoms that are still denied to so many. Attacks on foreigners *(ama-kwerekwere)* point to a rising tide of xenophobia, intensified by dire economic conditions and meager social resources. The debate over gay people and their marital, ecclesial, and economic rights challenges our deepest hidden prejudgments about sexual orientation. The policy of affirmative action, applied in many cases to the exclusion of persons who are "not black enough," challenges the "Africanization" agenda and opens the question of "black racism," seen by many as a contradiction in terms.

These are clearly not (South) African problems only. It is painfully easy to cite the many international examples of defective tribalism and other forms of dehumanization. Some are more explicit as in the Congo, Rwanda, and the Middle East; others are more refined, like the new immigration policies in Europe.

In the United States, for example, racism was a major factor in the 2008 presidential election campaign, eventually won by Barack Obama. Remarks by radio icon Don Imus and by movie star Mel Gibson demonstrate this claim.[48] Long after the civil rights movement, there is a contin-

45. Bonhoeffer, as discussed by de Gruchy, "Christian humanism," p. 52. See Schweiker, "Distinctive love," pp. 112-17, where he argues for the love commandments as a basis for humanism, though he does not develop an ecclesiological point of view in the way Bonhoeffer does.

46. Cornel West, *Race matters* (New York: Vintage Books, 1994), p. 20.

47. Maluleke, as quoted in Balcomb, "From liberation to democracy," p. 70.

48. See James Poniewozik's article "What the Imus implosion tells us about the bound-

ued need for a "black history month," and economic inequalities are evident from a simple observation of who makes use of public transport in Princeton. Black bodies are, according to James Cone, still being lynched today "whenever a people cry out to be recognized as human beings and society ignores them."[49] The naming of immigrants as "aliens" and immigration services as "homeland security" show the fear and even resentment of foreigners after 9/11; and the debates in the United States about the rights of gays to serve in the military speak for themselves.

A humanizing Christian theology can play a role in ensuring that exclusions and marginalizations, of whatever kind, are fought with the vision of Christ's inclusive grace, the openness of the church as hospitable community, and representative action to speak out for those who are voiceless.

In Christ "freedom in unity" is indeed a possibility.

---

aries of 'acceptable talk,'" *Time Magazine*, April 23, 2007, pp. 32-38, for an incisive analysis of freedom of speech and many other examples of racial and gender "slurring."

49. James H. Cone, "Strange fruit: The cross and the lynching tree," *Harvard Divinity Bulletin* 35 (Winter 2007): 47-55. He cites the criminal justice system, the aftermath of Hurricane Katrina, and the Iraq War as concrete examples. Racism "is still endemic to our society," and there is a general denial of history under the cloak of sentimental, Hollywood-style "universal culture," states William H. Willimon in "Why we all can't just get along: Racism as a Lenten issue," *Theology Today* 53, no. 4 (January 1997): 485-90.

Chapter 8

Reconciliation

Do not stigmatize people with AIDS. Show them care, support and, above all, love. You have to sympathize with them. It is your duty to be human.

— Nelson Mandela, AIDS Day speech, 2002[1]

One could choose many examples of enmity, fear, and prejudice for discussion in this chapter. For the sake of brevity, two issues are addressed under the heading of reconciliation, both relevant to the African context.[2] Can Belhar be called upon to establish true acceptance of and reconciliation between men and women? Second, can Belhar assist us in overcoming deep prejudices against people living with HIV and AIDS? Both are issues concerning gender relations and are of crucial importance for reconciliation and peace in church and society. As we deal with each of these topics, it is important to remember once again that Belhar should be read as one text, with each of its five articles woven intrinsically together.

---

1. Nelson Mandela, AIDS Day speech, December 1, 2002, Bloemfontein, South Africa.

2. For an ecclesiological view on the challenges of reconciliation, see Nico Koopman, "Reconciliation and the Confession of Belhar, 1986: Some challenges for the Uniting Reformed Church in Southern Africa," *Nederduitse Gereformeerde Teologiese Tydskrif* 48 (2007): 96-106.

Reconciled gender relations

For historical reasons, the focus of reconciliation in Belhar's third article is on "the enforced separation of people on *racial* basis" (my emphasis). However, Africa is a deeply patriarchal society, and gender bias — under the guise of tradition and culture — has terrible economic, educational, sexual, and psychological implications for young girls and adult women. The struggle for women's rights in the world and also in the ecumenical church requires us to consider whether Belhar can be legitimately called upon to aid in the struggle for gender reconciliation.

Despite different approaches and contrasting epistemologies, one can safely assert that much of feminist scholarship is focused on showing the powerful relationship between language (metaphors) and reality. A specific feature of feminist hermeneutics is its iconoclastic nature. For radical feminism,[3] it means the rejection of androcentric metaphors and the creation of an alternative symbolic world to the one expressed in the Christian canon. Reformist[4] and womanist[5] scholars see their task as recovering the liberative potential of a rereading of the canon from the perspective of women's experiences.

Whereas substantial feminist work has been done on a rereading of the canon or parts thereof, the creeds and confessions have, as far as I know, not yet received much attention. The reasons are simple: The canon is the founding document of the Christian church and the obvious site of a hermeneutical struggle for a feminist reinterpretation. The creeds and confessions are secondary expressions of the church's insight at a particu-

3. Well-known exponents of this paradigm are Mary Daly, Naomi Goldenberg, and Carol Christ.

4. The majority of feminist scholars fall into this paradigm and are represented by authors like Letty Russell, Sallie McFague, Rosemary Radford Reuther (all United States), Catharina Halkes (Netherlands), and Elizabeth Moltmann-Wendel (Germany). McFague's classic *Metaphorical theology: Models of God in religious language* (London: SCM Press, 1982) had the greatest formative influence on my own thinking in this regard. In South Africa one can refer to the work of Denise Ackermann (practical theology), Christina Landman (church history and, recently, pastoral care), Annalet van Schalkwyk (missiology), and Elna Mouton (New Testament).

5. Well-known representatives from this group who voice the concerns of African or African-American women are Dolores Williams, Katie Cannon, and bell hooks. Mercy Oduyoye and Isabel Phiri are the best-known African womanist theologians. For contributions and literature, see Ursula King, ed., *Feminist theology from the Third World: A reader* (Maryknoll, N.Y.: Orbis Books, 1994).

lar point in time and directed at particular heresies primarily (though not exclusively) relevant to that time. The creeds like Nicea and Athanasius, as well as the Apostles' Creed, are indeed ecumenical in nature but still not universally accepted or liturgically practiced in the same way in the various traditions. Confessions like Augsburg, the Belgic Confession, Barmen, and Belhar are strongly bound to the Protestant tradition.

It is thus natural for feminist scholarship to focus on the canon. However, because creeds and confessions witness to the apostolic faith in a specific time and have become part of the church's tradition, they are therefore important texts that require close scrutiny from a feminist perspective. We must ensure that they do not, by default, reinforce patriarchal images and oppressive practices. It would be strange to develop a critical feminist reading of the canon but allow the liturgical texts of the church their assumed androcentric bias!

This shifts the hermeneutical struggle from the canon to confessional texts. From a reformist perspective, the question is: If we accept the voice of the church at a specific moment in history but know already the androcentric bias of the church through the ages, do these texts have the potential to speak a "gendered truth"? Are confessions able to foster liberation when read from the perspective of sexist and related forms of patriarchal oppression? Let us therefore look at the emancipatory and feminist aspects of Belhar by focusing on the three middle articles regarding unity, reconciliation, and justice, and acknowledging the later inclusive-language versions of the confession.

It is clear from the rejection statements of the unity article that Belhar — true to its history and context — has the racial and cultural divisions of the church in mind. In Belhar's time, the danger was not perceived as sexism or gender discrimination, and thus no explicit rejection thereof appears in the text. But the text has too many explicit statements about an inclusive unity for it to be disregarded.

See for example article 2.4, which claims that unity in the church "must become visible so that the world may believe that separation, enmity and hatred between people and groups is sin which Christ has already conquered." This could include the deep suspicion against and exclusion of women in offices and leadership in the church. Belhar then clearly opens up an inclusive interpretation by saying that "anything [*alles* could also be translated "everything"] which threatens this unity [which could indeed be gender biases] may have no place in the Church and must be resisted." This finds an echo in article 2.5, where the community of believers is called upon to "fight against all which may threaten or hinder this unity." This hindrance is witnessed by many women, who find a distorted creation theology that prevents them from participating fully in the gifts of the Spirit.

If indeed some wish to argue for gender differentiation on grounds of culture, biology, or psychology, Belhar speaks clearly that such differences are, because of Christ's reconciliatory act, "opportunities for mutual service and enrichment within the one visible people of God" (art. 2.6). Although the gender issue is not specified, the text is clear in its intention to resist all forms and causes of disunity in the one church of Christ.

The article on reconciliation is also strong in its rejection of the idea of racial irreconcilability. It refers to the "enforced separation of people on a racial basis" (art. 3.3, with echoes also in 3.4). The rejection statement is also about "the forced separation of people on the grounds of race and color." But these references are embedded in more inclusive and general views of the church as salt and light, as peacemakers, and as an eschatological community that is a witness through word and deed "to the new heaven and the new earth in which righteousness dwells" (art. 3.1). This is followed by the confession of God's reconciling power through God's "lifegiving Word and Spirit," which overcame "irreconciliation and hatred, bitterness and enmity" to enable God's people to live as an example of a reconciled community in the world (see art. 3.2).

The fact that these fundamental expressions of God's reconciliation find application in one specific area of human life, namely race and culture, in no way precludes its application to other forms of irreconcilability such as gender divisions. The same could be confessed about sexist doctrines of subordination and exclusion, namely, "that any teaching which . . . is not prepared to venture on the road of obedience and reconciliation, but rather, out of prejudice, fear, selfishness and unbelief, denies in advance the reconciling power of the gospel, must be considered ideology and false doctrine" (art. 3.4). When the Bible and theology are used against women in order to keep them, in the name of the gospel, from exercising their spiritual gifts of teaching or leadership, they show exactly the same structure as a racist theology. With the rapid rise of evangelical and Pentecostal churches and their television reach around the globe, the struggle for gender reconciliation will intensify in the years to come. Churches with a fundamentalist hermeneutic struggle to read biblical texts with a view confirming that women should have the freedom to serve God according to the gifts of the Spirit.

Belhar's potential for an encompassing liberation that includes gender also lies in article 4, on justice. This article transcends the narrower application to race and culture that is evident in the former articles. Although God is named via traditional male metaphors, God is also described as "the One who wishes to bring about justice and true peace among men" (art. 4.1). This would include peace among different genders and, for that matter, among gay and straight Christians. How does God achieve this? By being "in a special way the God of the destitute, the poor and the wronged" (art. 4.1).

The examples in this passage, drawn from Scripture and the Lukan focus on the poor, explicitly mention the widow and the orphans twice. This should not be read as necessarily gender sensitive, but generically as a symbol for all those who are without legal recourse and legitimate voice in society. That is why people living with HIV and AIDS are included below. But the fact of the matter remains that, even in patriarchal societies, the message of a faultless religion before God is to stand by the orphans and widows in their suffering (Jas. 1:27). This surely opens the possibility to extend the categories of wronged peoples to include women and children, plus other voiceless ones who are physically poor or in other ways socially marginalized and shunned.

This is reinforced as the church is called to witness against "any form of injustice" (art. 4.2), including gender injustices, and against "all the powerful and the privileged who selfishly seek their own interests and thus control and harm others" (art. 4.3), as male-dominated church structures so often do. The rejection clause that ends article 4 is equally emphatic regarding "any ideology which would legitimate forms of injustice and any doctrine which is unwilling to resist such an ideology in the name of the gospel." It was relatively easy to see apartheid theology as an ideology. It is a little more difficult to deconstruct a patriarchal and heterosexual culture, supported by a fundamentalist reading of Scripture, as an equally vicious ideology that has to be resisted today.

The concluding article 5 is a source of encouragement for all who struggle against gender injustice. The church is called to confess and act on its confession, "even though the authorities and human laws might forbid them." I can see no reason why "authorities and human laws" — apart from referring to the sociopolitical order and laws denying women full access to human rights — could not also include ecclesial authorities, ordinances, and practices that continue to contradict both a confession and presumed commitment to gender freedom in the church.

In this way, Belhar, despite its limitations in terms of narrow racial focus and male-dominated theological metaphors in the original text, can indeed be a powerful tool to proclaim the church's true unity, God's encompassing reconciliation, and gendered justice in society.

Marginalization of people living with HIV and AIDS

Belhar was written before the full advent of the AIDS pandemic. One cannot live in Africa today and not take into account the plight of people living with HIV and AIDS. Words that Belhar uttered in relation to racial separation echo remarkably true when applied to the topic of AIDS.[6]

In 1998 the "hatred, bitterness and enmity" (art. 3.2) caused by fear-based stigma and discrimination of people with HIV resulted in the actual killing of a young woman by her own community.[7] In the view of those in this community, her declared HIV-status brought shame upon them. "Prejudice" (art. 3.4) against people with HIV leads to discrimination in the workplace and social marginalization elsewhere. "Fear" (art. 3.4) of people with AIDS, mixed with a lack of knowledge of how the virus is transmitted, means a life of isolation for many and is reminiscent of the social significance of leprosy in biblical times.

"I cannot attend any church commission meetings on a Saturday," says a colleague; "I need Saturdays for funerals — sometimes three on one day." Some cynical observers say that the most helpful function of a post-apartheid church is to bury people.[8]

It is indeed very difficult to communicate to an affluent, Western audience the vastness and the terrible impact of the AIDS pandemic on ordinary people's lives, not to mention the impact on various communities such as extended families in rural areas, churches, universities, the public sector workforce, and private sector production.[9] UNAIDS calculates that

6. A longer version of this section was earlier published in *Scriptura*; see Piet J. Naudé, "'It is your duty to be human': A few theological remarks amidst the HIV/AIDS crisis," *Scriptura* 89 (2005): 433-40.

7. See John Iliffe, *The African AIDS epidemic: A history* (Oxford: James Curry, 2006), p. 89.

8. See Olaf Derenthal, *AIDS in Afrika und die Rede von Gott* (Hamburg: Lit Verlag, 2002), p. 59.

9. By 2007 the estimated number of people living with HIV in South Africa was between 4.9 and 6.6 million, out of a total estimated population of approximately 48 million (UNAIDS, *Report on the global HIV/AIDS epidemic* [Geneva: United Nations, 2008], Annex

about US$15 billion is required annually to combat the disease in low- and middle-income countries.[10] Statistics and graphic images released by the media have a stunning effect on people, especially when disasters are depicted that happen "elsewhere." Reactions vary from shrugging of shoulders over this terrible sickness happening somewhere in dark Africa to an emotional block-out as a self-defense mechanism. Some people at least buy red ribbons on World AIDS Day (December 1) to help create awareness.

That the AIDS pandemic is a massive human catastrophe needs no further argument. That we need continued reflection on the anthropological and theological implications is equally clear. HIV and AIDS require the same reorientation of our theological thinking as was the case with three instances in the twentieth century: theology after the Holocaust, theology amid the possibility of nuclear devastation in the 1960s, and theology under and against apartheid in the period leading up to 1994. Any event or process or pandemic that claims 2 million lives each year must be a matter of serious concern. (One can only imagine what would have happened if a pandemic of this scale had hit Europe or the United States!) What is required is a "theology of AIDS" that will question and redefine each traditional locus of systematic theology from the doctrine of creation, the Trinity, and the human person, to ecclesiology, the sacraments, and eschatology. Tinyiko Maluleke recalls the language of the struggle era by saying that "the HIV/AIDS pandemic has ushered in a new kairos for the world in general and for the African continent in particular."[11]

A theology of AIDS indeed is required, as is clear from the illuminating point made in 1992 by Willem Saayman and Jacques Kriel (a missiologist and physician respectively) and repeated by Saayman in a 1999 retrospective evaluation: "The HIV/AIDS pandemic is not, like many previous pandemics such as the 1918 flu epidemic, maintained and contained

---

1). Two remarks put these figures in perspective. On the one hand, South Africa's relatively good public health infrastructure (good, at least when compared with other sub-Saharan African countries) secures higher levels of detection than in countries to the north. On the other hand, AIDS-related deaths are probably underreported because of the prevalence of diseases like tuberculosis and pneumonia, whose negative effects are increased because of a population with deficient immune systems.

10. UNAIDS, *Report on the global HIV/AIDS epidemic* (Geneva: United Nations, 2002).

11. Tinyiko Sam Maluleke, "The challenge of HIV/AIDS for theological education in Africa: Toward an HIV/AIDS sensitive curriculum," *Missionalia* 29, no. 2 (August 2001): 125. See Derenthal, *AIDS in Afrika*, pp. 79-88, for a brief outline of contributions from African theologians like John Waliggo, Laurenti Magesa, and Benezet Bujo.

by biological mechanisms (e.g. insect vectors, droplet spread or the development of immunity by the population), but by social behavioral patterns with essential religio-cultural dimensions."[12] They argue that the dominant biomedical model is reductionist,[13] as it deals only with the effect of the virus and is notoriously hesitant and slow to address the simple fact that the HIV virus is mostly spread by human behavior, specifically sexual patterns. This marks the disease as essentially sociocultural, which requires moral and ethical interventions, taking underlying religious worldviews into consideration.

What are the impediments hampering the development of an adequate theology to address the problem of AIDS? There are at least three reasons why Christian churches situated in societies where AIDS is a reality find the AIDS pandemic very difficult to deal with.

One reason relates to an inadequate reflective framework for in some way locating AIDS on the theological map. Crude ideas about sin and judgment are totally inadequate for dealing with the complexity of questions concerning God's position as Creator and "Keeper" of creation. The idea that HIV is God's rightful judgment on a promiscuous lifestyle is not only factually wrong; it is theologically dangerous and recalls Belhar's witness against false gospels that present prejudice against and separation from people on the grounds of (in this instance) their HIV status as the will of God. Other important theological themes are models of theodicy in relation to divine providence, the relation between Christ's suffering and the AIDS sufferer, models for being a church that welcomes people living with HIV or AIDS, and very literally, the question of hope and eschatology amid painfully slow physical deterioration and death.

The second reason for the difficulty in dealing with AIDS relates to the nature of AIDS as primarily a sexually related disease. Under normal conditions, churches are hesitant to address issues of sexuality publicly, except when campaigning against its "negative" manifestations in debates about pornography, abortion, prostitution, and sex before marriage. In societies

12. See Willem Saayman and J. Kriel, *AIDS — the leprosy of our time?* (Pretoria: Unisa, 1992); and Willem Saayman, "AIDS — still posing an unanswered question," *Missionalia* 29, no. 2 (August 1999): 212.

13. One could add: If the same amount of money available to the biological research community would be spent on AIDS education, a huge difference could be made in containing the disease. But, to be cynical, there is more money to be made from a "cure" or a "probable cure" than in investing in nondramatic educational efforts in clinics, villages, and schools, where the only return is a lower infection rate, with no direct monetary reward.

where sex as a public topic is considered a cultural taboo, and where actual sexual behavior is regulated by hierarchical and patriarchal social structures, the church is doomed to silence and is very cautious about sexually informed educational programs. Everybody whispers about who died of what, but nobody is able to speak up and speak out. "This silence is in effect a death sentence and the church needs to be called to accountability."[14]

The third reason has been intimated above. Churches struggle to address HIV and AIDS theologically because AIDS arises from issues of gender and sexism, which are still the Achilles' heels of many faith communities today. The much higher prevalence of HIV among young women than men of the same age is partly attributed to the social vulnerability of women in a patriarchal culture. "HIV/AIDS is ultimately a gender issue," writes Philippe Denis.[15] In this context, HIV represents another dramatic case of deeply unequal and destructive gender relations in need of transformation. Reflections by African women themselves are very important, as is evident from the publication *African women, HIV/AIDS, and faith communities.* In it, Isabel Phiri states, "We need to address the fact that physiological differences, social, cultural norms, economic and power relations between women and men have a big impact in the process of who gets infected."[16] Paul Germond remarks that "clergy are spending their time no longer at funerals of people who have died because of political violence, but at funerals where people have died of sexual violence, if we conceive the spreading of the HIV virus as an act of violence."[17]

Cumulatively, these three conditions — an inadequate theological interpretative framework, religio-cultural silence, and gender inequalities — create a terrible vacuum into which persons living with HIV or AIDS are cast. The consequences are predictable and real. AIDS has become the "leprosy of our time,"[18] with AIDS sufferers experiencing social marginalization and dehumanization that accompany views of persons with a dis-

14. Beverley Haddad, "Gender violence and HIV/AIDS: A deadly silence in the church," *Journal of Theology for Southern Africa* 114 (November 2002): 97.

15. Philippe Denis, "Sexuality and AIDS in South Africa," *Journal of Theology for Southern Africa* 115 (March 2003): 75.

16. Isabel Apawo Phiri, "African women of faith speak out in an HIV/AIDS era," in *African women, HIV/AIDS, and faith communities,* ed. Isabel Phiri, Beverley Haddad, and Madipoane Masenya, pp. 8-9 (Pietermaritzburg: Cluster, 2003).

17. Paul Germond, "Sex in a globalizing world: The South African churches and the crisis of sexuality," *Journal of Theology for Southern Africa* 119 (July 2004): 67-68.

18. Saayman and Kriel, *AIDS — the leprosy of our time?*

ease that is both incurable and infectious. Both these elements are driven by devastating myths that a cure is possible through sexual intercourse with babies or virgins, or that infections can occur via normal human interaction in the school, at work, or in the home. No wonder Nelson Mandela remarked: "Many who suffer from HIV and AIDS are not killed by the virus, but by stigma." He then added tellingly: "Do not stigmatise people with AIDS. Show them care, support, and above all, love. You have to sympathize with them. *It is your duty to be human.*"[19]

"It is your duty to be human" brings us to the anthropological question, again set in the context of theology and ecclesiology. There is obviously no room to develop a full theological framework in a few paragraphs. Here I start with a trinitarian note on God, Christ, and the Spirit. This is built on the opening line of the Belhar Confession, where the classic trinitarian faith of the church is repeated. The link with ecclesiology is established by a few observations about the church as a healing and embracing community.

God creates humans in God's image

The *imago Dei* is in no way diminished by a person's physical condition, including HIV status, because the image notion was never intended to express a "reflection of God" in a physical manner, and each human being's unique theological quality is not altered by accidental factors of race, gender, class, or even sickness or health. "Because humanity is created in God's image, all human beings are beloved by God and are held within the scope of God's concern and faithful care," notes the WCC report on AIDS.[20] As ethical guidance, the concept of *imago Dei* is of great significance: "because all human beings are created and beloved by God, Christians are called to treat every person as of infinite value."[21] The implication is that the personal worth of an HIV-infected person or AIDS sufferer, no matter in what stage of the illness he or she is, must be accepted in principle and confirmed in practice.

In a Constitutional Court case between the South African government

---

19. Mandela, AIDS Day speech (my emphasis).

20. World Council of Churches, *Facing AIDS: The challenge, the churches' response* (Geneva: WCC, 1997), p. 100.

21. World Council of Churches. *Facing AIDS,* p. 103.

and the Treatment Action Campaign (a coalition advocating the rights of people with HIV and AIDS), the ten judges of the court ruled unanimously on December 14, 2001, that the issue of treatment should be judged from a human rights perspective. Treatment was in this instance considered both a first-generation's innate right to life, as well as a second-generation's right to proper health care. As a positive obligation, this right, and specifically the provision of treatment at designated public clinics, is a programmatic right that requires a certain time frame for successful implementation. Clearly, respect in principle for people created in the image of God is meaningless without respectful action in practice, backed by human rights law.

Christ

The question "Where would Jesus go if he came to earth today?" was asked during the 2007 CNN Easter Sunday program (April 8, 2007). One participant, well-known pastor Rick Warren, answered: "There is no doubt we will find him among AIDS sufferers and their orphans."

The church is a Christian church, named after the Second Person of the Trinity. The office of Christ has its roots in the Old Testament messianic title of the "anointed one," reserved for prophets, kings, and priests. In the context of this chapter, I develop the priestly metaphor in correlation with the notion that the Trinity represents a cycle of perfect self-giving, which as Miroslav Volf rightly points out, cannot be simply repeated in the world of sin.[22] God's perfect love engages the world in the self-giving of Christ's incarnation, where this love is met with nonlove, resistance, deceit, and injustice. But God's love is nevertheless sustained amid, and sometimes against, cultural norms of social acceptability in Jesus' touching, healing, conversing, and eating with ritually impure and socially marginalized sinners.

For those who are co-anointed (Christians in the kingdom of priests, 1 Pet. 2:9), *imitatio crucis* implies a self-giving, sacrificial lifestyle that touches, heals, converses, and eats with those who are, in accordance with cultural-religious norms, socially marginalized through their HIV status. Indeed, "we are called to imitate the earthly love of that same Trinity that

---

22. Miroslav Volf, "'The Trinity is our social program': The doctrine of the Trinity and the shape of social engagement," *Modern Theology* 14, no. 3 (July 1998): 403-23.

led to the passion of the Cross, because it was from the start a passion for those caught in the snares of non-love." The imperative to "welcome one another . . . just as Christ has welcomed you" (Rom. 15:7) makes sense only if Christians, the co-anointed, imitate the divine welcome by making space for others, "prior to any judgement about others, except that of identifying them in their humanity."[23]

The Holy Spirit, Daughter of God, creates one body

The triune God's self-giving engagement with the world is not only via the incarnation, death, and resurrection of Christ, but it is given enduring historical significance in the outpouring of the Spirit. Proceeding from both the Father and the Son, the Spirit creates a faith community called the body of Christ. In this community the Spirit fills the hearts of the faithful with the love of God (Rom. 5:5), thus creating a sense of "being-in-communion," where individual members of the body find meaning in relation to the other members.

The double effect is that members share the joy of mutual enrichment: "If one member is honored, all rejoice together with it" (1 Cor. 12:26b). But they also share the pain of co-suffering with one another: "If one member suffers, all suffer together with it" (v. 26a). Instead of linking the signs of the Spirit to extraordinary signs, like speaking in tongues or laughing in the Spirit, the context of HIV and AIDS requires us to restore the vision that those who are filled with the Spirit show the "extraordinary" willingness to suffer with others and to develop practices of sympathy, overcoming social death before physical death. This provides a radical context for Belhar's view that reconciliation is established by God through the life-giving Spirit.

There is no longer a distinction between those living with HIV or AIDS and those who are not. We are all living with the disease and are affected by it in many ways. This claim is all the more radical if the church understands itself as one body. Only the Spirit can turn feelings of despair, as well as geographic-psychological distancing, into a practice of inhabiting the world of the suffering other. We are all living with the disease. If one part of the body suffers, the whole body as such is sick too. To say "the church has AIDS" is a pronouncement of this solidarity.

23. Volf, "The Trinity," pp. 415-16.

At the very beginning of its article 3, Belhar reminds us that the church has been entrusted with the message of reconciliation. In the context of death, in this case physical death, we proclaim that God has conquered "the powers of sin and death" by his lifegiving Word and Spirit. Through this Word and Spirit people are led to a new obedience "which can open new possibilities of life for society and the world" (art. 3.2). How does this apply to the church today? In the context of Belhar, how must the church understand itself if it is to stand where God stands?

Two metaphors that might express this ecclesiological notion are to view the church as a *healing community* and as an *embracing community*. Both images are attested to in Scripture, but the first image found specific resonance in the African Independent Churches, whereas the second has been reflected upon by Miroslav Volf in the Croatian situation of enduring ethnic conflict.

It is a well-known fact that, statistically speaking, African Independent Churches (AICs) are the fastest growing group of churches on the African continent. This pattern is strikingly unlike the growth patterns in mainline churches, even those with a predominantly black membership. This empirical observation immediately calls us to ask the reason for their growth. One of the most plausible explanations, supported by fieldwork studies, is that these churches address the issue of healing, the balancing of life and cosmic forces, in an encompassing way. This healing is reinforced through rituals and real forms of alternative community and identity that transcend all ethnic boundaries. AICs provide the communal setting for "coping-healing" in the widest sense of the word,[24] because the loss of an immune system (in the case of AIDS) can be "healed-and-coped" with only if there is not also a loss of the system of community interaction. Commenting on Zionist-type churches, Stephen Hays observes that "people are healed through the power of the Holy Spirit, acting either through a particular person with a healing ministry, or through the congregation as a whole."[25]

The WCC report on AIDS appropriately includes under pastoral care and counseling the observation: "By their very nature as communities of

24. This term has been developed by Stuart C. Bate, "Inculturation in process: Influence of coping-healing churches on the attitudes and praxis of mainline churches," *Missionalia* 31, no. 1 (April 2003): 177-207, in his study of inculturation and healing. It also is referred to by Saayman, "AIDS — unanswered question," p. 215.

25. Stephen Hayes, "African initiated church theology," in *Initiation into theology*, ed. Simon Maimela and Adrio König, p. 170 (Pretoria: Van Schaik, 1998).

faith in Christ, churches are called to be *healing communities*," because "the experience of love, acceptance and support within a community where God's love is made manifest can be a powerful healing force."[26]

We turn now to the church as an embracing community. Fear (to which Belhar refers in the context of race) is one of the dominant emotions of HIV-positive persons and AIDS sufferers — fear for loss of health and physical ability, fear that others might find out, fear of their reaction once it can no longer be hidden, fear of treatment (if it is even available), fear of loss of job and income, fear of death and of the future of those who remain behind. The Bible teaches us that fear is conquered only by love, and love is concretely expressed in embrace. Again, the structure of trinitarian thinking and ecclesiology serves us well.

When the Trinity turns to the world, writes Irenaeus in his *Against Heresies* (as cited by Volf),[27] the Son and the Spirit become the two arms of God by which humanity was made and taken into God's embrace. When God sets out to embrace humanity-as-enemy, the result is the cross: the arms of the crucified are open. "We, the others — we the enemies — are embraced by the divine persons who love us with the same love with which they love each other and therefore make space for us within their own eternal embrace."[28] In the act of grace, we are not only recipients but are constituted as a community of embraced, and therefore embracing, people. The context of HIV and AIDS requires us to radicalize Volf's explication of embrace and its phenomenology in two ways.[29]

First, we need to move from metaphor to the physical realm of actual embrace. Volf argues that "I am not interested here so much in the physical embrace itself as in the dynamic relationship between the self and the other that embrace symbolizes and enacts."[30] In our case, I am particularly interested in the physical embrace itself, as the reluctance to touch people living with HIV or AIDS embodies the marginalization caused by socio-

---

26. World Council of Churches, *Facing AIDS*, pp. 106-7, my emphasis.

27. Miroslav Volf, *Exclusion and embrace: A theological exploration of identity, otherness, and reconciliation* (Nashville: Abingdon, 1996).

28. Volf, *Exclusion and embrace*, p. 129.

29. One finds this "theology of embrace" scattered throughout Volf's work. See his article "Exclusion and embrace: Theological reflections in the wake of 'ethnic cleansing,'" *Journal of Ecumenical Studies* 29, no. 2 (1992): 230-48, as well as the structure of *Exclusion and embrace*, pp. 28-31 and 99-165, where the theology and phenomenology of embrace are well expounded.

30. Volf, *Exclusion and embrace*, p. 141.

cultural and religious taboos. Physical embrace imitates Jesus' ministry of touching those considered impure or socially outcast.

Second, Volf is at great pains to warn us to guard against both dissolving the self in the other and retaining the reciprocity of the embrace. Concerning the latter, he notes a "waiting" with open arms: before embrace can proceed, "it must wait for the desire to arise in the other and for the arms of the other to open,"[31] because others may sometimes simply want to be left alone. This makes sense in situations of reciprocity where the capacity for "desire to arise" is assumed. But this may not always be the case. In fact, in some cases prior confirmation may not be possible, because both the physical and social basis for such confirmation is simply not present.

The danger of turning the embrace itself into a means of self-assertion, thus overpowering the other, is obvious and real. It often happens that good work arises from asymmetrical power assumptions. In our situation, however, the danger is to open one's arms in anticipation of an embrace. Then, because of nonreciprocity, to turn away, satisfied that one has at least tried. On balancing the dangers between waiting and embracing, we must risk actual embrace, knowing that "a soft touch is necessary."[32]

Thus a truly Christian (Christlike) church will in effect be a healing and embracing community, a home for AIDS orphans, a refuge for the socially outcast, and a source of hope for a society in the grip of death. As a reconciling community, "the Church is witness both by word and by deed to the new heaven and the new earth in which righteousness dwells" (art. 3.1).

What message with regard to HIV and AIDS can we as African theologians give our colleagues in the North and the East? These colleagues would do well if they, with their considerable intellectual and infrastructural resources, participate in theological reflections on the AIDS pandemic. It is not necessary to live in our context in order to participate in theology and practice. There is still so much to do in creating adequate reflective frameworks. At the policy level, a huge stumbling block is the process of bringing the cultural-religious model on a par with the biomedical model. If the millions (rightly) spent on medical research were matched with money spent on information and education programs, in-

---

31. Volf, *Exclusion and embrace*, p. 142.

32. In *Exclusion and embrace*, p. 143, Volf's "soft touch" is used to show respect for the personhood and identity of the other: "I may not close my arms around the other too tightly." The reader will understand how apt these words are if taken slightly out of context, as I have done above.

fection rates may have decreased by now. In this case, prevention is essentially the only cure.

International pharmaceutical companies, some of which are listed on the world's important stock exchanges, have at least two particular responsibilities. The first is to maintain high ethical research standards and to refrain from capitalizing on the predicament of Africans. They should not use lax controls as an excuse for unwarranted, invasive biomedical trials. The second is to make antiretroviral medicine (so far the only answer to containing the human immunodeficiency virus) available at the cheapest sustainable prices.

It is imperative that the tragedy of the AIDS pandemic not be used in the promotion and reinforcement of Afro-pessimism. This is the easy way out. The Christian way is one of solidarity. We are all living with AIDS. There is no distinction. Shall we not, in the words of Belhar (art. 3.4), jointly "venture on the road of obedience and reconciliation"? Shall we not follow God in imitating his special love for women and people living with HIV and AIDS? Shall we not take seriously our duty to be human?

Chapter 9

Justice

I confess before you and before the Lord, not only my own sin and guilt . . . but vicariously I dare also to do that in the name of the DRC, of which I am a member, and for the Afrikaans people as a whole.

— Willie Jonker, "Understanding the church situation"[1]

It appears that it is better to be a cow in Europe than a poor person in a developing country.

— Joseph E. Stiglitz, *Making globalization work*[2]

This chapter concludes our reflections on the contemporary significance of the Belhar Confession. We turn our focus to article 4, on justice, looking particularly at restorative and distributive justice in the context of Africa and the global economic situation.

---

1. Willie Jonker, "Understanding the church situation and obstacles to Christian witness in South Africa," in *Road to Rustenburg*, ed. Louw Alberts and Frank Chikane, p. 92 (Cape Town: Struik, 1991).
2. Joseph E. Stiglitz, *Making globalization work* (New York: W. W. Norton, 2006), p. 85.

God is in a special way the God of the wronged:
Restorative justice

"In April 1994 South Africans experienced the miracle of a peaceful election, marking our transition to democracy. . . . Now, in order to nurture and to preserve our fledgling democracy, we have to deal with the legacies of the past. These legacies present an almost overwhelming agenda."[3] These words by South African feminist theologian Denise Ackermann touch on a theme of global importance: How do we deal with the overwhelming agenda of past legacies? To be concrete, how do people in Northern Ireland, Germany,[4] Australia, Belgium, Rwanda, the Congo, the Balkans, the Middle East, Russia — and in so many countries elsewhere — deal with past injustices? How do we construe restorative justice, and what theological considerations should lead us?[5]

Belhar was confessed when the inhumanities of South Africa's past were still in the making. It was a cry from the heart against injustice and enmity, and a call — in many cases a literal call — for the release of (political) prisoners and a rightful place for the oppressed, the destitute, the poor, and the wronged (art. 4.1). Especially this last category is of relevance here. Once political freedom is achieved, how is justice realized for "the wronged," the ones against whom oppression was unleashed and maintained through state force over many years? How are lost opportunities regained? How should guilt be apportioned and perpetrators of gross human rights violations be brought to justice?

People around the world know that South Africa chose to deal with its past injustices constructively via the now famous Truth and Reconciliation Commission (TRC), chaired by Archbishop Desmond Tutu. Established in terms of the significantly named "Promotion of National Unity and Reconciliation Act" (Act 34 of 1995), the commission completed its task by 2002. It submitted a final report, published in several volumes, the fourth of which deals specifically with faith communities.[6] Much theological re-

---

3. Denise Ackermann, "Take up a taunt song: Women, lament, and healing in South Africa," in *Reconstruction: The WCC assembly in Harare 1998 and the churches in Southern Africa,* ed. Leny Lagerwerf, p. 135 (Zoetemeer: Meinema, 1998).

4. In Germany the issue of "the past" had to be faced twice within the space of fifty years: after the Second World War and again after the fall of the Berlin Wall.

5. For an expanded version of this section on restorative justice, see Piet J. Naudé, "We cannot continue as if nothing has happened between us," *Scriptura* 82 (2003): 139-46.

6. *Truth and Reconciliation Commission of South Africa Report,* vol. 4 (Cape Town: The

flection accompanied the work of the commission, as South African theologians[7] and later German scholars[8] attempted to think through the complex issues of truth, reconciliation, collective guilt, the narrative structure of healing processes, and forgiveness. Much criticism was leveled against the commission,[9] described by Tutu himself as "a risky and delicate business, but still the only alternative to Nuremberg on the one hand and amnesia on the other."[10]

Two issues still need to be addressed after the work of the commission. The first is the question of amnesty, or alternatively, the criminal prosecution of those who did not divulge serious human rights abuses to the commission. If such prosecutions are not followed through, the unintended consequence will be general amnesty without either justice or truth. The second is the issue of reparation for victims of human rights violations. If that is not forthcoming, the consequence is "cheap" reconciliation in both the material and the moral sense of the word.

Both are important issues on the "overwhelming agenda" of dealing

---

Commission, 1998), pp. 59-92. This is imperative reading for any believer in South Africa, for, among other things, it reveals the deep ambiguity of religion as often being both oppressive and liberalizing.

7. For an introduction to the TRC for a German readership, with substantial bibliography, see Dirk J. Smit, "Keine Zukunft ohne Vergebung? Vom Umgang mit den 20. Jahrhundert in Südafrika," *Evangelische Theologie* 62, no. 3 (2002): 172-87. The list of South African contributions would be too long to include here. I merely refer to the important reflections by Tinyiko Sam Maluleke, "Truth, national unity, and reconciliation in Southern Africa," *Missionalia* 25, no. 1 (April 1997): 59-86; Maluleke, "'Dealing lightly with the wounds of my people'? The TRC process in theological perspective," *Missionalia* 25, no. 3 (November 1997): 324-43; and Annalet van Schalkwyk, "A gendered truth: Women's testimonies at the TRC and reconciliation," *Missionalia* 27, no. 2 (1999): 165-88.

8. I do not have a full list but did have access to the following: Geiko Müller-Fahrenholz, *The art of forgiveness: Theological reflections on healing and reconciliation* (Geneva: WCC, 1996); Theo Kneifel, *Zwischen Versöhnung und Gerechtigkeit. Südafrika — der Spagat der Kirchen nach der Apartheid* (Hamburg: Evangelisches Missionswerk in Deutschland, 1998); Ralf Carolus Wüstenberg, ed., *Wahrheit, Recht und Versöhnung. Auseinandersetzung mit der Vergangenheit nach den Politischen Umbruchen in Südafrika und Deutschland* (Frankfurt: Peter Lang, 1998); and Wüstenberg's habilitation thesis, as reflected in his article "Reconciliation with a new lustre: The South African example as a paradigm for dealing with the political past of the German Democratic Republic," *Journal of Theology for Southern Africa* 113 (2002): 19-40 (see this article for further German-related work).

9. Many points of concern were raised about the commission's work, but the one relevant here is that, in the absence of restoration, the TRC could amount to cheap reconciliation in the theological and material senses of the word.

10. *Sunday Times,* December 8, 1996; and Ackermann, "Taunt song," p. 134.

with the past.[11] Let us focus on the second issue, namely that of reparation — or in theological language, restorative justice, linked to the questions of memory, truth, and reconciliation. This may be of value to resolving the numerous "past agendas" all over the world that, if not dealt with theologically, may continue to infect relations between former victims and oppressors, or lead both to cheap forms of reconciliation and to continued injustices. It is even sadder to acknowledge that today there are present realities that are horrendous "pasts-in-the-making." These realities will ensure that, against people's best will and wishes, restorative justice will remain a crucial point on the churches' agenda, well into the twenty-first century.

What are some of the core theological considerations that could inform restorative justice? True restorative justice can grow only from its theological roots in God's inexplicable mercy. There is a strong tradition in the Old Testament that God restores relations with Israel at God's initiative. This restoration of the covenant happens despite God and Israel's knowledge that God could rightfully claim restoration for past injustices, but that God refrains from this claim. A good example is the exilic text in Jeremiah 31:31-34. After prophecies on the restoration of Israel, from chapter 30 onward, the announcement of a new covenant follows, despite Israel's obvious guilt in not keeping the old covenant (v. 32). In the new covenant, the law is written on their hearts. To make this new beginning possible, God does not demand restorative action from his people for their past misdemeanors but in fact frees them from that past: "I will forgive their iniquity, and remember their sin no more" (v. 34).

In the New Testament, the writer to the Hebrews takes this idea further. The community that is addressed is most probably a small Christian community of Jewish descent, living near Rome in about A.D. 60. They are under persecution both by the members of their former (Jewish) faith and by the Roman state. The writer goes to great lengths to explain the gospel of Christ in priestly and covenantal terms, which his readers would have been familiar with. To emphasize the continuity, but also the discontinuity, between high priests in the old order and Jesus' introduction of "a better covenant" (Heb. 8:6), the author twice quotes the Jeremiah text of God's surprising justice: "I will remember their sins no more" (Heb. 8:12; see also 10:17).

The startling point is that one of the crucial differences between the old and new covenants is that the continual sacrifices of the high priests were precisely to serve as a memory of sin (which in turn demanded con-

11. Ackermann, "Taunt song," p. 135.

tinued offerings for sin). However, the completeness of Christ's offering on the cross led to an *ephapaks* (once-for-all) that makes sacrifices for sins unnecessary (Heb. 10:14, 18). Through Christ, God will no longer remember our injustices and sins; in this sense, God remembers our sins only through God's "forgetfulness."

Any talk of restorative justice must therefore begin in the proclamation of God's gracious nonretributive justice in Christ, who carried past injustices while we were still helpless and wicked (Rom. 5:6).[12] In the Jeremiah and Hebrews texts, there is no reference to confession of sin as a condition set by God for covenantal restoration. God's work in Christ stands both before and outside our knowledge of sin and confession. It is exactly this proclamation of free grace that *results* in confession (see Acts 2:37-38). It is absolutely crucial to note, however, that both texts tell of the effect of free grace on those who know that God will no longer remember their past injustices.

Israel receives the Lord's love and grace in as constant a manner as the Lord sustains the regularity of the natural order of sun, moon, and stars. We thus see an inner relation between the created order and the moral order of the law (Jer. 31:35-36). And the Hebrew congregation, exactly because it now has the freedom to enter the Holy of Holies in the temple (previously the right of the high priest only), is set free from a guilty conscience and is thereby freed to love, do good works, and restore the community (Heb. 10:19-25). The people are indeed free to bring sacrifices that are pleasing to God, namely, continued love for one another, doing good, and helping in a sacrificial way (Heb. 13:1, 16); and they are free to extend their sacrifices beyond the boundaries of the congregation to welcome strangers into their homes, thereby welcoming angels without knowing it (Heb. 13:2).

Here, then, the act of "remembering" returns. This time, however, it is not to haunt or to declare guilty or to serve as a basis for new oppression;[13]

---

12. The text should be read as salvation-historical, not as politico-historical, but in the light of the political significance of the first (as explained below), I think the reading is not totally inappropriate.

13. We all cite the well-known phrase of George Santayana that those who forget the past are doomed to repeat it. But Dirk J. Smit's remarks about Afrikaner memories of British atrocities at the turn of the twentieth century ("Keine Zukunft") serve to remind us that there are forms of memory that are indeed dangerous — not in the Metzian sense, but in the sense that memory of oppression can blind one to repeat history in new forms of oppression. Politicians are extremely alert to this kind of memory — either to keep the opposition in a continued state of guilt and defense or to justify their present acts or commission of injustices.

rather, it is to "remember forward" by serving, by bringing restoration. "*Remember* those who are in prison, as though you were in prison with them; those who are being tortured, as though you yourselves were being tortured" (Heb. 13:3, my emphasis).

From a Reformed theological perspective, we find the pattern clearly revealed: if *sola gratia* and justification by faith alone are taken seriously, forms of restorative justice will flow "logically." This is what the Heidelberg Catechism says so eloquently in Question and Answer 64: Will free grace not breed people who treat good works lightly and consequently live without a conscience? No, teaches the catechism, *because it is impossible* for those who have received the grace in Christ not to bear the fruits of conversion (Matt. 7:18). If Reformed theology indicates that the faithful *must* bear fruit, this "must" is not explained deontologically as a moral imperative but ontologically as an expression of being, just as the relation between tree and fruit is "not a relation of ought but of is" ("kein Sollens-, sondern ein Seinszusammenhang").[14] The "logic of grace" lies in following Jesus and being obedient to the new law of love: "We know love by this, that he laid down his life for us — and we ought to lay down our lives for one another" (1 John 3:16). The impossible possibility is to receive God's grace and liberating justice — seeing God's open-heartedness in Christ — and then to close one's own heart to structural injustice[15] and to talk easily about love without corresponding deeds or truth.

Here "truth" returns as well, not as "narrative revelation about the past," like in the TRC, but accompanying our deeds of restoration as the criterion for Christlike love (1 John 3:16-18). In John's letters, this love is the mark of a truly just community, where people live in union with God and with one another, and where love has conquered fear (1 John 4:13-18).

The same pattern emerges from Belhar. Reconciliation, the prerogative of free grace from the triune God, is established in the church (art. 1). Where this reconciliation is accepted through faith, God's reconciliation is embodied in visible church unity (art. 2), peace among people (art. 3), and justice in society (art. 4). There is no doubt that article 4 includes restorative justice. It refers to specific "restorative" scriptural passages from Luke and Amos, and it calls the church to stand against the powerful and privileged who selfishly seek their own interests and discriminate against those over whom they exercise, or have exercised, control. This is an ide-

---

14. Wilfried Härle, *Dogmatik* (Berlin: Walter de Gruyter, 1995), p. 163.

15. In this case the Johannine reference is specifically about rich versus poor.

ology, says the article, which is to be resisted by those who follow the gospel message.

The theological structure remains clear. Restorative justice flows from an understanding of God's reconciliation with us in Christ and through the Spirit, which in turn is exemplified by the church. If this logic is overturned by a political discourse of vengeance, restorative justice becomes, theologically speaking, a law of the old covenant, no matter whether motivated by liberal human rights values, by quotations from Scripture, or by feelings of either vengeance or guilt. The same consequences as in the old covenant follow. No one can ever satisfy the law, and no matter how extensive your sacrificial actions, they do not liberate you but in actual fact continue reminding you of your guilt. So, riddled by guilt and vague feelings of inadequacy, you choose instead to withdraw and forget.

When seen from the perspective of Christ's priestly sacrifice, the opposite happens. Restorative justice, in the form of obedience and thankfulness, flows from the inner, irresistible logic of the gospel. Freed from a bad conscience (tellingly present in both Hebrews and 1 John), we are now able to bring sacrifices pleasing to God; furthermore, the more sacrifices we bring, the greater the joy in fulfilling the new law of love.[16]

The question naturally arises: What happens in cases of confrontation with suffering and injustice caused by our own wrongdoing or complicity? Even here, one must be careful not to lose sight of the distinct theological dimension that underlies the acts of restoration that are in turn significantly linked to justice. Psalm 51, a personal lamentation, reveals this structure. When David[17] was confronted by Nathan about his premeditated sins against Uriah and his family, the depth of the lament rises up from the confession before God:[18] "Against you, you

---

16. I have not seen a single white DRC congregation — and I have contact with many — that has closed its ears or its heart to this liberating gospel. The consequences in acts of material justice is a miracle from God, mostly unpublicized, as true grace should be. That said, I agree that white participation in, and success in living with, the TRC process was generally disappointing.

17. I do not wish to enter the debate about authorship or ascribed authorship, or the question as to whether the link with the Davidic events is indeed part of the original text.

18. Denise Ackermann's plea ("Take up a taunt song") to restore lament as theology and liturgy needs to be taken very seriously. Not only does it provide a constructive way to grieve, but it restores the dignity of the "unknown" sufferers, while giving women the initiative in the process.

alone, have I have sinned, and done what is evil in your sight" (Ps. 51:4). In the language of the letter to the Hebrews, if you see that you defiled the sacrifice of Christ in your dehumanization of others, it is before God that you stand. It is, according to the text, "a fearful thing to fall into the hands of the living God" if you keep sinning while knowing the truth (Heb. 10:31).

But once the writer of Psalm 51 stands before God in guilt and confession, there is a plea for the restoration of joy and for heart-cleansing (vv. 8, 10). Then the psalmist turns away in rededication to God. He will teach other sinners to convert (turn back: Heb. *suf*) to God (v. 13), and — most significantly — he will take God's justice on his lips (v. 14b). The sacrifice of a broken heart (guilt and confession) is more important than any other sacrifice that makes up the normal cultic duties (vv. 16-17). These sacrifices (extended in v. 19) include justice and only gain significance from the prior sacrifice of contrition.

Willie Jonker, influential South African systematic theologian, made a dramatic and moving confession to other South Africans on behalf of the DRC at the Rustenburg church convention late in 1990. His confession follows the same pattern as emerged from the biblical traditions:

> I confess before you and before the Lord, not only my own sin and guilt, and my personal responsibility for the political, social, economical and structural wrongs that have been done to many of you, and as a result of which you and our whole country are still suffering from, but vicariously I dare also to do that in the name of the DRC, of which I am a member, and for the Afrikaans people as a whole. I have the liberty to do just that because the DRC at its last synod declared apartheid a sin and confessed its own guilt of negligence in not warning against it and distancing itself from it long ago.[19]

"Before you and before the Lord. . . ." Confrontation with one's (premeditated) sin against others is confrontation with God himself because anthropological matters are indeed theological matters. Exactly because of this the opposite is also true: the theological reality of facing God always

19. See Jonker, "Understanding the church situation," p. 92. The confession is an extract from Jonker's speech at the national conference of churches in November 1990, held in the town of Rustenburg, South Africa. The speech is much richer than what is discussed here, as Jonker also raises issues of vicariousness and collective responsibility.

leads one back to human reality, specifically to talk (Ps. 51:14) and to do (Ps. 51:13) justice. Only then is costly reconciliation possible.[20]

We therefore can and must insist on restorative justice, in multiple senses. In the ritual of the TRC hearings,[21] which assumed "a definite socially representative function,"[22] the public recognition of victims' suffering, which assumed the form of narrative, dialogical, and healing truth,[23] served as moral compensation. This moral restoration is of immense symbolic value, though those who insist on factual-juristic truth so often underestimate it.

But the biblical tradition we investigated makes it clear that knowledge of suffering (truth and memory turned backward) must lead to sacrificial acts in all their materiality (truth and memory turned forward). There is the opening of homes to strangers (angels!) and the taking of the sufferings of others as our own as a sign that the love of God is in us.[24]

And let us not beat around the bush here. The Bible is clear that it is not enough to feel sorry for those who suffer (1 John 3:17). New governments who rule after oppressive pasts must indeed pay some financial compensation or grant some material relief. In most cases, this will not and cannot be exact financial compensation, and the latter will retain a symbolic function. The fact that the law cannot determine exact compensation for loss of opportunity and loss of dignity for millions of people, over decades, does not relieve us of sacrificial love in the most material sense of the word.

---

20. Piet Meiring stated, "For many, especially white South Africans, it was and still is extremely difficult to face the past, to acknowledge their responsibility, and to confess their guilt. But without that, there is still little chance of reconciliation" ("Reconciliation: Dream or reality?" *Missionalia* 27, no. 3 [November 1999]: 243-44).

21. Antjie Krog, Afrikaans poet and journalist, whose *Country of my skull* (Cape Town: Random House, 1998) is a moving literary account of the TRC that won her international acclaim, makes the incisive point that the TRC could be interpreted ritually. This opens the perspective of social representativeness, which releases the TRC from unrealistic expectations of dealing with every detail in each case. See Krog, "The Truth and Reconciliation Commission: A national ritual?" *Missionalia* 26, no. 1 (1998): 5-16.

22. See Wüstenberg, "Reconciliation," p. 34.

23. See Smit, "Keine Zukunft," p. 179.

24. Did not James relentlessly emphasize a material faith? "If a brother or sister is naked and lacks daily food, and one of you says to them, 'Go in peace; keep warm and eat your fill,' and yet you do not supply their bodily needs, what is the good of that?" (James 2:15-16). These "necessities of life" are the ultimate mark of reconciliation, wholesome shalom, a sign of pure and undefiled religion (James 1:27).

If churches follow Belhar, attempting to stand where God stands and resolutely trying to "witness against and strive against any form of injustice" (art. 4.2), they will have to call for sacrifices that make restorative justice possible. This is normally not popular among those who benefited from an unjust past. But if theological reflection does not enable such deeds of sacrifices pleasing to God, it is part of an interesting, but ultimately worthless, religion before God.

If there were ever a test case for *sola gratia*, this is it.

God is in a special way the God of the destitute and the poor: Economic justice

One could argue that apartheid was finally demolished by economic, and not so much political or ecclesial, forces. This is why sanctions, in which the ecumenical church played a crucial role, were so fiercely resisted by the apartheid government. Conversely, one of the prospects of political liberation was a renewed integration into the world's economy, with massive re-investment in order to undo the economic damage of the disinvestment that had taken place during the preceding decade. However, the idea of a "Marshall Plan" for South Africa after the collapse of apartheid did not materialize, among other reasons, because of the inherent "logic" of a global market economy into which South Africa had belatedly stepped in 1994.

Knowing the danger of not fully understanding the complexities of modern economics, as well as resisting the temptation to blame the international economic order for all woes, I nevertheless wish to make a few remarks here. Depending on one's hierarchical place in the system, the effect of globalism is deeply ambiguous.[25] If a country is classified as an "emerging economy" or a "Third World country," the following is true in most cases: its currency is left to the mercy of trader perceptions or international rating agencies, formed by factors over which it has absolutely no control — for example, a subprime banking crisis in the United States and elsewhere, a terrorist attack like 9/11, unconstitutional land-policies in Zimba-

25. I follow Ulrich Beck's distinction here between *globalization* as a process and *globalism* as the economic result of such a process. Globalism is expressed in the ideology of neoliberalism, where the multidimensionality of society is reduced to monocausal economic viewpoints. For Africans, the elimination of politics by the market leads to a serious loss of agency and creates new forms of dependencies. See Beck, *What is globalization?* (Cambridge: Polity Press, 2000), pp. 9-11.

bwe, or an election result in Kenya. A currency's relative value to the dollar, euro, or pound is not merely an interesting economic indicator, it has a material effect on the very livelihood of people. An example of this is the dramatic drop in the value of the South African rand over a few days in December 2001 and again in October 2008. This led to double-digit food inflation and a steep increase in the price of maize, the most basic food of poor South Africans.

The borrowing of money from international agencies is linked to enforced adjustment policies (normally dramatic privatization) that are not always suited to the social conditions of poor countries. This results in a deepening social malaise and erodes the very idea of autonomy in a nation-state. If a developing country does attract foreign direct (re)investment, it is mostly in liquid form, which enables a quick flight of capital at the press of a button somewhere in London or New York. This is hailed as the magic of digital capitalism.

When it comes to trade negotiations, many industrialized nations speak with a forked tongue on the liberalization of trade but yet act in their own interests whenever it suits their local election campaigns or sectional economic lobby-groups. This is especially the case with agriculture, steel, and intellectual property rights.

Poorer countries in the East and the South do not have the resources to combat the impact of global warming, caused mainly by the industrialized nations like the United States and countries with strong emerging economies like India and China. Unusual droughts and floods in poorer countries severely affect the majority of people reliant on subsistence farming. In a global context, these people are seen as recipients of "benevolent development aid," where such aid is dependent on the goodwill of the donor and is not seen as a case of co-responsibility for the environment.

The negative impact of global capitalism (there are obviously also advantages) leads to the deep paradox of "being accepted in the world" but simultaneously experiencing a loss of agency. In South Africa, it was exactly this sense of agency that was denied the country (politically speaking) over so many decades. Poor countries are deeply concerned by a lack of urgency by powerful agencies to create a more humane society where the very system of international trade and investment is reviewed to overcome forms of "invisible" marginalization and dehumanization.[26] The

26. The innovative work by economists like Amartya Sen and Joseph Stiglitz clearly challenges the traditional assumptions of neoliberal capitalism and the current trade re-

Accra Confession speaks in this regard of a resistance against an evil empire: "In using the term 'empire' we mean the coming together of economic, cultural, political and military power that constitutes a system of domination led by powerful nations to protect and defend their own interests" (AC art. 11).[27] A forceful passage from Calvin is perhaps apt at this point. In his exposition of the eighth commandment, he writes:

> There are very many kinds of theft. One consists in violence, . . . another in . . . the more hidden craft which takes possession of them with a semblance of justice; [another] in sycophancy, which wiles them away under the pretence of donation. But . . . we know that all the arts by which we obtain possession of the goods and money of our neighbours . . . are to be regarded as thefts. Though they may be obtained by an action at law, a different decision is given by God. He sees the long train of deception by which the man of craft begins to lay nets for his more simple neighbor, until he entangles him in its meshes. . . . [He] sees the harsh and cruel laws by which the more powerful oppresses and crushes the feeble . . . , though all these escape the judgment of man, and no cognisance is taken of them. . . . We defraud our neighbours to their hurt if we decline any of the duties which we are bound to perform towards them.[28]

It is not difficult to see why these words ring so true to an African reader.

Globalization not only poses the question of global economic justice. It raises crucial questions about how one understands personhood. South Africa's "joining the world" after the isolation of apartheid implied a radical and extremely swift immersion into the typical traits of personhood emanating from Western modernity, with its commendable values of freedom, individuality, rationality, questioning of authority, and secularity. South Africa's new constitution powerfully expresses these values.

But we know that each of these values can be and has been distorted in our present time: freedom turns into the unfettered power of arbitrary in-

---

gime. See, for example, Sen, *On ethics and economics* (Oxford: Blackwell, 1988), and, by Stiglitz, *Globalization and its discontents* (New York: W. W. Norton, 2002), *Making globalization work* (New York: W. W. Norton, 2006), and "Social justice and global trade," *Far Eastern Economic Review* 169, no. 2 (March 2006): 18-22.

27. World Alliance of Reformed Churches, *The Accra Confession: Covenanting for justice in the economy and the earth* (Geneva: WCC, 2004).

28. John Calvin, *Institutes of the Christian religion* (Grand Rapids: Eerdmans, 1957), 2.8.45.

dividual choice;[29] individuality becomes individualism, which inhibits community and weakens a striving for the common good; rationality and public argument turn into rationalism, which falls prey to scientism and hermeneutically naive positivism; a healthy questioning of authority turns into loss of cultural memory and tradition; and secularity in turn becomes secularism, with an impoverished ontology and antireligious attitudes.[30]

In South Africa (and other developing states), one unfortunately witnesses the inhuman consequences of a rising selfish individualism. This distorted value has been embraced by a new generation of black business people and public servants who openly say: "We are entitled to our enrichment" and "We did not join the struggle to be poor." It is also embraced by a new generation of young people (of all races) who religiously believe that money determines one's human destiny and social acceptability. Crass materialism has become deeply embedded as a guiding value, corruption based on greed is rife, and consumption has become an important form of personal and social therapy.

This individualism is a form of self-centered hedonism. It ravages a striving for the common good and relegates caring for those who stand very little chance of becoming part of the economic system to very low on the agenda. Belhar names these people the destitute, the poor, the wronged, the hungry, the downtrodden, and the stranger (art. 4.1). How shall we respond theologically to the two associated challenges of economic marginalization and rampant, self-referential individualism?

If our cue to be truly human lies in Jesus Christ, we must retain the vision of Jesus' earthly ministry in all its concreteness. We see how he transcends his own needs and, for the sake of others, does the will of the Father, even unto the cross. We see his openness to respond to the physical and spiritual needs of those marginalized by culture, religion, gender, or economics. We hear his teaching that it is better to give than to receive and that the eschatological judgment will be based on our action toward the weakest and the smallest. In the context of a self-serving agenda, Jesus teaches that those who cling to life will surely lose it, and that those who show mercy to others are blessed.

29. See Ellen T. Charry's discussion of freedom as understood in a sapiential sense (editorial, *Theology Today* 62 [2006]: 460).

30. See Schweiker's interesting remark that "overhumanization" is the combined effect of secularism and scientism (*Theological ethics and global dynamics* [Oxford: Blackwell, 2004], p. 202). This is an ideology and a social condition in which the maximizing of power becomes a good in itself.

The theological agenda of the "nonperson," the epistemological privilege of the poor, so forcefully argued for by Latin American (and later black) liberation theologians, and the revelation of God as "in a special way the God of the destitute, the poor and the wronged,"[31] so eloquently confessed in Belhar (art. 4.1), are now ecumenically accepted views, and adherence to them is as urgent as ever before.[32]

The vision of Christ-for-others tells of a man who not only shared gifts of friendship and healing but gave himself up. This vision should guide the church in its self-understanding as a holy church, gathered by Word and Spirit into a *sanctorum communio*. Belhar calls on the church to "witness against all the powerful and privileged who selfishly seek their own interests and thus control and harm others" (art. 4.3).

Holiness refers foremost to the church's state of justification, whereby believers receive Christ's holiness (1 Cor. 1:30), but it equally refers to our sanctification (Lev. 11:44; 1 Pet. 1:15) by following Christ. Both these dimensions need to be kept in focus. As holy people, the church is both (1) a distinct community set aside by and for God and (2) witnessing to Christ through an alternative lifestyle in the realities of the world (1 Pet. 2:11 and 3:15-16). "The church is sanctified," remarks Moltmann, "where it participates in the lowliness, helplessness, poverty and suffering of Christ."[33]

In a remarkable counterstatement to self-referential individualism, the Heidelberg Catechism explicates the *sanctorum communio* as "the obligation on each of us to use our God-given gifts freely and joyously for the

31. See Nico Koopman's excellent article "A basic and neglected conviction of (Reformed) theology?" in *350 years Reformed: 1652-2002*, ed. Pieter Coertzen, pp. 252-60 (Bloemfontein: CLF, 2002). For a more critical reflection on the "partisan" nature of God, see Mary Stewart van Leeuwen, "From Barmen to Belhar: Public theology in crisis situations," *Princeton Seminary Bulletin* 27, no. 1 (2006): 23-33, especially pages 25-26, where the justice article is discussed.

32. The philosophical translation of this partisan choice for the poor has been eloquently developed by John Rawls in his notion of distributive justice, whereby the position of the least-advantaged representative person and the most-burdened societies in the commonwealth of peoples serve as the criterion and reference point for establishing a just socioeconomic order. See the "domestic" version of Rawls's ideas in *A theory of justice* (Cambridge, Mass.: Harvard University Press, Belknap Press, 1972) and his "global" version in *The law of peoples* (Cambridge, Mass.: Harvard University Press, 1999). One of the best theological interpretations of Rawls is that of Heinrich Bedford-Strohm, *Vorrang für die Armen. Auf dem Weg zu einer theologischen Theorie der Gerechtigkeit* (Gütersloh: Gütersloher Verlagshaus, 1993).

33. Jürgen Moltmann, *The church in the power of the Spirit: A contribution to messianic ecclesiology* (London: SCM Press, 1977), p. 355.

benefit and welfare of others" (Question and Answer 55). This sharing obviously relates to spiritual gifts (1 Cor. 12–14), but the biblical teaching includes material gifts as well.

The early church is depicted in Acts 2 as a sharing community. They shared a common teaching, common prayers, common meals, common property, and a common doxology. The sharing included Greek widows (Acts 6), who in turn served as a basis for instituting the office of deacon, tasked to ensure that the needs of the needy were met. As the church spread beyond the borders of Jerusalem and the mother church itself was later plagued by poverty, the "mission" churches sent material help according to their ability. Paul uses the Eucharist as a basis to exhort not only unity but also the sharing of food (1 Cor. 11). An early church hymn interpreted the self-giving of Christ as a basis for the holy people of God to "let the same mind be in you that was in Christ Jesus," to count the interest of others higher than their own (Phil. 2:4-11).

There is no doubt that the church is a sharing communion of saints, a "community of concern" where members serve as "ministers of divine benefit."[34] What does that imply to being church in a complex, capitalist society, far removed from the social conditions prevailing at the time of the earliest churches? The answer lies in action at both global and local levels.

At a global level, the institutional church's witness against the systemically uneven distribution of economic goods in the world and the declaration of a confession like that of Accra should not be underestimated. Its ability to keep the issue of systemic injustices on the agenda of agencies like the G-8, the World Bank, the IMF, and the WTO is significant. More nuanced analyses are probably required rather than a mere dichotomy between "God" and "Mammon,"[35] but this witness remains a crucial contribution to what Gustafson referred to as "prophetic" ethical discourse.[36]

At regional and local levels, "prophecy" must be complemented by living the alternative christological narrative, where, to follow Stanley Hauerwas,[37] the church is a social ethic, embodying a community not

34. Kathryn Tanner, *Jesus, humanity, and the Trinity: A brief systematic theology* (Minneapolis: Fortress Press, 2001), p. 89.

35. See, for example, the variety of biblical traditions in Michael Welker and Michael Wolter, eds., "Gott und Geld," special issue, *Jahrbuch für Biblische Theologie* 21 (2006).

36. James Gustafson, *Varieties of moral discourse: Prophetic, narrative, ethical, and policy* (Grand Rapids: Calvin College and Seminary, 1988).

37. Stanley Hauerwas, *After Christendom? How the church is to behave if freedom, justice, and a Christian nation are bad ideas* (Nashville: Abingdon Press, 1991).

predicated upon the value of excessive greed presented by a neoliberal society. Belhar notes that God "blocks the path of the ungodly" (art. 4.1). The best way for the church to follow God in this blocking is to create "precedent communities" that establish noncompetitive forms of goods circulation, imitating the indiscriminate grace and good distributed by God to the entire creation.[38] Local or regional churches have proven themselves to be extremely effective redistributive agencies, playing indispensable roles in the lives of the poor, the hungry, the illiterate, the sick, and the marginalized.

To avoid the perceived "traditionalist" slant in Hauerwas[39] and to address Schweiker's concern about "the church" being an outpost of peaceableness in "alien lands,"[40] engagement with Gustafson's "ethical" and "policy" discourses is also required. This would imply, among other things, that economics (and not only science or philosophy) becomes a key disciplinary partner for theology. On a policy level, the most effective way for the church to be "the salt of the earth" is for ordinary Christians to follow their vocation concretely in business and the professions, where the real decisions affecting our world are made.[41]

In its position as the undisputed economic, military, and technologi-

38. Kathryn Tanner, "What does grace have to do with money? Theology within a comparative economy," *Harvard Divinity Bulletin* 30 (Spring 2002): 6-9.

39. See Jeffrey Stout, *Democracy and tradition* (Princeton: Princeton University Press, 2004), pp. 140-61, where he makes the specific point that Hauerwas and MacIntyre suffer from "excessive rhetoric" against liberal ideas and that Hauerwas presents a new traditionalism that is not helpful for sustaining a democratic political order. Hauerwas's response convinces me that his call on the church to be church is not a sectarian withdrawal from the world but a focus on the unique agency of the church to act as servant in the world. See Stanley Hauerwas, *Performing the faith: Bonhoeffer and the practice of nonviolence* (Grand Rapids: Brazos Press, 2004), pp. 215-41.

40. William Schweiker, "Humanity before God: Theological humanism from a Christian perspective," The Martin Marty Center for the Advanced Study of Religion: The Religion and Culture Web Forum, October 2003, p. 2, http://divinity.uchicago.edu/martycenter/publications/webforum/102003/commentary.shtml.

41. See Tanner, *Jesus, humanity, and the Trinity*, p. 68, who explicitly states: "My theological anthropology appears, indeed, to be a task- or vocation-oriented one." This must be read in the light of the strong link she forges between the Trinity and the vocation to spread the gifts that are ours in Christ. On vocation and the realities of business, see Shirley J. Roels, "The Christian calling to business life," *Theology Today* 60 (2003): 357-69. For broader discussions, see Kenneth R. Chase, ed., "Christian perspectives on business ethics: Faith, profit, and decision making," special issue of *Business and Professional Ethics Journal* 23, no. 4 (2004).

cal leader of the world, the United States, along with other developed nations, shoulders a heavy responsibility to use its immense power wisely and to see its own contextual challenges in a global, rather than a nationalistic, framework. A crucial task thus remains for theologians, ethicists, and church leaders in the United States and other developed nations to urge today's political powers to actively support global ecological initiatives. There is also a dire need to renegotiate the terms of global trade toward a fairer and more just system, such as in the (failed) Doha Development Rounds, where the notion of "special and differential treatment" of poor nations has been accepted. Theological ethics will have to show in what ways the debilitating effects of competitive structures "are maintained only by way of our own complicity in them,"[42] and what restitution would imply in a global context.[43]

In the first years of the twenty-first century, we saw the leader of the free world act unilaterally and engage in preemptive wars presumably to export freedom and democracy. If the Christian faith is called upon to legitimize these and similar actions, all of us in our small global village are in grave danger. Let us be reminded that the interrelatedness of security (which can easily appeal to "the war on terror" or "law and order"), patriotic politics ("our homeland and our nation"), and religion ("our God/god") were the main building blocks of National Socialism and apartheid in the twentieth century. We dare not repeat that history.

With Belhar we continue to confess that "we reject any ideology which would legitimate forms of injustice and any doctrine which is unwilling to resist such an ideology in the name of the gospel" (art. 4, rejection). Also with Belhar we remind ourselves that confession and action always go together. Those who dare to stand where God stands, namely against injustice and with the wronged, can expect resistance from the powerful and the privileged. Belhar therefore concludes that "the Church is called to confess and do all these things, even though the authorities and human laws might forbid them and punishment and suffering be the consequence" (art. 5.1).

"Jesus is Lord" (art. 5.2). Indeed, Jesus' lordship was not demonstrated by economic or military or political power but by his sacrificial love, given

42. Tanner, "What does grace have to do with money?" p. 9.
43. Restitution has been discussed above. This is an extremely emotive issue, but theologically it is an indispensable factor in the process of reconciliation and the peace (shalom) that accompanies it. Redistribution of land, writing off debt, and preferential trade conditions are all issues on the agenda, though not always cast in the context of restitution.

in order to restore the humanity of the weak, the poor, the wronged, and the marginalized. We are called by Belhar (art. 4.2) to stand where God stands and to follow Christ "so that justice may roll down like the waters, and righteousness like an ever-flowing stream."

Appendix A

The Belhar Confession, 1982

Article 1

1.1. We believe in the triune God, Father, Son and Holy Spirit,

1.2. . . . who gathers, protects and cares for his Church by his Word and his Spirit, as He has done since the beginning of the world and will do to the end.

Article 2

2.1. We believe in one holy, universal Christian Church, the communion of saints called from the entire human family.

Eph. 2:11-22
2.2. We believe that Christ's work of reconciliation is made manifest in the Church as the community of believers who have been reconciled with God and with one another;

This is the English version of the Belhar Confession as approved by the Dutch Reformed Mission Church in 1986. For historical reasons, this text was mainly used in this book. A slightly amended inclusive-language version of the confession was approved by the Uniting Reformed Church in Southern Africa in 2008. Both versions are available at www.urcsa.org.za under "confessions." For ease of reference, the articles have been broken into numbered subsections. The numbering of subsections is not part of the original text. An inclusive-language text of the confession prepared by the Presbyterian Church (USA), Office of Theology and Worship, is available at www.pcusa.org/theologyandworship/confession/belhar.pdf.

219

Eph. 4:1-16

2.3. . . . that unity is, therefore, both a gift and an obligation for the Church of Jesus Christ; that through the working of God's Spirit it is a binding force, yet simultaneously a reality which must be earnestly pursued and sought; one which the people of God must continually be built up to attain;

John 17:20, 23

2.4. . . . that this unity must become visible so that the world may believe that separation, enmity and hatred between people and groups is sin which Christ has already conquered, and accordingly that anything which threatens this unity may have no place in the Church and must be resisted;

Phil. 2:1-5; 1 Cor. 12:4-31; John 13:1-17; 1 Cor. 1:10-13; Eph. 4:1-6; Eph. 3:14-20; 1 Cor. 10:16-17; 1 Cor. 11:17-34; Gal. 6:2; 2 Cor. 1:3-4

2.5. . . . that this unity of the people of God must be manifested and be active in a variety of ways: in that we love one another; that we experience, practice and pursue community with one another; that we are obligated to give ourselves willingly and joyfully to be of benefit and blessing to one another; that we share one faith, have one calling, are of one soul and one mind; have one God and Father, are filled with one Spirit, are baptised with one baptism, eat of one bread and drink of one cup, confess one Name, are obedient to one Lord, work for one cause, and share one hope; together come to know the height and the breadth and the depth of the love of Christ; together are built up to the stature of Christ, to the new humanity; together know and bear one another's burdens, thereby fulfilling the law of Christ that we need one another and upbuild one another, admonishing and comforting one another; that we suffer with one another for the sake of righteousness; pray together; together serve God in this world; and together fight against all which may threaten or hinder this unity;

Rom. 12:3-8; 1 Cor. 12:1-11; Eph. 4:7-13; Gal. 3:27-28; Jas. 2:1-13

2.6. . . . that this unity can be established only in freedom and not under constraint; that the variety of spiritual gifts, opportunities, backgrounds, convictions, as well as the various languages and cultures, are by virtue of the reconciliation in Christ, opportunities for mutual service and enrichment within the one visible people of God;

2.7. . . . that true faith in Jesus Christ is the only condition for membership of this Church.

Therefore, we reject any doctrine which absolutizes either natural diversity or the sinful separation of people in such a way that this absolutization hinders or breaks the visible and active unity of the Church, or even leads to the establishment of a separate church formation;

. . . which professes that this spiritual unity is truly being maintained in the bond of peace whilst believers of the same confession are in effect alienated from one another for the sake of diversity and in despair of reconciliation;

. . . which denies that a refusal earnestly to pursue this visible unity as a priceless gift is sin;

. . . which explicitly or implicitly maintains that descent or any other human or social factor should be a consideration in determining membership of the Church.

Article 3

2 Cor. 5:17-21; Matt. 5:13-16; Matt. 5:9; 2 Pet. 3:13; Rev. 21–22
3.1. We believe that God has entrusted to his Church the message of reconciliation in and through Jesus Christ; that the Church is called to be the salt of the earth and the light of the world; that the Church is called blessed because it is a peacemaker; that the Church is witness both by word and by deed to the new heaven and the new earth in which righteousness dwells;

Eph. 4:17–6:23; Rom. 6; Col. 1:9-14; Col. 2:13-19; Col. 3:1–4:6
3.2. . . . that God by his lifegiving Word and Spirit has conquered the powers of sin and death, and therefore also of irreconciliation and hatred, bitterness and enmity; that God by his lifegiving Word and Spirit will enable his people to live in a new obedience which can open new possibilities of life for society and the world;

3.3. . . . that the credibility of this message is seriously affected and its beneficial work obstructed when it is proclaimed in a land which professes to be Christian, but in which the enforced separation of people on a racial basis promotes and perpetuates alienation, hatred and enmity;

3.4. . . . that any teaching which attempts to legitimate such forced separation by appeal to the gospel and is not prepared to venture on the road of obedience and reconciliation, but rather, out of prejudice, fear, selfishness and unbelief, denies in advance the reconciling power of the gospel, must be considered ideology and false doctrine.

Therefore, we reject any doctrine which, in such a situation, sanctions in the name of the gospel or of the will of God the forced separation of people on the grounds of race and colour and thereby in advance obstructs and weakens the ministry and experience of reconciliation in Christ.

Article 4

Deut. 32:4; Luke 2:14; John 14:27; Eph. 2:14; Isa. 1:16-17; Jas. 1:27; Jas. 5:1-6; Luke 1:46-55; Luke 6:20-26; Luke 7:22; Luke 16:19-31

4.1. We believe that God has revealed himself as the One who wishes to bring about justice and true peace among men; that in a world full of injustice and enmity He is in a special way the God of the destitute, the poor and the wronged and that He calls his Church to follow Him in this; that He brings justice to the oppressed and gives bread to the hungry; that He frees the prisoner and restores sight to the blind; that He supports the downtrodden, protects the stranger, helps orphans and widows and blocks the path of the ungodly; that for Him pure and undefiled religion is to visit the orphans and the widows in their suffering; that He wishes to teach his people to do what is good and to seek the right;

Ps. 146; Luke 4:16-19; Rom. 6:13-18; Amos 5

4.2. . . . that the Church must therefore stand by people in any form of suffering and need, which implies, among other things, that the Church must witness against and strive against any form of injustice, so that justice may roll down like waters, and righteousness like an ever-flowing stream;

4.3. . . . that the Church as the possession of God must stand where He stands, namely against injustice and with the wronged; that in following Christ the Church must witness against all the powerful and privileged who selfishly seek their own interests and thus control and harm others.

Therefore, we reject any ideology which would legitimate forms of injustice and any doctrine which is unwilling to resist such an ideology in the name of the gospel.

Article 5

Eph. 4:15-16; Acts 5:29-33; 1 Pet. 2:18-25; 1 Pet. 3:15-18

5.1. We believe that, in obedience to Jesus Christ, its only Head, the Church is called to confess and to do all these things, even though the authorities and human laws might forbid them and punishment and suffering be the consequence.

5.2. Jesus is Lord.

5.3. To the one and only God, Father, Son and Holy Spirit, be the honour and the glory for ever and ever.

Appendix B

The Nicene Creed, 381

We believe in one God,
the Father, the Almighty,
maker of heaven and earth,
of all that is, seen and unseen.

We believe in one Lord, Jesus Christ,
the only Son of God,
eternally begotten of the Father,
Light from Light,
true God from true God,
begotten, not made,
of one Being with the Father.
Through him all things were made.

For us all [man] and for our salvation
he came down from heaven:
by [the power of] the Holy Spirit
he became incarnate from the Virgin Mary,
and he was made man.

This wording of the Nicene Creed is from *Confessing the one faith: An ecumenical explication of the apostolic faith as it is confessed in the Nicene-Constantinopolitan creed (381)*, rev. ed., Faith and Order Paper 153 (Geneva: WCC, 1991), pp. 11-12. Words in brackets represent older translations that have been changed "in order to correspond better to the original text" (p. 12, n. 3).

For our sake he was crucified under Pontius Pilate;
he suffered [death] and was buried.
On the third day he rose [again] from the dead
in accordance with the scriptures;
he ascended into heaven
and is seated at the right hand of the Father.
He will come again in glory to judge the living
and the dead;
and his kingdom will have no end.

We believe in the Holy Spirit,
the Lord, the giver of life;
who proceeds from the Father.
Who with the Father and the Son is worshipped
and glorified,
who has spoken through the Prophets.

We believe in one holy catholic and apostolic Church.
We [acknowledge] confess one baptism for the forgiveness of sins.
We look for the resurrection of the dead,
and the life of the [world] age to come. Amen.

Appendix C

The Cottesloe Declaration, 1961

Part 1

We have met as delegates from the member churches in South Africa of the World Council of Churches, together with representatives of the World Council itself, to seek under the guidance of the Holy Spirit to understand the complex problems of human relationships in this country, and to consult with one another on our common task and responsibility in the light of the Word of God. Our worship, Bible study, discussion and personal contacts have led us to a heightened appreciation of one another's convictions and actions. Our next task will be to report to our several Churches, realizing that the ultimate significance of our meeting will consist in the witness and decisions of the Churches themselves in consequence of these consultations.

The general theme of our seven days together has been the Christian attitude towards race relations. We are united in rejecting all unjust discrimination. Nevertheless, widely divergent convictions have been expressed on the basic issues of apartheid. They range on the one hand from the judgment that it is unacceptable in principle, contrary to the Christian calling and unworkable in practice, to the conviction on the other hand that a

---

This version of the Cottesloe Declaration appears in *Between Christ and Caesar: Classic and contemporary texts on church and state*, ed. Charles Villa-Vicencio (Cape Town: David Philip; Grand Rapids: Eerdmans, 1986), pp. 211-13. Part 3 of the declaration was omitted from the version in *Between Christ and Caesar*. It is included here for the sake of making the full original text available to readers.

policy of differentiation can be defended from the Christian point of view, that it provides the only realistic solution to the problems of race relations and is therefore in the best interests of the various population groups.

Although proceeding from these divergent views, we are nevertheless able to make the following affirmations concerning human need and justice, as they affect relations among the races of this country. In the nature of the case the agreements here recorded do not — and we do not pretend that they do — represent in full the convictions of the member Churches.

The Church of Jesus Christ, by its nature and calling, is deeply concerned with the welfare of all people, both as individuals and as members of social groups. It is called to minister to human need in whatever circumstances and forms it appears, and to insist that all be done with justice. In its social witness the Church must take cognizance of all attitudes, forces, policies and laws which affect the life of a people; but the Church must proclaim that the final criterion of all social and political action is the principles of Scripture regarding the realization of all men of a life worthy of their God-given vocation.

We make bold therefore to address this appeal to our Churches and to all Christians, calling on them to consider every point where they may unite their ministry on behalf of human beings in the spirit of equity.

Part 2

1. We recognise that all racial groups who permanently inhabit our country are a part of our total population, and we regard them as indigenous. Members of all these groups have an equal right to make their contribution towards the enrichment of the life of their country and to share in the ensuing responsibilities, rewards and privileges.

2. The present tension in South Africa is the result of a long historical development and all groups bear responsibility for it. This must also be seen in relation to events in other parts of the world. The South African scene is radically affected by the decline of the power of the West and by the desire for self-determination among the peoples of the African continent.

3. The Church has a duty to bear witness to the hope which is in Christianity both to white South Africans in their uncertainty and to non-white South Africans in their frustration.

4. In a period of rapid social change the Church has a special responsibility for fearless witness within society.

5. The Church as the body of Christ is a unity and within this unity the natural diversity among men is not annulled but sanctified.

6. No one who believes in Jesus Christ may be excluded from any Church on the grounds of his colour or race. The spiritual unity among all men who are in Christ must find visible expression in acts of common worship and witness, and in fellowship and consultation on matters of common concern.

7. We regard with deep concern the revival in many areas of African society of heathen tribal customs incompatible with Christian beliefs and practice. We believe this reaction is partly the result of a deep sense of frustration and a loss of faith in Western civilization.

8. The whole Church must participate in the tremendous missionary task which has to be done in South Africa, and which demands a common strategy.

9. Our discussions have revealed that there is not sufficient consultation and communication between the various racial groups which make up our population. There is a special need that a more effective consultation between the Government and leaders accepted by the non-white people of South Africa should be devised. The segregation of racial groups carried through without effective consultation and involving discrimination leads to hardship for members of the groups affected.

10. There are no Scriptural grounds for the prohibition of mixed marriages. The well-being of the community and pastoral responsibility require, however, that due consideration should be given to certain factors which may make such marriages inadvisable.

11. We call attention once again to the disintegrating effects of migrant labour on African life. No stable society is possible unless the cardinal im-

portance of family life is recognized, and, from the Christian standpoint, it is imperative that the integrity of the family be safeguarded.

12. It is now widely recognized that the wages received by the vast majority of the non-white people oblige them to exist well below the generally accepted minimum standard for healthy living. Concerted action is required to remedy this grave situation.

13. The present system of job reservation must give way to a more equitable system of labour which safeguards the interest of all concerned.

14. Opportunities must be provided for the inhabitants of the Bantu races to live in conformity with human dignity.

15. It is our conviction that the right to own land wherever he is domiciled, and to participate in the government of his country, is part of the dignity of the adult man, and for this reason a policy which permanently denies to non-white people the right of collaboration in the government of the country of which they are citizens cannot be justified.

16. (a) It is our conviction that there can be no objection in principle to the direct representation of coloured people in Parliament. (b) We express the hope that consideration will be given to the application of this principle in the foreseeable future.

17. In so far as nationalism grows out of a desire for self-realization, Christians should understand and respect it. The danger of nationalism is, however, that it may seek to fulfill its aim at the expense of the interests of others and that it can make the nation an absolute value which takes the place of God. The role of the Church must therefore be to help to direct national movements towards just and worthy ends.

Part 3

1. Judicial commission on the Langa and Sharpeville incidents
The Consultation expresses its appreciation for the prompt institution of enquiries into the recent disturbances and requests the Government to publish the findings as soon as possible.

2. Justice in trial

It has been noted that during the recent disturbances a great number of people were arrested and detained for several months without being brought to trial. While we agree that abnormal circumstances may arise in any country necessitating a departure from the usual procedure, we would stress the fact that it belongs to the Christian conception of law, justice and freedom that in normal circumstances men should not be punished except after fair trial before open courts for previously defined offenses. Any departure from this fundamental principle should be confined to the narrowest limits and only resorted to in the most exceptional circumstances.

3. Position of Asians in South Africa

We assure the Indian and other Asian elements in the population that they have not been forgotten in our thoughts, discussions and prayers. As Christians we assure them that we are convinced that the same measures of justice claimed here for other population groups also apply to them.

4. Freedom of worship

Bearing in mind the urgent need for the pastoral care of non-white people living on their employer's premises, or otherwise unable without great difficulty to reach Churches in the recognized townships or locations, the Consultation urges that the State should allow the provision of adequate and convenient facilities for non-white people to worship in urban areas.

The Consultation also urges European congregations to cooperate by making their own buildings available for this purpose whenever practicable.

5. Freedom to preach the gospel

The Church has the duty and right to proclaim the Gospel to whomever it will, in whatever the circumstances, and wherever possible consistent with the general principles governing the right of public meetings in democratic countries. We therefore regard as unacceptable any special legislation which would limit the fulfillment of this task.

6. Relationship of churches

The Consultation urges that it be laid upon the conscience of us all that whenever an occasion arises that a church feels bound to criticize another church or church leader it should take the initiative in seeking prior consultation before making any public statement. We believe that in this way reconciliation will be more readily effected and that Christianity will not be brought into disrepute before the world.

7. Mutual information

The Consultation requests that means be found for the regular exchange of all official publications between the member Churches for the increase of mutual understanding and information. Furthermore, Churches are requested to provide full information to other Churches of their procedures in approaching the Government. It is suggested that in approaches to the Government, delegations, combined if possible, multi-racial where appropriate, should act on behalf of the Churches.

8. Co-operation in future

Any body which may be formed for co-operation in the future is requested to give its attention to the following:

(a) A constructive Christian approach to separatist movements;

(b) The education of the Bantu;

(c) The training of non-white leaders for positions of responsibility in all spheres of life;

(d) African literacy and the provision of Christian literature;

(e) The concept of responsible Christian society in all areas in South Africa, including the Reserves;

(f) The impact of Islam on Southern Africa.

9. Residential areas

The Consultation urges, with due appreciation of what has already been done in the provision of homes for non-white people, that there should be a greater security of tenure, and that residential areas be planned with an eye to the economic and cultural level of the inhabitants.

10. The Consultation urges the appointment by the Government of a representative commission to examine the migrant labour system, for the Church is painfully aware of the harmful effects of this system on the family life of the Bantu. The Church sees it as its special responsibility to advocate a normal family life for the Bantu who spend considerable periods of time, or live permanently, in white areas.

We give thanks to Almighty God for bringing us together for fellowship and prayer and consultation. We resolve to continue in this fellowship, and we have therefore made specific plans to enable us to join in common witness in our country.

We acknowledge before God the feebleness of our often divided witness to our Lord Jesus Christ and our lack of compassion for one another.

We therefore dedicate ourselves afresh to the ministry of reconciliation in Christ.

Appendix D

A Message to the People of South Africa, 1968

The Authorised Summary

In the name of Jesus Christ.

We are under an obligation to confess anew our commitment to the universal faith of Christians, the eternal Gospel of salvation and security in Christ Jesus alone.

The Gospel of Jesus Christ is the good news that in Christ God has broken down the walls of division between God and man, and between man and man.

The Gospel of Jesus Christ declares that Christ is the truth who sets men free from all false hopes of freedom and security.

The Gospel of Jesus Christ declares that God has shown himself as the conqueror of all the forces that threaten to separate and isolate and destroy us.

The Gospel of Jesus Christ declares that God is reconciling us to himself and to each other; and that therefore such barriers as race and nationality have no rightful place in the inclusive brotherhood of Christian disciples.

This version of "A Message to the People of South Africa, 1968" appears in *Between Christ and Caesar,* pp. 214-16.

The Gospel of Jesus Christ declares that God is the master of this world, and that it is to him alone that we owe our primary commitment.

The Gospel of Jesus Christ declares that the Kingdom of God is already present in Christ, demanding our obedience and our faith now.

The Gospel of Jesus Christ offers hope and security for the whole life of man, not just in man's spiritual and ecclesiastic relationships, but for human existence in its entirety. Consequently, we are called to witness to the meaning of the Gospel in the particular circumstances of time and place in which we find ourselves. In South Africa, at this time, we find ourselves in a situation where a policy of racial separation is being deliberately effected with increasing rigidity. The doctrine of racial separation is being seen by many not merely as a temporary political policy but as a necessary and permanent expression of the will of God, and as the genuine form of Christian obedience for this country. It is holding out to men a security built not on Christ but on the theory of separation and the preservation of racial identity; it is presenting the separate development of our race groups as the way for the people of South Africa to save themselves. And this claim is being made to us in the name of Christianity.

We believe that this doctrine of separation is a false faith, a novel gospel; it inevitably is in conflict with the Gospel of Jesus Christ, which offers salvation, both individual and social, through faith in Christ alone. It is keeping people away from the real knowledge of Christ; therefore it is the Church's duty to enable our people to distinguish between the demands of the South African state and the demands of Christian discipleship.

The Christian Gospel requires us to assert the truth proclaimed by the first Christians, who discovered that God was creating a new community in which differences of race, language, nation, culture, and tradition no longer had power to separate man from man. The most important features of a man are not the details of his racial group, but the nature which he has in common with all men and also the gifts and abilities which are given to him as a unique individual by the grace of God; to insist that racial characteristics are more important than these is to reject what is most significant about our own humanity as well as the humanity of others.

But, in South Africa, everyone is expected to believe that a man's racial identity is the most important thing about him: only when it is clearly settled can any significant decisions be made about him. Those whose racial classification is in doubt are tragically insecure and helpless. Without racial identity, it seems, we can do nothing; he who has it, has life; he who has not racial identity, has not life. This belief in the supreme importance of racial identity amounts to a denial of the central statements of the Christian Gospel. In practice, it severely restricts the ability of Christian brothers to serve and know each other, and even to give each other simple hospitality; it limits the ability of a person to obey Christ's command to love his neighbour as himself. For, according to the Christian Gospel, our brothers are not merely the members of our own race group. Our brother is the person whom God gives to us. To dissociate from our brother on the grounds of natural distinction is to despise God's gift and to reject Christ.

Where different groups of people are hostile to each other, this is due to human sin, not to the plan of the Creator. The Scriptures do not require such groups to be kept separate from each other; on the contrary, the Gospel requires us to believe in and to act on the reconciliation made for us in Christ. A policy of separation is a demonstration of unbelief in the power of the Gospel; any demonstration of the reality of reconciliation would endanger this policy. Therefore, the advocates of this policy inevitably find themselves opposed to the Church if it seeks to live according to the Gospel and to show that God's grace has overcome our hostilities. A thorough policy of racial separation must ultimately require that the Church should cease to be the Church.

The Gospel of Jesus Christ declares that God is love; separation is the opposite force of love. The Christian Gospel declares that separation is the supreme threat and danger, but that in Christ it has been overcome; it is in association with Christ and with each other that we find our true identity. But apartheid is a view of life and of man which insists that we find our identity in dissociation and distinction from each other; it rejects as undesirable the reconciliation which God is giving to us by his Son; it reinforces distinctions which the Holy Spirit is calling the people of God to overcome; it calls good evil. This policy is, therefore, a form of resistance to the Holy Spirit.

The Gospel of Jesus Christ declares that Christ is our master, and that to him all authority is given. Christians betray their calling if they give their highest loyalty, which is due to Christ alone, to one group or tradition, especially where that group is demanding self-expression at the expense of other groups. God judges us, not by our loyalty to a sectional group but by our willingness to be made new in the community of Christ. Christ is inevitably a threat to much that is called "the South African way of life"; many features of our social order will have to pass away if the lordship of Christ is to be truly acknowledged and if the peace of Christ is to be revealed as the destroyer of our fear.

And Christ is master of the Church also. If the Church fails to witness to the true Gospel of Jesus Christ it will find itself witnessing to a false gospel. If we seek to reconcile Christianity with the so-called "South African way of life" we shall find that we have allowed an idol to take the place of Christ. Where the Church abandons its obedience to Jesus Christ, it ceases to be the Church; it breaks the links between itself and the Kingdom of God. The task of the Church is to enable people to see the power of God at work, changing hostility into love of the brethren, and to express God's reconciliation here and now. For we are not required to wait for a distant "heaven" where all problems will have been solved. What Christ has done, he has done already. We can accept his work or reject it; we can hide from it or seek to live by it. But we cannot postpone it, for it is already achieved; and we cannot destroy it, for it is the work of the eternal God.

We believe that Christ is Lord, and that South Africa is part of his world. We believe that his Kingdom and its righteousness have power to cast out all that opposes his purposes and keeps men in darkness. We believe that the word of God is not bound, and that it will move with power in these days, whether men hear or whether they refuse to hear. And so, we wish to put to every Christian person in the country the question which we ourselves face each day; to whom, or to what, are you giving your first loyalty, your primary commitment? Is it to a subsection of mankind, an ethnic group, a human tradition, a political idea: or to Christ?

May God enable us to be faithful to the Gospel of Jesus Christ, and to be committed to Christ alone!

Bibliography

Ackermann, Denise. "Take up a taunt song: Women, lament, and healing in South Africa." In *Reconstruction: The WCC assembly in Harare 1998 and the churches in Southern Africa*, edited by Leny Lagerwerf, pp. 135-43. Zoetemeer: Meinema, 1998.

Adonis, H. C., and Dirk J. Smit. "Myth versus myth: Conflicting myths in South African religious discourse on violence." *Apologia*, 1991, pp. 21-38.

African Union Commission. *Strategic plan of the African Union Commission*. 3 vols. Addis Ababa: AUC, 2004.

Arens, Edmund. *Bezeugen und Bekennen. Elementäre Handlung des Glaubens*. Düsseldorf: Patmos, 1989.

Balcomb, Tony. "From liberation to democracy: Theologies of bread and being in the new South Africa." *Missionalia* 26, no. 1 (April 1998): 54-73.

Barth, Karl. *Church dogmatics*. I/2: *The revelation of God*. Edinburgh: T. & T. Clark, 1956. Originally published as *Kirchliche Dogmatik*, I/2 (Zürich: Evangelische Verlag, 1948).

——. *Church dogmatics*. III/4: *The doctrine of creation*. Edinburgh: T. & T. Clark, 1961. Originally published as *Kirchliche Dogmatik*, III/4 (Zürich: Evangelische Verlag, 1951).

——. "The desirability and possibility of a universal Reformed creed." In *Theology and Church: Shorter writings, 1920-1928*. With an introduction by T. F. Torrance. London: SCM Press, 1962.

——. *The humanity of God*. London: Collins, 1960.

——. *The knowledge of God and the service of God*. London: Hodder & Stoughton, 1938.

Bate, Stuart C. "Inculturation in process: Influence of coping-healing churches on the attitudes and praxis of mainline churches." *Missionalia* 31, no. 1 (April 2003): 177-207.

Beck, Ulrich. *What is globalization?* Cambridge: Polity Press, 2000.

Bedford-Strohm, Heinrich. *Vorrang für die Armen. Auf dem Weg zu einer theologischen Theorie der Gerechtigkeit*. Gütersloh: Gütersloher Verlagshaus, 1993.

Best, Thomas F. "Survey of church union negotiations, 1996-1999." *Ecumenical Review* 52 (January 2000): 3-6.

Beyers Naudé Centre. *The legacy of Beyers Naudé.* Beyers Naudé Centre Series on Public Theology. Stellenbosch: SUN Press, 2005.

Boesak, Allan. *Black and Reformed: Apartheid, liberation, and the Calvinist tradition.* Maryknoll, N.Y.: Orbis Books, 1984.

Bonhoeffer, Dietrich. *Creation and fall.* London: SCM Press, 1959.

―――. *Sanctorum communio: A theological study of the sociology of the church.* Minneapolis: Fortress Press, 1998.

Bosch, David J. "Nothing but a heresy." In *Apartheid is a heresy,* edited by John W. de Gruchy and Charles Villa-Vicencio, pp. 25-38. Cape Town: David Philip, 1983.

Bosch, David J., A. König, and Willem Nicol, eds. *Perspektief op die Ope Brief.* Cape Town: Human & Rousseau, 1982.

Botha, C. J. "Belhar — a century-old protest." In *A moment of truth: The confession of the Dutch Reformed Mission Church, 1982,* edited by G. Daan Cloete and Dirk J. Smit, pp. 66-80. Grand Rapids: Eerdmans, 1984.

Botha, Jan. "Aspects of the rhetoric of South African New Testament scholarship anno 1992." *Scriptura* 46 (1993): 80-99.

Botha, Johan, and Piet J. Naudé. *Op pad met Belhar. Goeie nuus vir gister, vandag en more.* Pretoria: Van Schaik, 1998.

Botman, Russel H. "The confession of Belhar and our common future." *Perspectives: A Journal of Reformed Thought* 23, no. 5 (May 2008): 14-16.

―――. "Is blood thicker than justice? The legacy of Abraham Kuyper for Southern Africa." In *Religion, pluralism, and public life: Abraham Kuyper's legacy for the twenty-first century,* edited by Luis E. Lugo, pp. 342-64. Grand Rapids: Eerdmans, 2000.

―――. "Who is 'Jesus Christ as community' for us today?" *Journal of Theology for Southern Africa* 97 (March 1997): 32.

Buckley, James J. "The hermeneutical deadlock between revelationists, textualists, and functionalists." *Modern Theology* 6, no. 4 (1990): 325-39.

Calvin, John. *Institutes of the Christian religion.* Grand Rapids: Eerdmans, 1957.

Charry, Ellen T. Editorial. *Theology Today* 62 (2006): 459-64.

Charta Oecumenica. *Ökumenische Rundschau* 48, no. 3 (1999): 275-95.

―――. *Ökumenische Rundschau* 50, no. 4 (2001): 506-14.

Chase, Kenneth R., ed. "Christian perspectives on business ethics: Faith, profit, and decision making." Special issue of *Business and Professional Ethics Journal* 23, no. 4 (2004).

Cilliers, J. H. "Die teologiese onderbou van die prediking." *Praktiese teologie in Suid-Afrika,* 1994, pp. 1-13.

Cloete, G. Daan, and Dirk J. Smit, eds. *A moment of truth: The confession of the Dutch Reformed Mission Church, 1982.* Grand Rapids: Eerdmans, 1984. Originally published as *'n Oomblik van waarheid* (Kaapstad: Tafelberg, 1984).

Comaroff, John L., and Jean Comaroff. "On personhood: An anthropological perspective from Africa." In *Die autonome Person — eine europäische Erfindung?* edited by

Klaus-Peter Köpping, Michael Welker, and Reiner Wiehl, pp. 67-82. Munich: Wilhelm Fink, 2002.

Cone, James H. "Strange fruit: The cross and the lynching tree." *Harvard Divinity Bulletin* 35 (Winter 2007): 47-55.

Cottesloe Consultation: The report of the consultation among South African member churches of the World Council of Churches, 7-14 December 1960 at Cottesloe, Johannesburg. Johannesburg, 1961.

Daniels, Andries. "Bybelgebruik in die Belharbelydenis se artikel oor 'eenheid.'" *Scriptura* 77 (2001): 193-209.

De Beer, Jan Mathys. "Die missionêre waarde van die Belhar Belydenis vir die N. G. Kerk. Instrument tot inheemswording." Doctoral thesis, University of Pretoria, 2008.

De Bruijn, Jan. "Abraham Kuyper as a romantic." In *Kuyper reconsidered: Aspects of his life and work,* edited by Cornelis van der Kooi and Jan de Bruijn, pp. 42-52. Amsterdam: V. U. Uitgeverij, 1999.

De Gruchy, John W. *Bonhoeffer and South Africa: Theology in dialogue.* Grand Rapids: Eerdmans, 1984.

―――. "Christian humanism: Reclaiming a tradition, affirming an identity." *Reflections: Centre of Theological Inquiry* 8 (Spring 2006): 38-65.

―――. *The church struggle in South Africa.* Cape Town: David Philip, 1979.

―――. *Liberating Reformed theology: A South African contribution to an ecumenical debate.* Grand Rapids: Eerdmans, 1991.

―――. "Recovering ecumenical vision and commitment in a post-ecumenical era." *Journal of Theology for Southern Africa* 102 (1998): 1-12.

―――. "Towards a confessing church." In *Apartheid is a heresy,* edited by John de Gruchy and Charles Villa-Vicencio, pp. 75-93. David Philip: Cape Town, 1983.

De Gruchy, John W., with Steve de Gruchy. *The church struggle in South Africa.* London: SCM Press, 2004.

De Gruchy, John W., and Charles Villa-Vicencio, eds. *Apartheid is a heresy.* Cape Town: David Philip, 1983.

De Klerk, W. A. *The Puritans in Africa.* London: Rex Collings, 1975.

Denis, Philippe. "Sexuality and AIDS in South Africa." *Journal of Theology for Southern Africa* 115 (March 2003): 63-77.

Department of Health, South Africa. *National HIV and syphilis antenatal seroprevalence survey in South Africa, 2004.* Pretoria: Department of Health, 2005.

Derenthal, Olaf. *AIDS in Afrika und die Rede von Gott.* Hamburg: Lit Verlag, 2002.

De Villiers, Etienne. "The influence on the DRC on public policy during the late 80s and 90s." *Scriptura* 76 (2001): 51-61.

Durand, Jaap J. F. "Afrikaner piety and dissent." In *Resistance and hope,* edited by Charles Villa-Vicencio and John W. de Gruchy, pp. 41-48. Cape Town: David Philip, 1985.

―――. "A confession — was it really necessary?" In *A moment of truth: The confession of the Dutch Reformed Mission Church, 1982,* edited by G. Daan Cloete and Dirk J. Smit, pp. 33-41. Grand Rapids: Eerdmans, 1984.

Engdahl, Hans. *Theology in conflict: Readings in Afrikaner theology.* Frankfurt: Peter Lang, 2006.

Enns, Fernando. "Elemente einer Kultur der gewaltfreiheit angesichts des globalisierten Terrorismus." In "Theologie und Gewalt." Special issue, *epd-Dokumentation* 6 (February 2002): 5-12.

————. "Impuls zur Gegenbewegung — eine Ökumenische Dekade. Das ÖRK Programm zur Überwindung von Gewalt vor und nach Harare." *Ökumenische Rundschau* 48, no. 2 (1999): 167-75.

————, ed. *Dekade zur Überwinding von Gewalt, 2001-2010. Impulse.* Frankfurt: Otto Lembeck, 2001.

Fage, J. D. *A history of Africa.* London: Unwin Hyman, 1998.

Germond, Paul. "Sex in a globalizing world: The South African churches and the crisis of sexuality." *Journal of Theology for Southern Africa* 119 (July 2004): 46-68.

Grundemann, Reinhold, *Missions-Studien und Kritiken.* 2 vols. Gütersloh: C. Bertelsmann, 1894-98.

Gustafson, James. *Varieties of moral discourse: Prophetic, narrative, ethical, and policy.* Grand Rapids: Calvin College and Seminary, 1988.

Haddad, Beverley. "Gender violence and HIV/AIDS: A deadly silence in the church." *Journal of Theology for Southern Africa* 114 (November 2002): 93-106.

Härle, Wilfried. *Dogmatik.* Berlin: Walter de Gruyter, 1995.

Hauerwas, Stanley. *After Christendom? How the church is to behave if freedom, justice, and a Christian nation are bad ideas.* Nashville: Abingdon Press, 1991.

————. *A community of character: Toward a constructive Christian social ethic.* Notre Dame, Ind.: University of Notre Dame Press, 1981.

————. *Performing the faith: Bonhoeffer and the practice of nonviolence.* Grand Rapids: Brazos Press, 2004.

Hauschild, Wolf-Dieter. "Nicäno-Konstantinopolitanisches Glaubensbekenntnis." *Theologische Realensiklopädie* 24 (1994): 444-56.

Hayes, Stephen. "African initiated church theology." In *Initiation into theology,* edited by Simon Maimela and Adrio König, pp. 159-78. Pretoria: Van Schaik, 1998.

Held, David, Anthony McGrew, David Goldblatt, and Jonathan Perraton. *Global transformations: Politics, economics, and culture.* Stanford, Calif.: Stanford University Press, 1999.

Hendricks, Jurgens H., ed. *Gemeentes vertel. Verandering in 'n Christelike geloofsgemeenskap.* Kaapstad: Lux Verbi, 1992.

Hesselink, I. John. *On being Reformed: Distinctive characteristics and common misunderstandings.* Ann Arbor, Mich.: Servant Books, 1983.

Hexham, Irving. *The irony of apartheid: The struggle for national independence of Afrikaner Calvinism against British imperialism.* New York: Edwin Mellen, 1981.

Heyns, Johan. "Burgerlike ongehoorsaamheid." *Skrif en Kerk* 12, no. 1 (1991): 36-53.

————. *Dogmatiek.* Pretoria: N. G. Kerkboekhandel, 1978.

————. *Die kerk.* Pretoria: N. G. Kerkboekhandel, 1977.

Hoekendijk, Johannes Christiaan. *Kerk en volk in de Duitse zendingswetenschap.* Amsterdam: Rodopi, 1948.

Bibliography

Hopewell, James. *Congregation: Stories and structures*. Worcester: SCM Press, 1987.

Hopkins, Dwight N. *Being human: Race, culture, and religion*. Minneapolis: Fortress Press, 2005.

———. "Black theology: The notion of culture revisited." *Journal of Theology for Southern Africa* 123 (November 2005): 74-83.

Houtepen, Anton. "Common confession." In *Dictionary of the ecumenical movement*, pp. 195-97. Geneva: WCC, 1991.

———. "Reception, tradition, communion." In *Ecumenical perspectives*, edited by Max Thurian, p. 145. Geneva: WCC, 1983.

Iliffe, John. *The African AIDS epidemic: A history*. Oxford: James Curry, 2006.

Isard, Peter. *Globalization and the international financial system*. Cambridge: Cambridge University Press, 2005.

Jonker, Louis C. "Israel en die nasies. 'n Kritiese nadenke oor die dokument *Ras, Volk en Nasie*." *Scriptura* 2 (2001): 165-84.

Jonker, Willie D. *Christus die Middelaar*. Pretoria: N. G. K. Uitgewers, 1977.

———. *Die Gees van Christus*. Pretoria: N. G. Kerkboekhandel, 1981.

———. "In gesprek met Johan Heyns." *Skrif en Kerk* 15, no. 1 (1994): 13-26.

———. "Kragvelde binne die kerk." *Aambeeld* 26, no. 1 (June 1998): 11-14.

———. "Die pluriformiteitsleer van Abraham Kuyper. Teologiese onderbou vir die konsep van aparte kerke vir aparte volksgroepe?" *In die Skriflig* 23, no. 3 (1989): 12-23.

———. *Die relevansë van die kerk*. Wellington: Lux Verbi, 2008.

———. *Selfs die kerk kan verander*. Cape Town: Tafelberg, 1998.

———. "Some remarks on the interpretation of Karl Barth." *Nederduitse Gereformeerde Teologiese Tydskrif* 29 (1988): 30-31.

———. "Understanding the church situation and obstacles to Christian witness in South Africa." In *Road to Rustenburg*, edited by Louw Alberts and Frank Chikane, pp. 87-98. Cape Town: Struik, 1991.

Jorns, Klaus-Peter. *Der Lebensbezug des Gottesdienst. Studien zu seinem kirchlichen und kulturellen Kontext*. Munich: Kaiser, 1998.

Kässmann, Margot. *Overcoming violence: The challenge to the church in all places*. Geneva: WCC, 1998.

Kelly, J. N. D. *Early Christian creeds*. London: Longman, 1972.

King, Ursula, ed. *Feminist theology from the Third World: A reader*. Maryknoll, N.Y.: Orbis Books, 1994.

Kinghorn, Johann. "Teologie en sosiaal-antropologie." In *Koninkryk, kerk en kosmos*, edited by P. F. Theron and Johann Kinghorn, pp. 112-29. Bloemfontein: Pro-Christo, 1989.

———, ed. *Die N. G. Kerk en apartheid*. Johannesburg: Macmillan, 1986.

Kinnamon, Michael. "Tough times." *Mid-Stream* 38, no. 3 (July 1999): 36-43.

Kneifel, Theo. *Zwischen Versöhnung und Gerechtigkeit. Südafrika — der Spagat der Kirchen nach der Apartheid*. Hamburg: Evangelisches Missionswerk in Deutschland, 1998.

König, Adrio. "Is versoening (te) goedkoop?" In *Koninkryk, kerk en kosmos,* edited by P. F. Theron and Johann Kinghorn, pp. 130-43: Bloemfontein: Pro-Christo, 1989.

Koopman, Nico. "A basic and neglected conviction of (Reformed) theology?" In *350 years Reformed: 1652-2002,* edited by Pieter Coertzen, pp. 252-60. Bloemfontein: CLF, 2002.

————. "Reconciliation and the Confession of Belhar, 1986: Some challenges for the Uniting Reformed Church in Southern Africa." *Nederduitse Gereformeerde Teologiese Tydskrif* 48 (2007): 96-106.

Köpping, Klaus-Peter, Michael Welker, and Reiner Wiehl, eds. *Die autonome Persone — eine europäische Erfindung.* Munich: Wilhelm Fink, 2002.

Kort, Wesley. *Bound to differ: The dynamics of theological discourses.* University Park: Pennsylvania State University Press, 1992.

Krog, Antjie. *Country of my skull.* Cape Town: Random House, 1998.

————. "The Truth and Reconciliation Commission: A national ritual?" *Missionalia* 26, no. 1 (1998): 5-16.

Kuhn, Ulrich. "Reception — an imperative and an opportunity." In *Ecumenical perspectives on the BEM,* edited by Max Thurian, pp. 136-74. WCC: Geneva, 1983.

Kuiper, D. T. "Groen and Kuyper on the racial issue." In *Kuyper reconsidered: Aspects of his life and work,* edited by Cornelis van der Kooi and Jan de Bruijn, pp. 69-82. Amsterdam: V. U. Uitgeverij, 1999.

Kuyper, Abraham. *Calvinism: Six lectures delivered in the Theological Seminary at Princeton. The L. P. Stone lectures from 1889 to 1899.* New York: Revell, 1899.

————. *Encyclopaedie der Heilige Godgeleerdheid.* 3 vols. Amsterdam: J. A. Wormer, 1894.

————. *De gemeene gratie.* 3 vols. Amsterdam: Höveker & Wormser, 1902-4.

————. *De hedendaagsche Schriftkritiek in hare bedenklijke strekking voor de gemeente des levenden Gods.* Amsterdam: J. H. Kruyt, 1881.

Lategan, Bernard. "History, historiography, and Reformed hermeneutics at Stellenbosch." In *Reformed theology: Identity and ecumenicity II; Biblical interpretation in the Reformed tradition,* edited by Wallace M. Alston Jr. and Michael Welker, pp. 157-71. Grand Rapids: Eerdmans, 2007.

Le Bruyns, Clint, and Gotlind Ulshöfer, eds. *The humanization of globalization: South African and German perspectives.* Frankfurt: Haag & Herchen, 2008.

Limouris, Gennadios. "Historical background of the apostolic faith today." In *Confessing the one faith,* pp. 105-11. Geneva: WCC, 1991.

————. "Nicene Creed." In *Dictionary of the ecumenical movement,* pp. 727-28. Geneva: WCC, 1991.

Loewe, Hartmurt. "Die Kirchen vor der Aufgabe der Rezeption von Ergebnissen ökumenischer Gespräche und Verhandlungen." In *Vernunft des Glaubens. Wissenschaftliche Theologie und kirchliche Lehre,* FS Wolfhart Pannenberg, pp. 637-51. Göttingen: Vandenhoeck & Ruprecht, 1988.

Loos, Marc. *De belijdenis van Belhar en haar betekenis voor ons.* Brussels: Verenigde Protestantse Kerk in België, 2001.

Loubser, J. A. *The apartheid Bible.* Cape Town: Tafelberg, 1987.

Lugo, Luis E., ed. *Religion, pluralism, and public life: Abraham Kuyper's legacy for the twenty-first century.* Grand Rapids: Eerdmans, 2000.

Maluleke, Tinyiko Sam. "The challenge of HIV/AIDS for theological education in Africa: Toward an HIV/AIDS sensitive curriculum." *Missionalia* 29, no. 2 (August 2001): 125-43.

―――. "'Dealing lightly with the wounds of my people'? The TRC process in theological perspective." *Missionalia* 25, no. 3 (November 1997): 324-43.

―――. "Truth, national unity, and reconciliation in Southern Africa." *Missionalia* 25, no. 1 (April 1997): 59-86.

Mandela, Nelson. "It is your duty to be human." Unpublished speech, World AIDS Day, December 1, 2002, Bloemfontein.

Marais, Frederick J., and Jurgens H. Hendricks. "What happens when congregations try to change their identity? Lessons from the stories of South African congregations." *Nederduitse Gereformeerde Teologiese Tydskrif* 37 (1996): 146-51.

Mau, Rudolph, ed. *Evangelische Bekenntnisse.* 2 vols. Bieleveld: Luther Verlag, 1997.

McFague, Sallie. *Metaphorical theology: Models of God in religious language.* London: SCM Press, 1982.

McGarrahan, Eunice T. *A study guide of the Belhar Confession and its accompanying letter.* Louisville, Ky.: PCUSA, Office of Theology and Worship, 2008.

Meiring, Piet. "Reconciliation: Dream or reality?" *Missionalia* 27, no. 3 (November 1999): 243-44.

Meyer, E. E. "Interpreting Luke with the confession of Belhar." *Scriptura* 72 (2000): 113-20.

Migliore, Daniel L. "Reformed theology in America." *Acta Theologica* 12, no. 1 (1992): 1-9.

Moltmann, Jürgen. *The church in the power of the Spirit: A contribution to messianic ecclesiology.* London: SCM Press, 1977.

Moody, T. Dunbar. *The rise of Afrikanerdom.* Berkeley: University of California Press, 1975.

Mosala, Itumeleng. *Biblical hermeneutics and black theology in South Africa.* Grand Rapids: Eerdmans, 1989.

Müller, Bethel A., and Dirk J. Smit. "Public worship: A tale of two stories." In *The relevance of theology for the 1990s*, edited by Johann Mouton and Bernard Lategan, pp. 385-408. Pretoria: Human Sciences Research Council, 1994.

Müller-Fahrenholz, Geiko. *The art of forgiveness: Theological reflections on healing and reconciliation.* Geneva: WCC, 1996.

Nash, Andrew. "Wine-farming, heresy trials, and the whole personality: The emergency of the Stellenbosch philosophical tradition, 1916-1940." *South African Journal for Philosophy* 16 (1997): 55-69.

Naudé, Piet J. "Die Belharstryd in ekumeniese perspektief." *Nederduitse Gereformeerde Teologiese Tydskrif* 38, no. 3 (1997): 226-43.

―――. "Between humility and boldness: Explicating human rights from a Christian perspective." *Nederduitse Gereformeerde Teologiese Tydskrif* 48, nos. 1-2 (2007): 139-49.

———. "Can our creeds speak a gendered truth? A feminist reading of the Nicene Creed and the Belhar Confession." *Scriptura* 86 (2004): 201-9.

———. "The challenge of cultural justice under conditions of globalisation: Is the New Testament of any use?" In *The New Testament interpreted: Essays in honour of Bernard C. Lategan,* edited by Cilliers Breytenbach, Johan C. Thom, and Jeremy Punt, pp. 267-87. Leiden: Brill, 2007.

———. "Confessing Nicea today? Critical questions from a South African perspective." *Scriptura* 79 (2002): 47-54.

———. "Confessing the one faith: Theological resonance between the creed of Nicea (325 A.D.) and the Confession of Belhar (1982 A.D.)." *Scriptura* 85 (2004): 35-53.

———. "The Dutch Reformed Church's role in the context of transition in South Africa: Main streams of academic research." *Scriptura* 76 (2001): 87-106.

———. "For South Africa, North America, and the church worldwide." *Perspectives: A Journal of Reformed Thought* 23, no. 5 (2008): 17-21.

———. "From pluralism to ideology: The roots of apartheid theology in Abraham Kuyper, Gustav Warneck, and theological Pietism." *Scriptura* 88 (2005): 161-73.

———. "'A gift from heaven' — the reception of the Belhar Confession in the period 1982-2000 and its ecumenical significance today." *Nederduitse Gereformeerde Teologiese Tydskrif* 44, nos. 3-4 (2003): 407-20.

———. "'It is your duty to be human': A few theological remarks amidst the HIV/AIDS crisis." *Scriptura* 89 (2005): 433-40.

———. "It is your duty to be human: Anthropological questions in a post-liberation South Africa." *Criterion: A Publication of the University of Chicago Divinity School,* Spring/Summer 2008, pp. 6-21.

———. "Reformed confessions as hermeneutical problem: A case study of the Belhar Confession." In *Reformed theology: Identity and ecumenicity II; Biblical interpretation in the Reformed tradition,* edited by Wallace M. Alston Jr. and Michael Welker, pp. 242-60. Grand Rapids: Eerdmans, 2007.

———. "Regaining our ritual coherence: The question of textuality and worship in ecumenical reception." *Journal of Ecumenical Studies* 35, no. 2 (1998): 235-56.

———. "The theological coherence between the Belhar Confession and some antecedent church witnesses in the period 1948-1982." *Verbum et ecclesia* 42, no. 1 (2003): 156-79.

———. "We cannot continue as if nothing has happened between us." *Scriptura* 82 (2003): 139-46.

———. "Would Barth sign the Belhar Confession?" *Journal of Theology for Southern Africa* 129 (2007): 4-22.

Naudé, Piet J., and Dirk J. Smit. "'Reception' — ecumenical crisis or opportunity for South African churches?" *Scriptura* 73 (2000): 175-88.

Nederduitse Gereformeerde Sendingkerk in Suid-Afrika. *Agenda en Handelinge van die drie en twintigste vergadering van die hoogeerwaarde sinode van die Nederduits Gereformeerde Sendingkerk in Suid Afrika, 22 September tot 6 Oktober 1982 en volgende dae in die N. G. Sendingkerk-Sentrum, Belhar.* Belhar: N. G. Sendingkerk, 1982.

Bibliography

————. *Konsepbelydenis van die N. G. Sendingkerk in Suid-Afrika.* Huguenot: Paarl Drukpers, 1982.

Niebuhr, Richard. *The social sources of denominationalism.* New York: Henry Holt, 1929.

Niemöller, J., ed. *Das Bekenntnis von Belhar und seine Bedeutung für die reformierten Kirchen in Deutschland.* Detmold: Reformierte Bund, 1998.

Niles, D. Preman. "Justice, peace, and the integrity of creation." In *Dictionary of the ecumenical movement,* pp. 557-59. Geneva: WCC, 1991.

————. *Resisting the threats to life: Covenanting for justice, peace, and the integrity of creation.* Geneva: WCC, 1989.

————, ed. *Between the flood and the rainbow: Essays interpreting the conciliar process of mutual commitment (covenant) to justice, peace, and the integrity of creation.* Geneva: WCC, 1992.

————, ed. *Justice, peace, and the integrity of creation: Documents from an ecumenical process of commitment.* Geneva: WCC, 1994.

Nolan, Albert. *God in South Africa: The challenge of the gospel.* Cape Town: David Philip, 1988.

Pakenham, Thomas. *The scramble for Africa, 1876-1912.* London: Abacus, 1991.

Perrone, Lorenzo. "Von Nicea (325) nach Chalcedon (451)." In *Geschichte der Konzilien. Vom Niceaum bis zum Vaticanum II,* edited by Alberigo Guiseppe, pp. 22-83. Düsseldorf: Patmos, 1993.

Peters, Christian. "Pietismus." *Lexikon für Theologie und Kirche* 8 (1999): 291-93.

Phiri, Isabel Apawo. "African women of faith speak out in an HIV/AIDS era." In *African women, HIV/AIDS, and faith communities,* edited by Isabel Phiri, Beverley Haddad, and Madipoane Masenya, pp. 3-20. Pietermaritzburg: Cluster, 2003.

Plasger, Georg. *Die relative Autorität des Bekenntnisses bei Karl Barth.* Neukirchen: Neukirchener Verlag, 2000.

Plou, Dafne. *Peace to the cities: Creative models of building community amidst violence.* Geneva: WCC, 1998.

Poniewozik, James. "What the Imus implosion tells us about the boundaries of 'acceptable talk.'" *Time Magazine,* April 23, 2007, pp. 32-38.

Prior, Andrew, ed. *Catholics in apartheid society.* Cape Town: David Philip, 1982.

Raiser, Konrad. "Gewalt Überwinden. Ökumenische Reflexionen zu einer 'Kultur aktiver und lebensfreundlicher Gewaltfreiheit.'" In *Dekade zur Überwindung von Gewalt, 2001-2010. Impulse,* edited by Fernando Enns, pp. 11-30. Frankfurt: Otto Lembeck, 2001.

Rawls, John. *The law of peoples.* Cambridge, Mass.: Harvard University Press, 1999.

————. *A theory of justice.* Cambridge, Mass.: Harvard University Press, Belknap Press, 1972.

Ritschl, Dietrich. *Zur Logik der Theologie.* Munich: Kaiser, 1984.

Ritschl, Dietrich, and Hugh Jones. *"Story" als Rohmaterial der Theologie.* Munich: Kaiser, 1976.

Ritter, Adolf Martin. "Arianismus." *Theologische Realensiklopädie* 3 (1978): 693-719.

Roels, Shirley J. "The Christian calling to business life." *Theology Today* 60 (2003): 357-69.

Rusch, William. *Reception — an ecumenical opportunity.* Philadelphia: Fortress Press, 1988.

Saayman, Willem. "AIDS — still posing an unanswered question." *Missionalia* 29, no. 2 (August 1999): 208-19.

Saayman, Willem, and J. Kriel. *AIDS — the leprosy of our time?* Pretoria: Unisa, 1992.

Sauter, Gerhard. "Die Rechtfertigungslehre als theologische Dialogregel. Lehrentwicklung als Problemgeschichte?" *Ökumenische Rundschau* 48, no. 3 (1999): 275-95.

Schlink, Edmund. *Der kommende Christus und die kirchlichen Traditionen.* Göttingen: Vandenhoeck & Ruprecht, 1961.

———. *Ökumenische Dogmatik. Grundzüge.* Göttingen: Vandenhoeck & Ruprecht, 1983.

———. *Schriften zu Ökumene und Bekenntnis.* Vol. 2: *Ökumenische Dogmatik.* Göttingen: Vandenhoeck & Ruprecht, 2005.

Schreiter, Robert. *Constructing local theologies.* Maryknoll, N.Y.: Orbis Books, 1985.

Schweiker, William. "Distinctive love: Gratitude for life and theological humanism." In *Humanity before God: Contemporary faces of Jewish, Christian, and Islamic ethics,* edited by William Schweiker, Michael A. Johnson, and Kevin Jung, pp. 91-117. Minneapolis: Fortress Press, 2006.

———. "Humanity before God: Theological humanism from a Christian perspective." The Martin Marty Center for the Advanced Study of Religion: The Religion and Culture Web Forum, October 2003, http://divinity.uchicago.edu/martycenter/ publications/webforum/102003/commentary.shtml.

———. *Theological ethics and global dynamics.* Oxford: Blackwell, 2004.

———. "We are not our own: On the possibility of a new Christian humanism." In *Loving God with our minds: The pastor as theologian,* edited by Michael Welker and Cynthia A. Jarvis, pp. 31-49. Grand Rapids: Eerdmans, 2004.

Schwöbel, Christoph, and Colin E. Gunton, eds. *Persons, divine and human: King's College essays in theological anthropology.* Edinburgh: T & T Clark, 1991.

Sen, Amartya. *On ethics and economics.* Oxford: Blackwell, 1988.

Seubold, Gunther. "Romantik." *Lexikon für Theologie und Kirche* 8 (1999): 1268-69.

Sieben, Hermann Josef. *Die Konzilidee der alten Kirche.* Paderborn: Ferdinand Schöningh, 1979.

Sjollema, Baldwin. "Programme to Combat Racism." In *Dictionary of the ecumenical movement,* pp. 825-27. Geneva: WCC, 1991.

Smit, Dirk J. "Barmen and Belhar in conversation — a South African perspective." *Nederduitse Gereformeerde Teologiese Tydskrif* 47, nos. 1-2 (2006): 291-302.

———. "Das Bekenntnis von Belhar. Entstehung, Inhalt, Rezeption, Relevanz." In *Das Bekenntnis von Belhar und seine Bedeutung für die reformierten Kirchen in Deutschland,* edited by J. Niemöller, pp. 17-33. Detmold: Reformierte Bund, 1998.

———. "In a special way the God of the destitute, the poor, and the wronged." In *A moment of truth: The confession of the Dutch Reformed Mission Church, 1982,* edited by G. D. Cloete and Dirk J. Smit, pp. 53-65. Grand Rapids: Eerdmans, 1984.

———. "Keine Zukunft ohne Vergebung? Vom Umgang mit den 20. Jahrhundert in Südafrika." *Evangelische Theologie* 62, no. 3 (2002): 172-87.

Bibliography

————. "Reformed theology in South Africa: A story of many stories." *Acta Theologica* 12, no. 1 (1992): 88-110.

————. "Social transformation and confessing the faith? Karl Barth's views on confession revisited." *Scriptura* 72 (2000): 67-85.

————. "Südafrika." *Theologische Realensiklopädie* 32 (2000): 322-32.

————. "Views on Calvin's ethics: Reading Calvin in the South African context." *Reformed World* 57, no. 4 (2007): 306-44.

————. "What does *status confessionis* mean?" In *A moment of truth: The confession of the Dutch Reformed Mission Church, 1982,* edited by G. D. Cloete and Dirk J. Smit, pp. 7-32. Grand Rapids: Eerdmans, 1984.

Soyinka, Wole. *The Blackman and the veil: A century on, and beyond the Berlin Wall.* Accra: SEDCO: W. E. B du Bois Memorial Centre for Pan-African Culture, 1993.

————. *Climate of fear.* London: Profile Books, 2004.

Stiglitz, Joseph E. *Globalization and its discontents.* New York: W. W. Norton, 2002.

————. *Making globalization work.* New York: W. W. Norton, 2006.

————. "Social justice and global trade." *Far Eastern Economic Review* 169, no. 2 (March 2006): 18-22.

Stout, Jeffrey. *Democracy and tradition.* Princeton: Princeton University Press, 2004.

Strauss, Piet J. "Abraham Kuyper, apartheid, and the Reformed churches in South Africa in their support of apartheid." *Theological Forum* 23, no. 1 (March 1995): 4-27.

Szesnat, Holger. "The concept of 'class' and social-scientific interpretation of the New Testament." *Nederlands Gereformeerde Teologiese Tydskrif* 38, nos. 1-2 (1997): 70-84.

Tanner, Kathryn. *Jesus, humanity, and the Trinity. A brief systematic theology.* Minneapolis: Fortress Press, 2001.

————. "What does grace have to do with money? Theology within a comparative economy." *Harvard Divinity Bulletin* 30 (Spring 2002): 6-9.

Thomas, Hugh. *The slave trade: The history of the Atlantic slave trade, 1440-1870.* London: Macmillan, 1997.

Thornton, John. *Africa and Africans in the making of the Atlantic world, 1400-1800.* Cambridge: Cambridge University Press, 1998.

Truth and Reconciliation Commission of South Africa Report, vol. 4. Cape Town: The Commission, 1998.

UNAIDS. *Report on the global HIV/AIDS epidemic.* Geneva: United Nations, 2002.

Van der Bent, Ans, ed. *Breaking down the walls: WCC statements and actions on racism, 1948-1985.* Geneva: WCC, 1986.

Van der Kooi, Cornelis. "A theology of culture: A critical appraisal of Kuyper's doctrine of common grace." In *Kuyper reconsidered: Aspects of his life and work,* edited by Cornelis van der Kooi and Jan de Bruijn, pp. 95-101. Amsterdam: V. U. Uitgeverij, 1999.

Van der Kooi, Cornelis, and Jan de Bruijn, eds. *Kuyper reconsidered: Aspects of his life and work.* Amsterdam: V. U. Uitgeverij, 1999.

Van der Merwe, Willem Jakobus. *The development of missionary attitudes in the Dutch Reformed Church in South Africa.* Cape Town: Nasionale Pers, 1936.

Vandervelde, George. "The meaning of 'apostolic faith' in World Council of Churches' documents." In *Apostolic faith in America,* edited by Thaddeus Horgan, pp. 20-25. Grand Rapids: Eerdmans, 1988.

Van Huyssteen, Wentzel. *Unique in the world? Human uniqueness in science and theology.* Grand Rapids: Eerdmans, 2006.

Van Leeuwen, Mary Stewart. "From Barmen to Belhar: Public theology in crisis situations." *Princeton Seminary Bulletin* 27, no. 1 (2006): 23-33.

Van Niekerk, A. C. J. "Moet ons die belydenis van Belhar (1986) as 'n nuwe belydenisskrif aanvaar?" *Skrif en Kerk* 12, no. 2 (1996): 443-55.

Van Schalkwyk, Annalet. "A gendered truth: Women's testimonies at the TRC and reconciliation." *Missionalia* 27, no. 2 (1999): 165-88.

Velema, W. H. "Kuyper as theoloog. Een persoonlike evaluatie na dertig jaar." *In die Skriflig* 23, no. 91 (September 1989): 56-73.

Verster, Pieter. "Politiek en teologie. Oos-Europa 1990 — Barth agterhaal?" *Nederduitse Gereformeerde Teologiese Tydskrif* 32, no.4 (1991): 614-21.

Villa-Vicencio, Charles, ed. *Between Christ and Caesar: Classic and contemporary texts on church and state.* Cape Town: David Philip; Grand Rapids: Eerdmans, 1986.

————, ed. *On reading Karl Barth in South Africa.* Grand Rapids: Eerdmans, 1988.

Vischer, Lukas. "The process of 'reception' in the ecumenical movement." *Mid-Stream* 23 (1984): 221-33.

Volf, Miroslav. *After our likeness: The church as the image of the Trinity.* Grand Rapids: Eerdmans, 1998.

————. *Exclusion and embrace: A theological exploration of identity, otherness, and reconciliation.* Nashville: Abingdon, 1996.

————. "Exclusion and embrace: Theological reflections in the wake of 'ethnic cleansing.'" *Journal of Ecumenical Studies* 29, no. 2 (1992): 230-48.

————. "'The Trinity is our social program': The doctrine of the Trinity and the shape of social engagement." *Modern Theology* 14, no. 3 (July 1998): 403-23.

Vorster, J. M. "Die belydenis van Belhar in dogma-historiese perspektief." *In die Skriflig* 32, no. 4 (December 1998): 469-85.

Wainwright, Geoffrey. "Lex orandi, lex credendi." In *Dictionary of the ecumenical movement,* pp. 600-604. Geneva: WCC, 1991.

Warneck, D. Gustav. *Evangelische Missionslehre. Ein missionstheorethischer Versuch.* Part 3: *Der Betrieb de Sendung.* Gotha: Berthes, 1897.

Welker, Michael, and Cynthia A. Jarvis, eds. *Loving God with our minds: The pastor as theologian.* Grand Rapids: Eerdmans, 2004.

Welker, Michael, and David Willis, eds. *Reformed identity and ecumenicity.* Grand Rapids: Eerdmans, 2003.

West, Cornel. *Prophesy deliverance! An Afro-American revolutionary Christianity.* Philadelphia: Westminster, 1982.

————. *Race matters.* New York: Vintage Books, 1994.

Wilkens, Klaus, ed. *Gemeinsam auf dem Weg. Offizieller Bericht der Achten Vollversammlung des Ökumenischen Rat der Kirchen. Harare 1998.* Frankfurt: Otto Lembeck, 1999.

Bibliography

Willimon, William H. "Why we all can't just get along: Racism as a Lenten issue." *Theology Today* 53, no. 4 (January 1997): 485-90.

Wilson, Francis, and Mamphela Ramphele. *Uprooting poverty: The South African challenge; Report for the Second Carnegie Inquiry into Poverty and Development in Southern Africa.* Cape Town: David Philip, 1989.

World Alliance of Reformed Churches. *The Accra Confession: Covenanting for justice in the economy and the earth.* Geneva: WCC, 2004.

World Council of Churches. *Baptism, Eucharist, and Ministry, 1982-1990.* Faith and Order Paper 149. Geneva: WCC, 1990.

————. *Church and world: The unity of the church and the renewal of human community.* Faith and Order Paper 151. Geneva: WCC, 1990.

————. *A common account of hope.* Faith and Order Paper 92. Geneva: WCC, 1978.

————. *Confessing the one faith.* Faith and Order Paper 140. Geneva: WCC, 1987. New revised version, Faith and Order Paper 153. Geneva: WCC, 1991.

————. *Facing AIDS: The challenge, the churches' response.* Geneva: WCC, 1997.

————. *The nature and purpose of the church.* Faith and Order Paper 181. Geneva: WCC, 1998.

Wüstenberg, Ralf Carolus. "Reconciliation with a new lustre: The South African example as a paradigm for dealing with the political past of the German Democratic Republic." *Journal of Theology for Southern Africa* 113 (2002): 19-40.

————, ed. *Wahrheit, Recht und Versöhnung. Auseinandersetzung mit der Vergangenheit nach den Politischen Umbruchen in Südafrika und Deutschland.* Frankfurt: Peter Lang, 1998.

Zizioulas, John. *Communion as being: Studies in personhood and the church.* Crestwood, N.Y.: St. Vladimir's Seminary Press, 1985.

Index

ABRECSA. *See* Alliance of Black Reformed Christians in Southern Africa

Accompanying Letter: apolitical nature of, 15, 23-24; confessing against oneself in, 102; hermeneutical key of, 117; introduction to, 1-2; and the need to confess, 91; as proclamation against false doctrine, 97; on reading the "signs of the times" in, 162; statement on conversion in, 98; and *status confessionis,* 57

Accra Confession: comparing Belhar with, 161-64; introduction to, 161-62; resists effects of globalization, 212, 215

Africa: AIDS in, 190-91, 199, 200; colonialism in, 171-74; as cradle of mankind, 170; identity of Africans in, 180-84; justice in, 212; slavery in, 171-73

Afrikaners: and British rule, 28-29, 30, 47; DRC provides moral legitimacy to political leaders of, 44; and nationalism, 30, 31, 42; neo-Calvinist influence on, 77, 78; Pietism and the social vision of, 42; "sacred history" of, 30

AIDS: Christian churches struggle with the problem of, 192-94; discrimination of people living with, 190; *imago Dei* and the Trinity in relation to, 194-200; theology of, 191

Alliance of Black Reformed Christians in Southern Africa (ABRECSA): and Christ's lordship, 65-67; on church unity, 63, 68; confessional stance of, 56; definition of "black" by, 72; and obedience to Christ alone, 67; white Reformed theology challenged by, 59, 60

Apartheid: building blocks of, 217; DRC confesses its support for, 139, 208; DRC Open Letter against, 72; economic forces and, 210; the false gospel of, 24, 87n.25, 93, 97, 192; Group Areas Act and, 111; Immorality Act and, 70; no reference in Belhar to, 46, 73; as sin, 56, 60; *status confessionis* destroys Christian canopy of, 58; theological resistance against, 51; theology (of) supporting, 24, 40, 67-68, 70-71, 93, 101, 189

Apostles' Creed: not accepted by all traditions, 187; Belhar Confession's bond with, 6, 120-21, 150; the *status confessionis* of the, 80; and the Trinity, 6

Athanasian Creed: and confessions of

the Protestant Reformation, 108; ecumenical nature of, 187; and the Trinity, 6

Augsburg Confession: and Barth's opposition to the Formula of Concord, 90; Belhar influenced by the, 55; as Lutheran expression of faith, 135, 154

Bam, Gustav: on commission to prepare Belhar Confession, 82; speech after acceptance of the *status confessionis,* 79-81

Baptism: Belhar and unity in, 153; Eucharist, Ministry, and, 152; forgiveness of sins and, 126-27; Nicene Creed as formula for, 118; role of creed in rite of, 112; sin and death conquered by, 13

Barmen Declaration: apolitical stance of, 97; Barth as composer of, 81, 84; Belhar's relation to, 94; deconstruction of apartheid and the, 44; German study comparing Belhar with, 136; *status confessionis* and the, 80

Barth, Karl: on a creed defining Christian community, 99; on criteria for confession, 81; DRC theology destabilized by Christology of, 78-79; influence of, on Belhar Confession, 77-79, 81-85; statement on "no" of confession by, 23; and the theology behind confession, 87-103

Belgic Confession: ABRECSA's relation to, 60, 66; Belhar's relation to, 5-7; reception of Belhar and the, 144

Boesak, Allan: as assessor at DRMC General Synod (1982), 57; and the Belydende Kring, 137; on commission to prepare Belhar Confession, 82; as confessional leader of the Mission Church, 56; and Kuyper's theology, 31; as president of WARC, 56, 141; on racism and apartheid, 56

Bonhoeffer, Dietrich: on Christ, church, and ethics, 177; and dismantling

ideological pluralism, 44; *ubuntu* and the Christology of, 181, 182

Botman, Russel: on Bonhoeffer's Christology and *ubuntu,* 181; and Kuyper's theology, 31; on the reception of Belhar, 131-32

British: Afrikaner resistance to colonization by, 28-30, 47; War (1899-1902) with Afrikaners, 30, 42

Calvin: ambiguity of "old Calvin" versus "young," 30; Kuyper's common grace and general grace of, 29; on self-knowledge and knowledge of God, 176

Calvinism: Afrikaner, and Kuyper, 29; "imperial," and Kuyper, 31; and Kuyper's thinking, 25-26

Canons of Dort: developed from *status confessionis,* 80; election without merit in, 7; reception of Belhar and the, 144

Catholic bishops. *See* SACBC

Charta Oecumenica, 157-59

Christian Institute. *See* Naudé, Beyers

Christian rehumanization (humanism), 175-78

Christology: and Bonhoeffer's definition of community, 181, 182; divinity and humanity in, 121-23; Durand on, 78; and the indivisibility of the body of Christ, 68; and the lordship of Jesus Christ, 65-67

Colonization, 171-72, 174

Confession: accompanying letters of a, 117; and baptism, 126-27; Barth's criteria for, 81; Belhar and the Accra, 161-64; biblical and theological roots of, 50, 88-90; church called to act on its, 189, 217; as a common expression of faith, 104-9; comparing Nicea and Belhar, 117-18; as confessing Jesus Christ, 87; as a counterstatement against heresy, 112-14; *credo in,* 118; and eschatology, 127-28; feminist reinterpretation of, 186; four theses of the reception of (the Belhar), 139-48; free grace results in, 205; God's revelation and the role of, 90-92; for outsiders and insiders, 99-103; reception of a, 114-17; reception of Belhar as, 131-38; as redefinition of self-understanding and identity, 102; role of context in the formulation of a, 94-95; spontaneous statement of, 92-94; and trinitarian theology, 119-26; of Willie Jonker, 208; the will of God as expressed by, 96-99

Cottesloe: origins of, 54n.14; social commentary of, 59, 71; unity, inclusivity, and spiritual unity in, 62

De Gruchy, John: on Afrikaner "sacred history," 30; on Christian humanism, 175; and Kuyper's theology, 31

DRC. See Dutch Reformed Church

DRMC. See Dutch Reformed Mission Church

Dutch Reformed Church (DRC): Accompanying Letter on the, 2, 5; apartheid laws requested by, 111; Barth, theology, and Pietism in, 78-79; Belhar and Canons of Dort in, 44; Belhar does not mention, 73; confesses its sins, 139; division and Holy Communion (Eucharist) in, 57, 152; Federal Mission Policy of, 34, 39; and hermeneutical trap, 43-44; as mother church of the DRMC, 100, 150; Pietism and, 42; racial attitudes of, 32; reception of Belhar in, 82, 138-48; reconciliation in Open Letter of, 65-66, 72; separate churches in the, 11, 111, 150; visible unity in Open Letter of, 63; Warneck's missiology and separate churches in, 35; Willie Jonker's confession on behalf of, 208

Dutch Reformed Church, Synods of: 1824, 1826, 1829, 33; 1857, 33, 46, 100; 1880, 34; 1990, 116, 140-41

Dutch Reformed Church in Africa: and the formation of the Uniting Reformed Church in Southern Africa, 138; foundation of, 34; reunification of, 136

Dutch Reformed Mission Church (DRMC): acceptance of Belhar by, 5-6, 50; Belhar provides theological worth to, 102; and the Circuit of Wynberg on apartheid, 52n.9, 70; confession and Barth in the context of, 79, 90; establishment of, 34, 100, 144, 150; on the irreconcilability of apartheid, 64; as "object" of Belhar, 141; refuses to share Lord's Table with DRC, 143, 152; Synod (1982) of, 57, 60, 94, 111, 115, 136; Synod (1986) of, 82, 136; see also Mission Church

Ecclesiology: anthropology in the context of theology and, 194; based on spiritual unity and ABRECSA, 63; Belhar and preeminence of, 64, 69; built on "God-willed" differentiation, 46; direct link between sociology and, 74; humans intrinsically related to theology and, 176; and reconciliation and healing, 197-98; subjectivism in Kuyper's, 30; as theological and social locus for renewal, 161; Trinity, unity, and, 121; and visible unity, 62-64

Ecumenism: Charta Oecumenica, 157-59; and church dialogue, 133; and confession and identity, 146; and gender reconciliation, 186; Joint Declaration on the Doctrine of Justification, 153-55; and recognition of Belhar, 134-35, 149-50; and renewal of humanity, 160-61; and role of liturgy, 142

Enlightenment: Christian humanism and the values of the, 175; and ubuntu, 180-81

Eschatology: Christ's lordship, 66; and hope of Belhar, 127-28; and interecclesial reconciliation, 155, 188

Eucharistic: fellowship and unity, 105,

150-53, 215; *also see* Holy Communion

Faith and Order: Conferences, 105-6; and unity, 150, 160-61; and WCC, 151
Feminist: hermeneutics, 186; scholarship, 186, 187

Gender: and HIV and AIDS, 193; reconciliation, 186-90
Global: capitalism, 211; warming, 211
Globalization: Accra addresses, 163, and black liberation theology, 179; and economic justice, 210-18; impact of, on Africa, 173-74
Grace: common (general), 26-29, 40; free, 205, 206; special (particular), 26-28

Heidelberg Catechism: Belhar's relation to, 5-8, 10, 86, 121; on self-referential individualism, 214; *sola gratia* in, 206
Hermeneutics: and ideological pluralism, 40, 43, 44; and separate churches, 43, 44; struggle with feminism, 187, 188; of suspicion, 141
Historical criticism: and Pietism, 43; and scholarship, 41-42; and Stellenbosch University, 43
HIV and AIDS: *imago Dei*, the Trinity, and people living with, 194-200; marginalization of people living with, 190-94
Holy Communion: not shared by DRMC and DRC members in Ottawa, 57, 127, 143; and the racial divide, 33, 46, 57, 64, 152

Identity: community and, 180; confession and redefinition of, 102; through disassociation, 64; of the DRC, 146-48; globalization and, 179; national and religious, 41; and *ubuntu*, 180-83; unity and, 178; Volf on, 179

Ideology: Christianity as, 24; as counterposition of apartheid, 141-42; to legitimate injustice, 18, 47, 69, 112, 164, 189, 217; racial separation as, 14, 15; and reconciliation denied, 153, 188
Individualism: and Africa, 180-81; distorted, 213; Heidelberg Catechism on, 214-15; and Kuyper, 30
Injustice: Belhar against, 202; gender, 189; God opposed to, 16-18; as God's will, 47; social and economic, 47-48

Joint Declaration on the Doctrine of Justification, 153-55
Jonker, Willie: on Barth, 79; confesses on behalf of DRC, 208; on Kuyper, 30, 38; Ottawa speech by, 57
Justice: Belhar and, 61, 86, 88, 89, 125; charity and, 54, 58; and the church, 64-65; economic and social, 47-48, 210-18; ecumenical initiatives and, 157-64; equal but separate, 31; God as source of, 15-18; Open Letter on, 72, 73; restorative, 201-10
Justice, Peace, and the Integrity of Creation, 159, 162. *See also* World Council of Churches

Kuyper, Abraham: common and special grace of, 26-29, 40; cosmology of, 26, 29, 42-43, 78; ecclesiology of, 26, 27, 30; influence of, on DRC theology, 25-32; on modern biblical scholarship, 43; social development of, 27-28

Liberation theology, 16, 89, 116, 141, 142, 179
Lordship of Christ: Belhar and obedience to, 23; Christology and, 65-67; confession of, 19; divinity and, 122; social order and, 71
Lutheran Church: and the Augsburg Confession, 55, 90; and Barth on Formula of Concord, 90; *Joint Declaration on the Doctrine of Justification*, 153-55; and the Lutheran World Federation, 55, 154

Message to the People of South Africa:
and apartheid anthropology, 68; biblical authority of, 59; Christ's lordship in, 65, 67, 71; confessional theme of, 55; opposition to apartheid by, 64
Missiology, 32-41
Mission Church. *See* Dutch Reformed Mission Church

Naudé, Beyers: founder of Christian Institute, 44n.71, 55, 94; and ideological pluralism, 44
Neo-Calvinism: Afrikaner civil religion and Kuyperian, 78; as ideological and theological basis for apartheid, 30, 67, 79, 87, 101, 111; Kuyper and, 25
Nicene Creed: Belhar and trinitarian nature of, 6; bond between Belhar and, 6; ecumenical nature of, 187; "signs" (marks) of the church in, 7; unity in faith and the, 105-28, 150, 158

Open Letter, 52-53n.11, 60n.27, 63, 65, 72. *See also* Dutch Reformed Church

Personhood: Comaroffs on, 181; globalization and, 212; and the Trinity, 119
Pietism, 41-43
Presbyterian Church in the USA, 137
Protestantism: Barth and Scripture in, 88; confessions and tradition in, 187; greater diversity of churches in, 33; history and revelation in, 85; Reformation and confessions in, 108; Reformation and "faith alone" in, 12

Racism: Justice, Peace, and the Integrity of Creation stands against, 159; SACBC on, 54; in the United States, 183; WARC stands against, 56; and xenophobia in South Africa, 183
Reconciliation: in Christ, 4-5, 8, 11-15, 45, 46-47, 86; diversity and, 178, 183; and ecumenism, 153-55; gender and, 186-90; and healing embrace, 197-99; HIV and AIDS and, 190-94; and jus-

tice, 124, 125, 156-59; the Trinity and, 194-97; and unity, 161; and violence, 155-57
Reformed churches: Belhar as "common confession" of, 135; Belhar does not mention white, 97; Belhar and the tradition of, 83; National Party and, 70; Pietism and, 41-43; *status confessionis* in, 56; suspension of, 56
Reformed Church in America, 115, 137
Reformed creed: Barth on, 84-85, 94-99; as confessional cry, 44; and Scripture, 85; universal, 83, 94
Reformed theology: black Reformed Christians challenge white face of, 59; and "catholicity of persons," 182; many faces of, 144; retrieval of critical, 79; *sola gratia* and, 206; Word-tradition argument of, 60
Reformed tradition: apartheid and, 56; Barth on dogma in, 96; confessions and Scripture in, 88; critical reformed theology enriches, 79; and Enlightenment values, 175; false and true interpretation of, 59-60, 66; on judging confessions in, 89; justice and reclaiming of, 59; will of God in, 26
Roman Catholic Church: *Joint Declaration on the Doctrine of Justification,* 153-55; and WCC, 151. *See also* SACBC

SACBC. *See* Southern African Catholic Bishops' Conference
Sacraments: separate, 33, 100; and "theology of AIDS," 191; unity and, 95, 152-53
Schweiker, William, 175, 181, 216
Slavery, 170-74
Smit, Dirkie: and Adonis on fear of social change, 147; on commission to prepare confession, 82; rebuttal against Marxist influence in Belhar, 89
South African Council of Churches, 55,

64, 94. *See also Message to the People of South Africa*

Southern African Catholic Bishops' Conference (SACBC): on charity and justice, 54, 58, 70; condemns apartheid, 53-54; on social change, 70-71

Status confessionis: Bam on, 79-81; Barth's theology and, 79, 81, 83-84, 91; Belhar a result of, 91; DRC identity and, 147; DRMC accepts, 115; and DRMC's refusal to share the Lord's Table, 143, 152; ethical situation brings about, 98; first accepted in Ottawa, 143; introduction to, 55-58, 60; justice and, 157; and liberation theology, 141; and pietistic spirituality, 144

Three Formulae of Unity, 51, 82, 102, 139

Trinity: Belhar and, 5, 6, 19; church unity and, 41, 118-24; and embrace, 198; *imago Dei* and, 194-96; and similarities between Belhar and *Charta Oecumenica,* 159

Truth and Reconciliation Commission: Accompanying Letter as prefiguring, 98; on faith communities, 145; and restorative justices, 202-9

Ubuntu, 180-82

United States: global warming and, 211; racism in, 183-84; and subprime crisis, 210; as world leader, 217

Uniting Reformed Church in Southern Africa: and Barth, 79; division between DRC and, 144; and schism, 138; and unification of DRMC and Dutch Reformed Church in Africa, 115, 136; and Verenigde Protestantse Kerk in België, 137

Unity: apartheid theology and, 67-68; Belhar and, 120-24, 126, 128, 137-38, 144-45, 150-53, 163-64, 187, 189-90, 206; *Charta Oecumenica* and, 158;

through Christ, 124; between church and society, 69; as church's task, 23; confession of faith and, 97-98; DRC and, 34, 138, 144-45, 148; ecumenism and, 160; eucharistic fellowship and, 105, 215; Kuyper on, 27-28; Nicene Creed and, 105, 106, 110-11, 117, 119-21; and Promotion of National Unity and Reconciliation Act, 202; spiritual (invisible) and eschatological, 11, 40-41, 45, 63, 101, 150, 178; the Trinity and, 86; visible, 9-12, 62-64, 98, 112, 178

Volf, Miroslav: on exclusion and embrace, 197-99; on identity, 179; on the Trinity, 195-96

Volk: ethnographic (ethnological) pluralism, 38-40; and Israel, 41; myth of, 147; and structure of society, 35

WARC. *See* World Alliance of Reformed Churches

Warneck, Gustav, 34-40

WCC. *See* World Council of Churches

World Alliance of Reformed Churches (WARC): and apartheid, 68-69; Boesak elected president of, 56; "Boesak's confession" and, 141; meeting of, in Accra, 161-62; meeting of, in Ottawa, 60, 152; Reformed churches suspended from, 56

World Council of Churches (WCC): on AIDS, 197-98; confessing one faith by, 115, 135; and Decade to Overcome Violence, 155-57; formation of, 151; and Justice, Peace, and the Integrity of Creation, 159-60, 162; and Program to Combat Racism, 157; on those who suffer, 125-26; visible unity as main aim of, 105, 150-51, 160-61

World Council of the Alliance of Reformed Churches: Barth on creed at, 84, 94, 103